Race, Ethnicity, and Gender in the United States

THE PINE FORGE PRESS SOCIAL SCIENCE LIBRARY

The Sociology of Work: Concepts and Cases *by Carol J. Auster*

Adventures in Social Research: Data Analysis Using SPSS for Windows *by Earl Babbie and Fred Halley*

Race, Ethnicity, Gender, and Class: The Sociology of Group Conflict and Change *by Joseph F. Healey*

Sociology: Exploring the Architecture of Everyday Life, *by David M. Newman*

Sociology: Exploring the Architecture of Everyday Life (Readings), *by David M. Newman*

The Production of Reality: Essays and Readings in Social Interaction, 2nd ed., *by Jodi O'Brien and Peter Kollock*

Diversity in America *by Vincent N. Parrillo*

The McDonaldization of Society, Rev. ed., *by George Ritzer*

Shifts in the Social Contract: Understanding Change in American Society *by Beth A. Rubin*

The Pine Forge Press Series in Research Methods and Statistics
edited by Kathleen S. Crittenden

Investigating the Social World: The Process and Practice of Research *by Russell K. Schutt*

A Guide to Field Research *by Carol A. Bailey*

Designing Surveys: A Guide to Decisions and Procedures *by Ronald Czaja and Johnny Blair*

How Sampling Works *by Richard Maisel and Caroline Hodges Persell*

Sociology for a New Century
A Pine Forge Press Series edited by Charles Ragin, Wendy Griswold, and Larry Griffin

Global Inequalities *by York W. Bradshaw and Michael Wallace*

How Societies Change *by Daniel Chirot*

Cultures and Societies in a Changing World *by Wendy Griswold*

Crime and Disrepute *by John Hagan*

Gods in the Global Village: The World's Religions in Sociological Perspective *by Lester Kurtz*

Waves of Democracy: Social Movements and Political Change *by John Markoff*

Development and Social Change: A Global Perspective *by Philip McMichael*

Constructing Social Research *by Charles C. Ragin*

Women and Men at Work *by Barbara Reskin and Irene Padavic*

Cities in a World Economy *by Saskia Sassen*

The Pine Forge Press Series in Crime and Society
edited by George S. Bridges, Robert D. Crutchfield, Joseph G. Weis

Volume 1: Crime

Volume 2: Juvenile Delinquency

Volume 3: Criminal Justice

Race, Ethnicity, and Gender in the United States

Inequality, Group Conflict, and Power

Joseph F. Healey

Department of Sociology
Christopher Newport University

Pine Forge Press

Thousand Oaks, California ■ London ■ New Delhi

For information, address:

 Pine Forge Press
A Sage Publications Company
2455 Teller Road
Thousand Oaks, California 91320
(805) 499-4224
E-mail: sdr@pfp.sagepub.com

Sage Publications Ltd.
6 Bonhill Street
London EC2A 4PU
United Kingdom

Sage Publications India Pvt. Ltd.
M-32 Market
Greater Kailash I
New Delhi 110 048 India

Production Management: Scratchgravel Publishing Services
Designer: Lisa S. Mirski
Photo Researcher: Monica Suder
Cover Design: Paula Shuhert and Graham Metcalfe

Printed in the United States of America
96 97 98 99 00 10 9 8 7 6 5 4 3 2 1

Library of Congress Cataloging-in-Publication Data
Healey, Joseph F., 1945–
    Race, ethnicity, and gender in the United States: inequality,
group conflict, and power / Joseph F. Healey.
        p.   cm.
    "Abridged and updated version of Race, ethnicity, gender, and
class"—Preface.
    Includes bibliographical references and index.
    ISBN 0-7619-8520-4 (acid-free paper)
    1. Minorities—United States.   2. United States—Race relations.
3. United States—Ethnic relations.   4. Racism—United States.
5. Ethnicity—United States.   I. Healey, Joseph F., 1945–   Race,
ethnicity, gender, and class.   II. Title.
E184.A1.H414   1996
305.8'00973—dc20
                                                    96-15614
                                                    CIP

About the Author

Joseph F. Healey is Professor of Sociology at Christopher Newport University in Virginia. He received his Ph.D. in Sociology and Anthropology from the University of Virginia. He has written a statistics textbook and articles on minority groups, the sociology of sport, social movements, and violence.

About the Publisher

Pine Forge Press is a new educational publisher, dedicated to publishing innovative books and software throughout the social sciences. On this and any other of our publications, we welcome your comments and suggestions.

Please call or write us at:

Pine Forge Press
A Sage Publications Company
2455 Teller Road
Thousand Oaks, California 91320
(805) 499-4224
E-mail: sdr@pfp.sagepub.com

BRIEF CONTENTS

CONTENTS

5 African Americans: From Segregation to Modern Institutional Discrimination and Racism / 115

8 Asian Americans: Modes of Incorporation / 203

O f all the challenges confronting the United States today, those relating to minority groups may be the most urgent and the most daunting. Discrimination and racial inequality are part of our national heritage, and prejudice and racism are among our oldest values. Minority group issues penetrate every aspect of the society, and virtually every item on the national agenda—balancing the federal budget, welfare and health care reform, crime and punishment, the future of the family, even defense spending and foreign policy—has some connection with dominant-minority relations.

These issues will not be resolved easily or quickly. Feelings are intense and controversy, acrimony, and bitter debate are common. As a society, we have little hope of resolving these dilemmas unless we confront them openly and honestly: They will not disappear and they will not resolve themselves.

This textbook contributes to the ongoing discussion by presenting information, raising questions, and probing issues. My intent is to help students increase their fund of information, improve their understanding of the issues, and clarify their thinking regarding matters of race and ethnicity. This text has been written for undergraduate students—sociology majors and nonmajors alike. It makes minimal assumptions about knowledge of history or sociological concepts, and the material is presented in an accessible and coherent way.

A unified set of themes and concepts is used throughout the text. The analysis is consistent and continuous, even as it examines a variety of points of view. The conceptual focus is on power, inequality, and group conflict, and the analysis is generally in the tradition of conflict theory. However, other issues of interest to students, such as ethnic identity and assimilation, are also raised, and other perspectives are introduced and applied. My goal is to present the sociology of minority group relations in a way that students will find understandable as well as intellectually challenging, and to deal with the issues and tell the stories behind the issues in a textbook that is both highly readable and a demonstration of the power and importance of thinking sociologically.

The bulk of the conceptual framework is introduced in the first four chapters. These concepts and analytical themes are then applied in a series of five case studies of minority groups in contemporary America. In the final chapter, main points and themes are summarized and reviewed and the analysis is brought to a conclusion.

This text explores the diversity within each minority group and, in particular, the differences in the experiences of minority group males and females. The ways in which gender differences crosscut ethnic and racial differences are examined, and the point that these sources of inequality and injustice are independent of each other is stressed. Solving one set of problems (e.g., prejudice and racial discrimination) will not automatically or directly solve the other (e.g., sexism and gender inequalities).

Finally, I emphasize the ways in which American minority groups are inseparable from American society. The relative success of this society is due no less to the contributions of minority groups than to those of the dominant group. The nature of the minority group experience changed as the larger society changed and to understand America's minority groups is to understand some elemental truths about America. To raise the issues of race and ethnicity is to ask what it means, and what it has meant, to be an American.

This text is an abridged and updated version of *Race, Ethnicity, Gender, and Class: The Sociology of Group Conflict and Change,* also published by Pine Forge Press. The larger volume contains greater detail and more explanations and examples, and includes a series of debates on current issues. This shorter volume has been slightly reorganized to enhance clarity and focus. It retains the individual case studies of minority groups and, most important, the conceptual framework for the analysis of group relations developed in the larger text. Thus, this briefer version can be used in conjunction with other materials or as a supplement in courses other than those concerned solely with minority relations.

I wish to thank Jeremy Hein, University of Wisconsin at Eau Claire, for critical comments and suggestions, and Becky Smith for editorial assistance. As always, the staff at Pine Forge Press has been remarkably professional, friendly, and helpful. Thanks especially to Rebecca Holland for all her help and support and to Steve Rutter for the inspiration and the opportunity. The time necessary to complete this volume was made possible by a sabbatical leave and by the support of the administration and faculty of Christopher Newport University. Thanks in particular to my colleagues in the Department of Sociology, Robert Durel and Lea Pellett.

I dedicate this book to my mother, Mrs. Alice Theresa Healey. Her life has begun to assume legendary proportions of late and has been chronicled in movie, music, and the written word. In one essay, a son thanked her for her love and support: "No one believed I could succeed . . . except my mother" (Tom Healey). In another essay, a granddaughter described her selflessness and devotion to family as "a love that asks only that you know it's there" (Kirsten Madden). Another granddaughter captured her sense of humor and her famous laugh: "Imagine a witch cackling and then take away the mean part" (Katie Chiotos). Dearly beloved by family and friends, she understands what truly matters in life: not wealth or fame or things but, simply, others.

Acknowledgments

For permission to reprint from the following, grateful acknowledgment is made to:

HarperCollins Publishers, Inc. for Figure 2.1, "The Vicious Cycle" from *An American Dilemma: The Negro Problem and Modern Democracy* by Gunnar Myrdal, copyright © 1944, 1962 by Harper & Row, Publishers, Inc.

Population Reference Bureau for Table 1.1, "Groups in American Society" from Philip Martin and Elizabeth Midgley, "Immigration to the United States: Journey to an Uncertain Destination," *Population Bulletin* (Vol. 47, No. 4), 1994; Figure 5.3, "Occupation by Race and Sex, 1990," Figure 6.3, "American-Indian, Aleut, and Eskimo Population of U.S. Counties, 1990," Figure 6.4, "Occupational Distribution of Native Americans and Whites, 1990," Figure 7.2, "Hispanic Population of U.S. Counties, 1990," Figure 8.3, "Asian and Pacific Islander Population by U.S. Counties, 1990," from William O'Hare, "America's Minorities: The Demographics of Diversity," *Population Bulletin* (Vol. 47, No. 4), 1992; Table 5.2, "Residential Patterns by Race," from William O'Hare et al., *African Americans in the 1990s*, 1991.

Prentice Hall for Table 4.1, "Characteristics of Three Systems of Group Relationships" from Farley, John, *Majority-Minority Relations*, 2/E, © 1988, pp. 18, 81. Adapted by permission of Prentice Hall, Inc., Englewood Cliffs, New Jersey.

Simon & Schuster for Figure 2.1, adapted with the permission of The Free Press, a Division of Simon & Schuster, from *Social Theory and Structure* by Robert K. Merton. Copyright © 1968, 1967 by Robert K. Merton.

The University of Chicago Press for Table 2.2, "Results of American Social Distance Rankings of Other Groups, 1926–1977" from Tom Smith and Glen Dempsey, "The Polls: Ethnic Social Distance and Prejudice," *Public Opinion Quarterly* 47, p. 588, 1983. Copyright © 1980, 1983 The University of Chicago Press.

Grateful acknowledgment is also made to the following for use of the photos in this book:

page 59, slave auction poster (#B-TPM-0443), © Topham/The Image Works; *page 60,* Harriet Tubman (LC-USZ62-7816), Library of Congress; *page 60,* cotton plantation, Miss., Library of Congress; *page 61,* Chinese railroad laborers (#PG.17187), © Corbis-Bettman; *page 61,* capture of Sitting Bull (#IND005 CP001 032), © Culver Pictures; *page 62,* Mexican-American cotton pickers (UPI #24 EFL), © Corbis-Bettman; *page 62,* segregated drinking fountains (#8022263bft), © Elliott Erwin/Magnum Photos; *page 63,* immigrant ship arriving in New York, © Ernst Haas/Magnum Photos; *page 261,* a field laborer, © Eve Arnold/Magnum Photos; *page 262,* workers in a sweatshop (#BO141-2/80), © Bill Owens/Jeroboam; *page 262,* Mexicans crossing the U.S. border, © Alex Webb/Magnum Photos; *page 263,* San Francisco Chinatown (#9445-10), © Phiz Mezey; *page 263,* Navajo women at bus stop, © Henri Cartier Bresson/Magnum Photos; *page 264,* Little Havana, Miami (#BGTS0005BC), © Granitsas/The Image Works; *page 265,* children eating meal, © Kit Hedman/Jeroboam; *page 265,* college students in cafeteria, © Shmuel Thaler/Jeroboam.

Race, Ethnicity, and Gender in the United States

CHAPTER 1

Diversity and Unity in U.S. Society
Questions and Concepts

What does it mean to be an American? Recent controversies about immigration, cultural diversity, ethnicity, and race indicate that this question is far from settled. Many people fear our society will splinter into conflicting groups with no core of common values or language. How much diversity can we tolerate before national unity is threatened? How should we respond to the challenge of living in a diverse society (and a diverse world)? Should we stress our similarities and insist on conformity, and or should we celebrate our differences and encourage diversity?

These questions are crucial but they are not new. They have been debated in one form or another over and over in our past. We are a nation of immigrants, and we have been arguing, often passionately, about exclusion and inclusion, unity and diversity, since the infancy of American society. Each wave of newcomers raises these issues once again, evoking the same fears and alarms, eliciting the same questions and concerns.

Our immigrant heritage and our cultural diversity have made us a nation of both groups and individuals. Some of us feel intensely connected with the groups to which we belong and identify closely with our heritage. For others the group connection is tenuous and distant. Regardless of our subjective sense of the connection, our group memberships influence our lives and our perceptions. They help to shape who we are and how we fit in with the larger society.

The groups to which we belong have their own histories and, very often, different perspectives on the present and agendas for the future. Any discussion of the future of American group relations is unlikely to be meaningful, profitable, or even mutually intelligible without some understanding of this variety of viewpoints and experiences.

Some minority groups have been a part of U.S. society for centuries and still face systematic exclusion, widespread injustice, and oppressive inequality. In fact, there is considerable evidence that the problems of African Americans, Native Americans, Mexican Americans, and other groups are just as formidable today—or even more so—as they were a generation ago.

Other groups are more recent additions to the American mix and bring new traditions, new perspectives, and new questions. U.S. society is, at present, in a period of increasing diversity. Over the past three decades, the number of immigrants arriving in the United States each year has increased from fewer than 300,000 to more than a million (U.S. Immigration and Naturalization Service, 1992, p. 25). The current wave of newcomers includes groups from all over the globe.

As one simple way of gauging the dimensions of diversity in our nation, consider recent changes in the group makeup of American society. Table 1.1 shows the relative size of various groups in 1980 and 1993. Two different size projections for the year 2050 are also supplied. The highest growth rates, associated with Asians and Pacific Islanders and Hispanics, are the results of high birth rates as well as high rates of immigration.

Perhaps the most striking feature of the table is that white Americans declined in percentage of the population from almost 80% to less than 75% by 1993. As Table 1.1 makes clear, it will not take too many generations before "non-Hispanic whites" may be a numerical minority of the population. In fact, in some American cities such as

Table 1.1 Groups in American Society

	Percentage of the Population		Projected Percentage of the Population in 2050	
	1980	1993	With No Immigration	With Immigration of 800,000 per Year
Asians and Pacific Islanders	2	3	4	10
Hispanics	7	10	18	22
Native Americans/ Eskimos/Aleuts	1	1	1	1
African Americans	12	12	17	14
Non-Hispanic Whites	80	74	61	52

Sources: 1980 data from the U.S. Bureau of the Census, 1993, p. 18; 1993 data and projections from Martin and Midgley, 1994, p. 9.

Miami, they already constitute less than a majority of the population. Does this matter? What are the implications of these growth patterns for the future of our society? Can U.S. society deal successfully with this diversity of cultures, languages, and races? Does this changing group structure threaten the primacy of traditional white middle-class American values and lifestyles? Does it provide an opportunity to express other, equally legitimate, value systems?

A number of questions have been raised in the preceding paragraphs. The goal of this text is to help you develop some thoughtful, informed positions on these issues. You should be aware from the beginning that the questions we address are complex and that the answers we seek are not obvious or easy. Indeed, there is no guarantee that U.S. society will be able or willing to resolve its myriad problems of intergroup relations. Progress will never be made in this area, however, unless the issues are confronted honestly and with an accurate base of knowledge and understanding. These problems certainly will not resolve themselves or disappear if we ignore them.

In addition to raising questions, this chapter introduces and defines many of the sociological concepts and themes that guide this text. In the chapters that follow, we explore prejudice and discrimination, America's past relations with minority groups, and the current situation of American minority groups. The final chapter summarizes the major themes of the text, draws some conclusions, and speculates about the future.

What Is a Minority Group?

Before we can begin to sort out the issues, we need common definitions and a common vocabulary for discussion. We begin with the term **minority group**, which is a bit misleading. Taken literally, the term has a mathematical connotation implying that the group so defined is small. In reality, a "minority" group can be quite large and can even be a numerical majority of the population. Women, for example, are sometimes considered to be a separate minority group, but they are a numerical majority of the U.S. population.

Minority status has more to do with the distribution of resources and power than with simple numbers. Our definition of minority group is based on Wagley and Harris (1958). According to this definition, a minority group has five characteristics:

1. The members of the group experience a pattern of disadvantage or inequality.
2. The members of the group share a visible trait or characteristic that differentiates them from other groups.

3. The minority group is a self-conscious social unit.

4. Membership in the group is usually determined at birth.

5. Members tend to marry within the group.

Each of these defining characteristics is examined below. The first two—inequality and visibility—are the most important and are examined in greater detail in the following sections.

The first and most important defining characteristic of a minority group is inequality; that is, some pattern of *disability and disadvantage.* The nature of the disability and the degree of disadvantage are variable. At one end of the spectrum might be exploitation, slavery, and **genocide** (the extermination of the group). At the other end might be such slight irritants as a lack of desks in classrooms for left-handed students. (Note, however, that if you are the left-handed student awkwardly taking notes at a right-handed desk, you would probably not agree that the irritant is slight.)

Whatever the scope or severity, the pattern of disadvantage is the key defining characteristic of a minority group. Because the group has less of what is valued by society, a term synonymous with minority group is subordinate group. Inequality between minority and dominant groups might exist in their shares of wealth, jobs, housing, political power, police protection, health care, or schooling. More important, the pattern of disadvantage is the result of the actions of another group that benefits from and tries to sustain the existing arrangement. This group can be called the core group, the majority group, or the **dominant group.** Since it reflects the patterns of inequality and the power realities of minority group status, the last term will be most commonly used throughout this text.

The second defining characteristic of a minority group is the possession of some *visible trait or characteristic* that the dominant group holds in low esteem. The trait could be either cultural (e.g., language, religion, speech patterns, or dress styles), physical (e.g., skin color, stature, or facial features), or both. Groups defined primarily by their cultural characteristics are called **ethnic minority groups.** Examples of such groups would be Irish Americans or Jewish Americans. Groups defined primarily by their physical characteristics are **racial minority groups,** such as African Americans or Native Americans. Note that these categories can overlap. So-called ethnic groups may have distinguishing physical characteristics (e.g., the stereotypical Jewish nose) and racial groups often have cultural traits different from those of the dominant group (e.g., differences in dialect or religious values).

These traits, whatever they may be, are used to establish group boundaries and to identify members of the minority group. The traits operate like an outward sign that marks group membership and reinforces the patterns of disadvantage. The dominant group has (or, at one time, had) sufficient power to select the identifying characteristic, create and maintain the distinction between groups, and thus solidify a higher position for itself. These markers of group membership usually are not important in and of themselves but become crucial features of any dominant-minority relationship. Without such visible signs, it would be difficult or impossible to identify who was in which group.

Third, minority groups are *self-conscious social units,* aware of their differentiation from the dominant group and of their shared disabilities. The shared social status can provide the basis for strong intragroup bonds and a sense of fellowship. Also, the experience of being in a minority group can lead to a view of the world that is quite different from that of the dominant group and other minority groups.

Recent events provide a dramatic illustration of the extent to which perceptions can vary from group to group. In June 1994, O. J. Simpson, a well-known sports star and celebrity, was arrested and charged with the murder of his ex-wife, Nicole Brown Simpson, and her friend Ronald Goldman. The trial that followed was one of the most closely observed and widely watched events in U.S. history but was viewed in vastly different ways by black and white Americans.

Public opinion surveys showed that the two groups differed in their opinions of Simpson's probable guilt, the justice of his acquittal, and virtually every other aspect of the trial. One survey showed that 85% of black Americans but only 32% of white Americans agreed with the jury's verdict of not guilty. Also, whereas 80% of black Americans thought the jury was fair and impartial, only 50% of white Americans agreed (Whitaker, 1995, pp. 30–34).

The fourth defining characteristic is that, in general, minority group membership is an **ascribed status**, one that is acquired at birth. The trait identifying minority group membership typically cannot be easily changed and minority group status is usually involuntary and for life.

Finally, minority group members tend to *marry within their own group.* This act is voluntary in part, but is sometimes dictated by the dominant group. It was only a generation ago in America that the law in many states forbade members of different racial groups to marry. The state laws against **miscegenation**, or interracial marriage, were declared unconstitutional in the late 1960s by the U.S. Supreme Court (Bell, 1992, p. 71).

This is a lengthy definition, but notice how inclusive it is. Clearly, it encompasses the "traditional" American minority groups such as African Americans and Native Americans. With perhaps a little stretching, it also can be applied to groups that usually are not regarded as minorities. For example, women arguably fit the first four criteria and can be analyzed with many of the same concepts and ideas that guide the analysis of other minority groups. Also, gay and lesbian Americans, Americans with disabilities, left-handed Americans, and very short, very tall, or very obese Americans could fit the definition of minority group without much difficulty. Thus, the analysis developed in this text can be applied more generally than you might realize at first. If you think of these other people as "minority groups," you may generate some fresh insights into their situations and your own feelings and experiences.

Inequality

Inequality is the most important defining characteristic of a minority group. In fact, one reason minority groups are important is that they are associated with the general patterns of inequality in society. Minority group membership can affect access to jobs, education, wealth, health care, and housing. It is associated with a lower (often much lower) proportional share of valued goods and services and more limited (often much more limited) opportunities to improve one's situation.

Stratification, or the unequal distribution of valued goods and services, is a basic feature of society. Every human society, except perhaps the simplest hunter-gatherer society, is stratified to some degree. That is, the resources of the society are distributed so that some get more and others less of whatever is valued. Societies are divided into horizontal layers (or strata), often called **social classes,** which differ from one another in terms of the amount of resources they command. Many criteria (e.g., education, age, gender, or talent) may affect a person's social class position and his or her access to goods and services. Minority group membership is one of these criteria and it has had a powerful, even a controlling, impact on the distribution of resources.

This section begins with a brief consideration of theories about the nature and important dimensions of stratification and then focuses on how minority group status relates to stratification. This discussion identifies several concepts and themes used throughout this text.

Theories of Inequality

Sociologists have been concerned with stratification and human inequality since the formation of the discipline in the 19th century. An early and important contributor to our understandings of social inequality was Karl Marx. He coauthored *The Communist Manifesto* in 1848 with Friedrich Engels and was the primary architect of a political, economic, and social philosophy that has played a major role in world affairs for nearly 150 years. Marxism is an elaborate theory of history and social change in which inequality is a central concept and concern.

Marx proposed that the most important source of inequality in society was related to control or ownership of the system of economic production. More specifically, he focused on the **means of production,** or the materials, tools, resources, and organizations by which the society produces and distributes goods and services. In an agricultural society, the means of production include land, draft animals, and plows. In an industrial society, the means of production include factories, commercial enterprises, banks, and transportation systems such as railroads.

All societies include two important social classes that struggle over the means of production. One class consists of those who own or control the means of production. In industrial society, this elite or ruling class is, in Marx's terms, the **bourgeoisie.** The other class is the working class, or the **proletariat.** Marx believed that conflict between these classes was inevitable and that the ultimate result of this class struggle would be the victory of the working class and the creation of a utopian society without exploitation, coercion, or inequality—in other words, a classless society.

Although modern social science owes a great deal to Marx, it is also clear that his analysis was limited in many ways. Max Weber (1864–1920), a German sociologist, was a significant critic of Marx. He thought Marx's view of inequality was too narrow. While Marx saw social class as entirely a matter of economic position or relationship to the means of production, Weber noted that inequality involved more dimensions than just the economic. Individuals could be members of the elite in some ways but not in others. For example, a major figure in the illegal drug trade could enjoy substantial wealth but be held in low esteem otherwise.

Weber recognized two additional sources of stratification besides economic position. He noted that people (and groups) can vary in **prestige** or the amount of honor, esteem, or respect accorded by others. Prestige might be determined by wealth, family lineage, or even physical appearance. In the United States, prestige is influenced by the groups to which we belong. Members of minority groups typically receive less prestige than members of the dominant group.

Weber's third system of inequality is **power,** defined as the ability to influence others, have an impact on the decision-making process of society, and achieve one's goals. One measure of power is a person's standing in politically active organizations, such as labor unions or pressure groups, which lobby state and federal legislatures.

Some politically active groups have access to great wealth and can use their riches to promote their cause. Other groups may rely more on their size and their ability to mobilize large demonstrations to achieve their goals.

Typically, these three dimensions of stratification go together, and wealthy, prestigious groups will be more powerful (more likely to achieve their goals or protect their self-interest) than low-income groups or groups with little prestige. It is important to realize, however, that power is a separate dimension from prestige and economic position and even very impoverished groups have found ways to express their concerns and pursue their goals.

A third contribution to our understanding of inequality was made by Gerhard Lenski, a contemporary sociologist who follows Weber and distinguishes among class (or control of property), prestige, and power. Lenski analyzes stratification in the context of societal evolution, or the **level of development** of a society. He argues that the nature of inequality (e.g., the degree of inequality or the specific criteria affecting one's position) is closely related to **subsistence technology**, the means by which the society satisfies basic needs such as hunger and thirst. A preindustrial agricultural society relies on human and animal labor to generate the calories necessary to sustain life. Inequality in this type of society centers on control of land and labor, since they are the most important means of production.

In an industrial society, however, land ownership is not as crucial as ownership of factories and other manufacturing and commercial enterprises. At the industrial level of development, control of capital is more important than control of land, and the nature of inequality changes accordingly.

We are entering still another level of development, often referred to as the postindustrial society. In this type of society, economic growth will be powered by developments in new technology, computer-related fields, information processing, and scientific research. It seems fairly safe to speculate that economic success at this next level of development will be closely related to familiarity with new technologies and education in general (Chirot, 1994, p. 88; see also Bell, 1973).

These changes in subsistence technology, from agriculture to industrial to the "information society," alter the stratification system. As the sources of wealth, success, and power change, so does the nature of the relationships between minority and dominant groups.

Minority Group Status and Stratification

There are at least three important relationships between minority groups and stratification. First, as we have already noted, minority group status affects access to property, prestige, and power. In the

United States, this status has been a powerful determinant of life chances, health and wealth, and success.

Second, stratification and minority group membership, although correlated, are separate social realities. The degree to which one is dependent on the other varies from group to group. Today, for example, some American minority groups face formidable barriers to equality, whereas others, even groups that were massively victimized in the past, face only minor limitations on their social mobility.

Also, each minority group can be internally divided by the three dimensions of stratification. Different members of the same groups can have very different life experiences. Some might be economically successful, wield great political power, or enjoy high prestige even as the vast majority of their group languish in poverty and powerlessness. Of course, just as minority group members vary in terms of inequality, social classes can be split by ethnic and racial factors.

A third connection between stratification and minority group status brings us to group conflict. We shall see repeatedly in the pages to come that minority-dominant group relationships are created as a result of a struggle over the control of valued goods and services. Minority group structures (such as slavery) emerge so that the dominant group can control commodities such as land or labor, maintain its position in the stratification system, or eliminate a perceived threat to its well-being. Struggles over property, prestige, and power lie at the heart of every minority-dominant relationship.

The Visibility Factor

In this section, we focus on the second defining characteristic of minority groups: the visible traits that denote one's membership in an ethnic or a racial group. The marks of membership that become important in a society reflect the outcomes of previous struggles between dominant and minority groups. The identifying trait is selected as a convenient and visible way for the dominant group to identify the minority group and maintain a boundary. These marks of group membership, it should be stressed, are arbitrary. They are chosen as a result of a social process, not because they are important in any other sense.

The most socially visible mark of group membership in U.S. society is **race**, which is both a biological and a social concept. Biologically, a race is an isolated, inbreeding population that has a distinctive genetic heritage (Harris, 1988, p. 98; see also Montagu, 1972). Race became a matter of concern for Western Europeans only in the recent past, when their curiosity about race was aroused by their increasing contact with the peoples of Africa, Asia, and the Americas. Europeans also conquered, colonized, and sometimes destroyed the non-Caucasian peoples and cultures they encountered. From the beginning, the European awareness of race was linked to notions of inferior and superior (conquered vs. conquering) peoples. For centuries, the European tradition has been to see race in this political and military context and to intermix the biological realities with judgments about the relative merits of the various races.

Scientific and biological investigations of race have focused for the most part on the construction of racial typologies or taxonomies, systems of classification that ideally would provide a category for every race and every person. Some of these typologies are quite elaborate, use multiple criteria, and recognize many races and sub-races. For example, the Caucasian race was often subdivided into Nordics (blond, fair-skinned Northern Europeans), Mediterraneans (dark-haired Southern Europeans), and Alpines (those between the first two categories).

Even the most elaborate of these racial taxonomies failed to establish clear dividing lines between racial groups, primarily because of the ambiguous and indeterminate nature of race. Because of migration patterns and crossbreeding, there are few, if any, isolated and "pure" races left. The genes that determine racial characteristics (e.g., skin color or hair texture) have been spread around the globe and occur in every possible combination. Most racial traits run gradually from one extreme to the other. In skin color, for example, there are no clear or definite points at which "black" skin color stops and "white" (or brown or yellow or red) skin color begins. Many people fit into more than one racial category or none at all. This ambiguity makes it impossible to establish racial categories that are nonarbitrary, and the attempt to do so has been abandoned by the huge majority of scientists.

Even though race is not regarded as important biologically, it is still an important social concept; it is seen as a significant way of differentiating among people. Race, along with gender, is one of the first things people note about one another. In the United States, we tend to see race as a simple, unambiguous matter of skin color alone and to judge everyone as belonging to one and only one group. People are seen as either black, red, brown, yellow, or white, and the realities of multiple ancestry and ambiguous classification are ignored.

Objectively, skin color is derived from melanin, a pigment that everyone, except albinos, has. The amount of melanin in the skin is thought to relate to climate and, specifically, to the amount of sunlight characteristic of a given ecology. In areas with intense sunlight (i.e., at or near the equator), melanin acts as a screen and protects the skin against the ultraviolet (UV) rays of the sun which cause sunburn and, more significantly, skin cancer. Thus, higher levels of melanin and darker skin colors are found in peoples who are adapted to equatorial ecologies.

In peoples who are adapted to areas with less sunlight (i.e., farther away from the equator), the amount of melanin is lower and skin color is therefore lighter. The lower concentration of melanin, or lighter skin color, is also an adaptation to a particular ecology. It maximizes the synthesis of vitamin D, which is important for the absorption of calcium and protection against disorders such as rickets. Thus, the skin color of any group (the amount of melanin) is an adaptation to climate and represents a balance between the need for vitamin D and the need for melanin to protect against the UV rays of the sun. (See Harris, 1988, pp. 98–114.)

From a scientific point of view, that's all there is to skin color. Our most visible marker of minority group membership is a superficial and relatively unimportant biological trait. In the United States, race is a social, not a biological, reality, and racial minority groups are creations of historical and social, not biological, processes. (See Omi & Winant, 1986; Smedley, 1993.) Who belongs to which racial group is largely a matter of social definitions and traditions, not biological reality.

Membership in ethnic minority groups is even more arbitrary and subjective than membership in racial minority groups. The former are distinguished by stigma that are typically less visible (language, religion, or customs) and more changeable than skin color.

The Role of Gender

Minority groups are not homogeneous. They can be divided along lines of wealth, prestige, and power, region of residence, religion, and any number of other criteria. One important source of variation within minority groups is gender. As a physical and biological trait, gender is like race; it is highly visible and can be a convenient way of judging people. It is common for societies to separate adult work roles by gender and to socialize boys and girls differently in preparation for these adult roles. In hunting-and-gathering societies, for example, boys train for the role of hunter, while girls learn the skills necessary for successful harvesting of vegetables, fruits, and other foodstuffs.

Gender roles and relationships vary across time and societies, but throughout history women have commonly occupied a subordinate status. Human societies are typically stratified on the basis of gender, with men claiming more property, prestige, and power than women. The societies of Western Europe and the United States, like most, have a strong tradition of **patriarchy**, or male dominance. In patriarchal societies, women possess many characteristics (e.g., a pattern of disadvantage based on group membership marked by physical characteristics) of a minority group.

Given these patterns of inequality and visibility, women could be, and in many ways probably should be, treated as a separate minority group. In this text, however, gender has been incorporated into the discussion of each minority group. This approach allows us to see that both the history and the present situation of members of minority groups vary by gender. Often, the bonds of gender are weaker or less controlling than the bonds of ethnicity or race. For example, the modern women's liberation movement has been largely a white, middle-class phenomenon (Ladner, 1971). Although the movement raises issues of concern to all women, the major problem for minority group females is not just sexism but the entire system of racial and ethnic stratification that defines, stigmatizes, and controls the minority group as a whole. Thus, male and female minority group members often face different barriers and limitations in their dealings with the larger society.

Also, part of the price of being in a minority group is a kind of enforced silence. History has been and is written from the standpoint of the "winners"—that is, those in power. The experiences of minority group members are less likely to be recorded, and the voices of minority group members who are also female are doubly suppressed. Hence, the experiences of minority women are much less well known and documented than those of the male members of their groups. While this text concentrates on minority groups as single social units, it also strives to recognize and articulate the experiences of women within that broad category.

Key Concepts in Dominant-Minority Relations

This section introduces six concepts that are used to guide our analysis of minority-dominant relations. The discussion here is introductory and is supplemented in later chapters.

Prejudice, Discrimination, Ideological Racism, and Institutional Discrimination

In the pages to come, we often discuss how individuals from different groups interact as well as how the groups themselves relate to one another. Even though the distinction between groups and individuals can be arbitrary and artificial (you can't have groups without individuals and vice versa), we need to distinguish between what is true for individuals (i.e., the psychological level of analysis) and what is true for groups or society as a whole (the sociological level of analysis). Beyond that, we must attempt to trace the connections between the two levels of analysis.

A further distinction on both the individual and group levels can be made. At the individual level, there can be a difference between what people think and feel about other groups and how they actually behave toward members of that group. For example, a person may express negative feelings about another group in private but deal fairly with members of that group in face-to-face interaction. Groups and entire societies may display this same kind of inconsistency. A society may express support for equality in its codes of law while simultaneously treating minority groups in unfair and destructive ways. For example, compare the commitment to equality stated in the Declaration of Independence ("All men are created equal") and the actual treatment of slaves, Anglo-American women, and Native Americans at that time.

At the individual level, we will refer to the "thinking/feeling" dimension as prejudice and the "doing" part as discrimination. At the group level, the terms *ideological racism* and *institutional discrimination* reflect a parallel distinction. Table 1.2 displays these four concepts, organized by level of analysis and dimension.

Prejudice is the tendency of an individual to think about other groups in negative ways and to attach negative emotions to other groups. Individual prejudice has two different aspects: the **cognitive**, or thinking, aspect and the **affective**, or feeling, part. A prejudiced person thinks about other groups in terms of **stereotypes**, generalizations that are thought to apply to members of the group. Examples of familiar American stereotypes include such notions as "Jews are stingy," "blacks are lazy," and "Irish are drunks." At the extreme, the prejudiced person believes that the stereotypes accurately characterize all members of the group. In addition to stereotypes, the prejudiced person experiences negative emotional responses to other groups, including contempt, disgust, and hatred.

People vary in their levels of prejudice, and levels of prejudice in the same person can vary over time. We can say, however, that people are prejudiced to the extent that they use stereotypes in their thinking about other groups and/or experience negative emotions in reaction to other groups.

Table 1.2 Relationships Between Concepts

	Level of Analysis	
Dimensions	**Individuals**	**Group/Societal**
Thinking/feeling	Prejudice	Racism
Doing	Discrimination	Institutional discrimination

The cognitive and affective dimensions of prejudice can be independent of each other. One person might think entirely in stereotypes but have little emotional reaction to other groups. Another person may feel strong aversion toward a group but be unable to articulate a clear mental image of that group.

Discrimination, unlike prejudice, refers to behavior and may be defined as the unequal treatment of a person or persons based on group membership. An example of discrimination would be an employer who does not hire an individual because he or she is African American (or Puerto Rican, Jewish, Chinese, etc.). If the unequal treatment is based on the group membership of the individual, the act is discriminatory.

Just as the cognitive and affective dimensions of prejudice can be independent, discrimination and prejudice do not necessarily occur together. Even highly prejudiced individuals may not act on their negative thoughts or feelings. On the one hand, in social settings regulated by strong egalitarian codes or laws (e.g., restaurants and other public facilities), people who are highly bigoted in their private thoughts and feelings may abide by the codes when they are in their public role.

On the other hand, situations in which prejudice is strongly approved and supported might evoke discrimination in otherwise non-prejudiced individuals. For example, in the American South during the height of segregation, it was usual and customary for white people to treat black people in discriminatory ways. Regardless of a person's actual level of prejudice, there was strong social pressure to conform to the patterns of racial superiority and participate in acts of discrimination.

Both the "thinking/feeling" dimension and the "doing" dimension can be found at the level of groups or entire societies. The former involves **ideological racism**, a belief system that asserts that a particular group is inferior. Whereas individual prejudice is an attitude, a set of feelings and stereotypes, racism is a set of ideas used to legitimize or rationalize the inferior status of a group. An example of a racist ideology would be the elaborate system of beliefs and ideas that attempted to justify slavery in the American South in terms of the innate racial inferiority of blacks.

Unlike individual prejudice, ideological racism is incorporated into the culture of a society, separate from the individuals who may inhabit the society at a specific point in time. It is a system of ideas that can be passed from generation to generation like any other part of the cultural heritage (See & Wilson, 1988, p. 227).

What is the relationship between individual prejudice and ideologies of racism? We explore this question in later chapters, but for now we can make what is probably an obvious point: people socialized into societies with strong racist ideologies are likely to absorb racist ideas and be highly prejudiced. It should not surprise us that a high level of prejudice existed among whites in the antebellum American South or in other highly racist societies such as South Africa. At the same time, we need to remember that ideological racism and individual prejudice are different systems with different causes and different locations in the society. Racism is not a prerequisite for prejudice and prejudice may exist even in the absence of an ideology of racism.

For groups or societies, the "doing" dimension involves **institutional discrimination,** or patterns of unequal treatment based on group membership that are built into the institutions and daily operations of society. The public schools, the criminal justice system, and political and economic institutions can operate in ways that put members of some groups at a disadvantage.

Institutional discrimination can be obvious and overt. During the era of racial segregation in the American South, African Americans were prevented from voting. Elections and elected offices were limited to whites only until well after World War II by practices such as poll taxes and rigged literacy tests. The purpose of this blatant pattern of institutional discrimination was obvious and widely understood by black and white Southerners alike: it existed to disenfranchise the black community and keep it politically powerless.

At other times, institutional discrimination may operate in more hidden and unintended ways. If public schools use "aptitude" tests that are biased in favor of the dominant group, decisions about who does and who does not take college preparatory courses may be made on racist grounds even if everyone involved sincerely believes that objective criteria are being applied in a rational way. If a decision-making process has unequal consequences for dominant and minority groups, institutional discrimination may well be at work.

Note that whereas a particular discriminatory policy may be implemented by individuals, the policy is more appropriately thought of as an aspect of the operation of the institution as a whole. Election officials in the South during segregation or public school administrators today do not have to be personally prejudiced themselves in order to implement these discriminatory policies.

Institutional discrimination is one way in which members of a minority group can be denied access to valued goods and opportunities. That is, institutional discrimination helps to sustain and reinforce the unequal positions of racial and ethnic groups in the stratification system.

How are these four concepts related? A major thesis of this text is that *both racist ideologies and institutional discrimination are created in order to sustain the respective positions of dominant and minority groups in the stratification system.* The relative advantage of the dominant group is maintained from day to day by widespread institutional discrimination. Members of the dominant group who are socialized into communities with strong racist ideologies and a great deal of institutional discrimination are likely to acquire high levels of personal prejudice and to routinely practice acts of discrimination. The respective positions of dominant and minority groups are preserved over time through the mutually reinforcing patterns of prejudice, racism, and discrimination at both the individual and institutional levels.

Assimilation Versus Pluralism

Throughout much of this text, we are concerned with assimilation and pluralism: two possible relationships between groups and two different pathways of development for group relations in society. **Assimilation**, on the one hand, is a process in which formerly distinct and separate groups merge and become one. When a society undergoes assimilation, differences between groups decrease. **Pluralism**, on the other hand, exists when groups maintain their individual identities. In a pluralistic society, groups are separate and their cultural and social differences persist over time.

In some ways, assimilation and pluralism are contrary processes, but they are not mutually exclusive. They may occur together in a variety of different combinations within a particular society or group. Some segments of a society may be assimilating, while other segments may be maintaining (or even increasing) their differences. For example, some Native Americans are pluralistic. They live on or near reservations, are strongly connected to their heritage, and speak their native language. Other Native Americans are more assimilated and live in urban areas, where they speak English only (Snipp, 1989). Both assimilation and pluralism are important forces in the everyday lives of Native Americans and most other minority groups.

Of course, groups may pursue goals other than assimilation and pluralism. Minority groups may seek **separatism** or work toward **revolution** (Wirth, 1945). A separatist group goes well beyond pluralism and wants to sever *all* ties (political, cultural, geographic, and so forth) with the larger society. Separatism has been a goal of many Native American tribes and some African-American organizations such as the Nation of Islam (sometimes known as the Black Muslims). A revolutionary minority group wishes to switch places with the dominant group and become the ruling elite. This goal is relatively rare for minority groups in the United States. It is more commonly found in situations such as that in colonial Africa, where one nation conquers and controls another racially or culturally different nation.

The dominant group may also pursue goals other than assimilation and pluralism, including forced migration, genocide, and continued subjugation of the minority group. Native Americans have been the victims of the first of these goals. In the 1830s, all tribes living east of the Mississippi were forced to migrate to new territory in the west. The most infamous example of genocide is the Holocaust of Nazi Germany, during which 6 million Jews were murdered. The dominant group pursues continued subjugation when, as in slavery in the antebellum South, it attempts to maintain the status quo. A dominant group may simultaneously pursue different policies with different minority groups and may, of course, change policies over time.

Assimilation

Assimilation is a general term for a process that can occur in a variety of ways. One form of assimilation is expressed in the metaphor of the **melting pot**, a process in which different groups come together and contribute in roughly equal amounts to a common culture and a new, unique society.

Although the melting pot continues to be a powerful image in American life, it has definite limits. It does not accurately describe the experiences of many minority groups, past and present (Abrahamson, 1980, pp. 152–154). Racial minorities, including African Americans and Native Americans, have been excluded from the "melting" process. In fact, the melting pot has had a distinctly Anglocentric flavor, favoring the white Anglo-Saxon Protestant tradition above all others (Schlesinger, 1992).

Contrary to the myth of the melting pot, assimilation has been a one-sided process that is better described by the terms **Americanization** and **Anglo-conformity**. This kind of assimilation was designed to maintain the predominance of the British-type institutional patterns established during the early years of American society. Under Anglo-conformity there was relatively little sharing of cultural traits, and immigrant and minority groups were expected to abandon their traditions and adapt to Anglo-American culture as fast as possible. Historically, Americanization has been a precondition for access to better jobs, higher education, and other opportunities. Although some groups have been eager to assimilate, even at the expense of losing their heritage, Americanization for other groups generated conflict, anxiety, demoralization, and resentment.

The Process of Assimilation. It is not unusual for sociological theories to reflect and incorporate the climate of opinion in which they were created. Assimilation has been a strong value in American culture (even though racial minority groups have been excluded from the process) and is often seen as natural, inevitable, and desirable. Many theories of assimilation developed by sociologists reflect this view. For example, some earlier theorists argued that since the United States is a political democracy based on fairness and equality and an industrializing economy in which people tend to be judged on ability alone, the petty prejudices of the past would eventually disappear and the primordial dividing lines of race and culture would dissolve. (See Park & Burgess, 1924.)

A distinct step forward in our understanding of assimilation was made by Milton Gordon in his book *Assimilation in American Life* (1964), in which he divided assimilation into a number of subprocesses. The first three of these subprocesses are particularly useful for our examination of American minority groups and will be the focus of our attention.

Gordon called the first stage of assimilation **cultural assimilation**, or **acculturation**. During acculturation, members of the minority group learn the culture of the dominant group. **Culture** encompasses all aspects of the way of life associated with a group of people. It includes language, religious beliefs, customs and rules of etiquette, and the values and ideas people use to organize their lives and interpret their existence. Thus, the process of acculturation might include learning English, adopting new value systems, or altering the spelling of the family name.

During the second stage of assimilation, called **structural assimilation**, or **integration**, the minority group enters the **social structure** of the larger society: the network of social relationships, groups, organizations, stratification systems, communities, and families. The social structure organizes the work of the society and connects individuals to one another and to the larger society.

It is common in sociology to further distinguish between primary and secondary sectors of the social structure. The **primary sector** of the social structure includes relationships that are intimate and personal, such as those in families and groups of friends. Groups in the primary sector are small. The **secondary sector** includes organizations that are more public, task oriented, and impersonal. Organizations in the secondary sector are often very large. Examples include businesses, factories, schools and colleges, and bureaucracies in general.

According to Gordon, integration typically begins in the secondary sector and, after a time, moves into the primary sector. That is, before members of different groups can form friendships with one another (integration in the primary sector), they must first become acquaintances. The initial contact between groups often occurs in public institutions such as schools and workplaces (integration in the secondary sector).

The extent to which a particular minority group is integrated in the secondary sector can be assessed by comparing it with the dominant group on the three dimensions of stratification: income and property, prestige, and power. The greater the equality between the minority and dominant groups, the greater the integration in the secondary sector.

Once a group has entered the institutions and public sectors of the larger society, the other stages of assimilation will follow inevitably, although not necessarily quickly. Integration in the secondary sector will eventually lead to integration in the primary sector. Measures of integration in the primary sector would include the extent to which people had acquaintances, close friends, or neighbors from other groups.

When integration in the primary sector becomes substantial, the basis for Gordon's third stage of assimilation, **marital assimilation**, or intermarriage, is established. People are likely to select spouses from among their primary relationships, and thus, in Gordon's view, primary structural integration typically precedes intermarriage.

Gordon argued that acculturation is virtually a prerequisite for integration. Given the stress on Anglo-conformity, a member of an immigrant or a minority group would not be able to compete for jobs or other opportunities in the secondary sector of the social structure until he or she had learned the dominant group's culture. But Gordon also argued that acculturation is no guarantee of integration. Just because a group has successfully acculturated does not ensure that it will begin the integration phase. Even while insisting on acculturation, the dominant group may exclude the minority group from its institutions and limit the opportunities available to the group. Gordon argued that "acculturation without integration" (or Americanization without equality) is a common situation for many minority groups, especially racial minority groups.

Since the publication of Gordon's work, some 30 years of additional research and thinking have called many of his conclusions into question. In more contemporary writings, the individual subprocesses that he saw as linked in a certain order are often found to occur independently of one another (Yinger, 1985, p. 154). A group may integrate before acculturating or combine the subprocesses in a variety of other ways. Also, many researchers no longer think of the process of assimilation as necessarily linear or one-way (Greeley, 1974). Groups (or segments thereof) may "reverse direction" and, over time, become less assimilated, revive their traditional cultures, relearn the old languages, or revitalize ethnic organizations or associations. More recent work has identified a variety of additional courses that a group might take through the maze of adjustment to American society. One of these is, of course, pluralism.

Pluralism

Sociologists and the public in general have become more interested in pluralism and ethnic diversity in the past few decades. Interest has been stimulated by the fact that the assimilation predicted by so many has not materialized. Perhaps we simply haven't waited long enough, but as the 21st century approaches, the racial minority groups in our society show few signs of disappearing; in fact, many of these groups are questioning the very desirability of assimilation.

A more surprising development is that many of the European ethnic groups—the descendants of European immigrants—have also failed to disappear. In the 1960s, there actually was a revival of ethnicity (an apparent increase in the strength and salience of group ties) among white ethnic groups. Many "unmelted" white ethnic groups remain a formidable and organized force in politics, religion, and other sectors of American life.

An additional reason for the increased interest in pluralism, no doubt, is the high rate of immigration since the mid-1960s, as reflected in Table 1.1. The focus on pluralism, in part, reflects this everyday reality of increased social and cultural diversity and perceived threats to unity and Americanization (assimilation).

Finally, interest in pluralism and ethnicity in general has been stimulated by developments around the globe. Several nation-states have recently disintegrated into smaller units based on language, culture, race, and ethnicity. Recent events in the former U.S.S.R., the former Yugoslavia, Rwanda, Quebec, and the state of Chiapas, Mexico (just to mention a few), have provided dramatic, often tragic, evidence of the persistence of ethnic identities and enmities through decades or even centuries of submergence and suppression in larger national units.

Pluralism has become more prominent because domestic cultural diversity has increased and because ethnic groups, both in the United States and elsewhere, have persisted as consequential forces in modern industrialized society. In contemporary debates, discussions of diversity and pluralism are often phrased in the language of **multiculturalism,** an umbrella term for a variety of programs and ideas that stress mutual respect for all groups and for the multiple heritages that shaped and built the United States. Some aspects of multiculturalism are controversial and have evoked strong opposition. In many ways, however, the current debates over diversity merely echo what has been a continuing, decades-long argument about the character of American society.

Types of Pluralism. We can distinguish among various types of pluralism by using some of the concepts introduced in our discussion of assimilation. **Full** or **cultural pluralism** exists when groups have neither acculturated nor integrated. In this situation, the differences between groups are at a maximum. They might speak different languages, practice different religions, have different value systems, and belong to different networks of social relations, groups, and organizations. The groups are part of the same society and might even live in adjacent areas but, in some ways, they live in different worlds. Many Native American tribes are fully pluralistic, maintaining their traditional language and culture and living on isolated reservations. The Amish, also known as the Pennsylvania Dutch, are another example of a fully pluralistic group. This religious community is committed to a traditional way of life organized around farming. (See Hostetler, 1980; Kephart & Zellner, 1994.)

A second type of pluralism exists when a group has acculturated but has not integrated (i.e., the group has adopted the Anglo-American culture but does not have full and equal access to the institutions of the larger society). In this situation, called **structural pluralism**, cultural differences are minimal, yet the groups occupy different locations in the social structure. The groups might speak with the same accent, pursue the same goals, and subscribe to the same values; however, they would also maintain separate organizational lives that include different churches, clubs, schools, and neighborhoods. Under structural pluralism, the various groups practice a common culture but do so in different social locations and with minimal interaction across group boundaries.

A third type of pluralism reverses the order of Gordon's first two phases: integration without acculturation. This situation is exemplified by a group that has had some material success (measured by wealth or income, for example) but has not Americanized (learned much English or adapted American values and norms). Two different situations illustrate this pattern. An **enclave minority** establishes its own neighborhood, and its economic survival generally relies on small businesses owned by members of the group. Some businesses serve the group while others serve the larger society. The Cuban-American community in south Florida (discussed in chapter 7) is an enclave minority (Portes & Bach, 1985). A similar pattern of adjustment, the **middleman minority**, also relies on small businesses, but the businesses are more dispersed throughout an area rather than concentrated in a specific locale. Some Chinese-American communities fit this pattern (Portes & Manning, 1986).

The economic success of enclave and middleman minorities is partly due to the strong ties of cooperation and mutual aid within their groups. The ties are based, in turn, on cultural bonds that would weaken if assimilation took place. Therefore, the success of these groups is due to the fact that they have *not* Americanized, contrary to the idea that acculturation is a prerequisite to integration (Bonacich & Modell, 1980; Kitano & Daniels, 1988; Portes & Manning, 1986).

The situation of enclave and middleman minorities—integration without acculturation—can be considered either a type of pluralism (emphasizing the absence of acculturation) or a type of assimilation (emphasizing the high level of economic equality). Keep in mind that assimilation and pluralism are not opposites but can occur in a variety of combinations. It is best to think of acculturation, integration, and the other stages of assimilation (or pluralism) as independent processes.

Perspectives on Pluralism. Contrary to popular myths and biased views of our history, the United States has been a multicultural society from the beginning, incorporating traditions and peoples from a variety of European cultures as well as the cultures of Africa and the Western Hemisphere (Parrillo, 1996). Attempts to examine and understand this diversity have created a tradition of pluralist thought that counterpoints the stronger and more voluminous assimilation thread. As long ago as 1915, Horace Kallen argued that people should not have to surrender their culture and traditions in order to become full participants in American society. He rejected the Anglo-conformity of his day and argued that American society could be a federation of diverse groups, a mosaic of harmonious and interdependent cultures and peoples (Kallen, 1915a, 1915b).

Contemporary scholars have also questioned and criticized the assimilationist school of thought and have tried to understand the persistence of ethnicity and white ethnic groups in America. The persistence of racial minority groups, with more visible identifying characteristics and centuries of rejection, exploitation, prejudice, and racism in their past, is less difficult to explain.

Although their analysis varies in many ways, most pluralist writers conclude that ethnic groups persist because of the functions they perform for members. For example, Glazer and Moynihan, in their influential study, *Beyond the Melting Pot* (first published in 1963), found that white ethnic groups retained a vital significance for their members in spite of massive acculturation over the decades. The groups helped to shape the self-image of their members and provided a means of belonging to the larger society. They linked members to one another and provided the basis of organization for political action and for conflict with other groups.

In a 1974 study of ethnicity, Greeley came to similar conclusions. He criticized the assimilationist idea that differences among groups would diminish over time in a simple, straightforward process of homogenization to the Anglo-American norm. He concluded that a person's ethnic identity can vary in strength, salience, and even content from time to time and that ethnic differentiation can occur alongside the process of assimilation.

To illustrate, Greeley introduced the concept of **ethnogenesis,** a process in which new minority groups are formed from combinations of a variety of traditions, including Anglo-American traditions. As one example, he cited the possible emergence of a national Spanish-speaking ethnic group as opposed to the various, largely unconnected Hispanic groups (e.g., Mexican Americans, Puerto Ricans, Cuban Americans, Colombians, and so forth) that exist at present (Greeley, 1974, pp. 295–296). Greeley concluded that "ethnicity is not a residual social force that is slowly and gradually disappearing; it is, rather, a dynamic, flexible social mechanism that can be called into being rather quickly and transformed and transmuted to meet changing situations and circumstances" (1974, p. 301).

Thus, for Greeley and for Glazer and Moynihan, minority group membership is neither fixed, nor constant, nor diminishing in importance. The pressure to assimilate can be resisted and may actually create more, rather than less, diversity. The salience and meaning of a person's group membership are, at least in part, variable and dependent on situational factors.

What social forces might cause groups to become more cohesive? In what kinds of situations might people come to identify more strongly with their ancestral groups? In his book *The Ethnic Myth* (1981), Steinberg contends that increasing ethnic diversity and strength of group identification may be a result of group conflict over valued goods and services, a way of defending privilege and position. He argues that the ethnic revival of the 1960s resulted from the fear of white ethnics that they were losing their position or status to other groups. White ethnic groups became more interested in their heritage essentially as a defensive reaction to the perceived advances of African Americans and other racial minorities. White ethnics organized around their common heritage to strengthen their solidarity and protect their control of resources.

Although some of their conclusions differ, Glazer and Moynihan, Greeley, and Steinberg all find the assimilationist point of view inadequate. Ethnic groups play important roles in intergroup conflicts and can remain viable and important social entities, even though they may change form and function as the surrounding society changes. New groupings may appear even as old groups decline in importance. In the current era of multiculturalism, ethnicity is frequently celebrated and people are encouraged to know and express their heritage. Pluralism is seen as sophisticated and progressive because it seems to be associated with a higher tolerance for diversity and respect for all peoples and ways of life. Steinberg, in particular, reminds us that ethnicity and strong identification with one's group can be negative as well as positive. It may be the result of conflict and a disguise for denying opportunity to other groups.

Conclusion

This first chapter has introduced many of the terms, concepts, and themes that form the core of this text. We can begin our exploration and conclude this chapter by making several points.

First, minority group status has much more to do with power, prestige, and the distribution of resources than with simple numbers. Inequality and differentials in status are also linked to prejudice, racism, and both individual and institutional discrimination. To discuss minority groups, we must be prepared to discuss the way society does business, makes decisions, and distributes income, jobs, and opportunity.

A second area of concern in the following pages is the question of how our society should develop. Assimilation and pluralism, with all of their variations, define two broad directions. Each has been extensively examined and discussed by social scientists, by leaders and decisionmakers in U.S. society, and by ordinary people from all groups and all walks of life. I have introduced the concepts of assimilation and pluralism early in this text because I wanted to point out the diversity of the goals and agendas found among American minority groups. It has simply been assumed too often in the past that all minority groups desired to assimilate. By recognizing the variety of goals pursued by minority groups, we can begin to sense the multiplicity of alternatives for the future.

Our society faces enormous unsolved problems of racial and ethnic inequality. In addressing these issues today, we have the opportunity to avoid the mistakes and cruelties of the past. A candid and complete understanding of the realities of America's often dismal and racist past is necessary for an intelligent consideration of the choices before us now.

MAIN POINTS

- The United States is becoming more diverse even as many historic grievances of minority groups remain unresolved. Debates about what it means to be an American are common and intense.

- A minority group has five defining characteristics, primary among which are inequality and visibility.

- Stratification systems have three dimensions, and the nature of inequality in a society varies by its level of development. Minority group status is correlated with stratification, and the struggle for prestige, power, and the control of resources is central to every minority-dominant relationship.

- Race is a widely used criterion to identify minority group members. Although largely abandoned as a biological concept, race retains a powerful influence on the way we classify and think about one another.

- Six central concepts in the analysis of dominant-minority relations are prejudice, discrimination, ideological racism, institutional discrimination, assimilation, and pluralism. Historically, assimilation (Anglo-conformity) has been dominant in the United States. In recent decades, there has been increased interest in pluralism, stimulated by both international and domestic events.

FOR FURTHER READING

Alba, Richard. 1990. *Ethnic Identity: The Transformation of White America*. New Haven, CT: Yale University Press.

Baca Zinn, Maxine, & Dill, Bonnie Thorton. 1994. *Women of Color in U.S. Society*. Philadelphia: Temple University Press.

Feagin, Joe R., & Feagin, Clarice B. 1978. *Discrimination American Style: Institutional Racism and Sexism*. Englewood Cliffs, NJ: Prentice Hall.

Gordon, Milton. 1964. *Assimilation in American Life*. New York: Oxford University Press.

Montagu, Ashley. 1972. *Statement on Race*. 3rd ed. New York: Oxford University Press.

Portes, Alejandro, & Bach, Robert L. 1985. *Latin Journey: Cuban and Mexican Immigrants in the United States*. Berkeley: University of California Press.

Schlesinger, Arthur. 1992. *The Disuniting of America: Reflections on a Multicultural Society*. New York: Norton.

Prejudice

What causes prejudice? Why do some people discriminate? How widespread is prejudice in the United States? Is it declining? Is it possible to eliminate prejudice?

The concepts of prejudice and discrimination were introduced in chapter 1 in combination with the concepts of ideological racism and institutional discrimination (see Table 1.2). The latter, more sociological, pair of concepts is our primary concern in the chapters to come. Chapter 2 is devoted to the individual level of analysis and the more psychological concepts of prejudice and discrimination. Remember that there is no sharp dividing line between the individual and sociological levels of analysis, and as you will see, many of the theories discussed in this chapter incorporate "sociological" concepts. Prejudice is complex and multifaceted and a broad perspective is required to explain it fully.

This chapter examines the nature of individual prejudice and many of the theories that have been proposed to explain its causes. We also observe how U.S. prejudice has changed over the past several decades and consider the factors that may be responsible for those changes. Let's begin the analysis by sharpening the distinction between prejudice and discrimination.

Recall from chapter 1 that prejudice, on the one hand, is the tendency of individuals to think and feel in negative ways about members of other groups. Discrimination, on the other hand, is a behavior in which someone or some group receives unequal treatment because of group membership. While discrimination and prejudice are obviously related, they are two different things and do not always occur together or even necessarily have a causal relationship with each other.

Table 2.1   Robert Merton's Typology of the Relationships Between Individual Prejudice and Discrimination

	Does Not Discriminate	Does Discriminate
Unprejudiced	Unprejudiced nondiscriminator (All-Weather Liberal)	Unprejudiced discriminator (Fair-Weather Liberal)
Prejudiced	Prejudiced nondiscriminator (Timid Bigot)	Prejudiced discriminator (All-Weather Bigot)

Source: Merton, 1968.

Table 2.1 presents four possible relationships between prejudice and discrimination. In two cases, the relationship is consistent. The "All-Weather Liberal" is not prejudiced and does not discriminate, while the "All-Weather Bigot" is prejudiced and does discriminate. The other two combinations illustrate the independence between these two concepts: the "Fair-Weather Liberal" discriminates without prejudice, while the "Timid Bigot" is prejudiced but does not discriminate. We have several occasions in this chapter to further explore the relationship between these two concepts.

Prejudice and Stereotypes

The prejudiced person assumes that members of certain groups have certain personality characteristics ("Asians are clannish") or behavioral tendencies ("Italians are hot-tempered"). These generalizations or assumptions are **stereotypes,** one of the basic components of individual prejudice.

What makes stereotypes different from other generalizations is that they are exaggerated, overly simplistic, and resistant to disproof (Pettigrew, 1980, p. 822). Stereotypes are overgeneralizations that stress a few traits that are assumed to apply to *all* members of the group. Highly prejudiced people will maintain their stereotypes even in the face of massive evidence that their views are wrong.

Once a stereotype is learned, it can shape perceptions to the point that individuals pay attention only to information that confirms their stereotypes. **Selective perception,** the tendency to see only what one expects to see, can reinforce and strengthen stereotypes to the point that the highly prejudiced individual screens out any information that is not consistent with his or her biases.

Categorization

For the prejudiced person, stereotyping is a way of categorizing people. We all continually identify and "sort" the impressions we receive from our environment into categories. We judge people as well as things and sometimes we categorize others based on a quick appraisal of their most obvious characteristics.

When classifying people, why do we tend to see certain traits (gender, skin color) and not others? One answer is that our attention is drawn to the characteristics that have come to identify the dividing lines between groups. Racial characteristics such as skin color aren't necessarily any more obvious than other traits (like hair length or size of nose), but they are one of the first and, for many, most important pieces of information we recognize about one another. Our perceptions and impressions in the present are conditioned by the dividing lines that reflect group relations in the past. Our "knowledge" that skin color can be used to judge others, and our sensitivity to this characteristic, reflects our socialization into a race-conscious society with a long history of racial stratification.

Attribution Theory and Stereotypes

Attribution theory tries to explain how we perceive and make judgments about one another. We don't just observe the people around us; we try to analyze and understand why they behave as they do. Sometimes we explain behavior by attributing actions to personality traits or internal dispositions ("She didn't offer to pay for lunch because she's stingy"). At other times, we may see behavior as a response to a particular situation or to external factors ("He was rude because of all the pressure he's under at work") (Ashmore & del Boca, 1976).

Stereotypes provide one way of accounting for the behavior of others. People typically give members of their own group the benefit of the doubt and attribute positive actions to internal factors ("She did it because she has a good heart") and negative actions to external or situational factors ("He only did it because he had to under the circumstances") (Pettigrew, 1980, p. 824). This pattern of attribution allows us to maintain positive thoughts about people with whom we identify, even when their behavior is offensive to us.

Members of other groups are not accorded the benefit of the doubt. Negative or threatening behaviors are seen as motivated by internal or personality characteristics ("That's just the way they are"), and positive behaviors are seen as exceptional or caused by situational factors ("He's polite, not like all the others"). This tendency helps maintain stereotypical thinking even in the face of contrary evidence (Pettigrew, 1980, p. 824). Any challenge to the stereotype is dismissed as exceptional or situational, and the highly prejudiced individual sees only the behaviors and characteristics that confirm his or her stereotypes as valid representations of the character of members of other groups.

Types of Stereotypes

Stereotypes arise from the process of sorting and absorbing information gleaned from the environment, and even the most simplistic or derogatory stereotype can reflect, to a certain extent, the actual situation of the group (Pettigrew, 1980, p. 823). For example, in situations in which the dominant group is attempting to control and exploit the minority group, as in slavery in the antebellum South, it is common to find stereotypes alleging that the minority group is inferior.

A different kind of stereotype is found in situations where the minority group has had some success in the struggle for control of resources. In such cases the attribution of inferiority doesn't fit and, instead, the success of the group is seen in negative terms: they are *too* smart, *too* materialistic, *too* crafty, or *too* ambitious. This stereotype has been attached to Eastern European Jews who immigrated between the 1880s and 1920s and to several different groups of Asian Americans.

Thus, stereotypes don't "just happen." They characterize minority groups in ways consistent with dominant group policies of exclusion, control, or discrimination. Keep in mind, however, that we are on the psychological level of analysis. On this level, stereotypes and prejudice can exist apart from any need to rationalize or justify dominant group advantage. Research shows that some individuals will readily stereotype groups about which they have little or no information (e.g., Turks, Eskimos). One study showed that people will express prejudice toward groups that don't even exist (Hartley, 1946)!

Stereotypes and Emotions

In addition to the cognitive dimension, individual prejudice has an emotional or affective dimension. The distinction between these dimensions is dramatically made by Robert Merton, a prominent American sociologist. Merton analyzed American stereotypical perceptions of Abe Lincoln, Jews, and Japanese. In the following passage, he argues that the three "stereotypes" are identical in content but vastly different in emotional shading.

> The very same behavior undergoes a complete change of evaluation in its transition from the in-group Abe Lincoln to the out-group Abe Cohen or Abe Kurokawa. Did Lincoln work far into the night? This testifies that he was industrious, resolute, perseverant, and eager to realize his capacities to the full. Do the out-group Jews or Japanese keep these same hours?

This only bears witness to their sweatshop mentality, their ruthless undercutting of American standards, their unfair competitive practices. Is the in-group hero frugal, thrifty, and sparing? Then the out-group villain is stingy, miserly, and penny-pinching. All honor is due to the in-group Abe for his having been smart, shrewd, and intelligent, and, by the same token, all contempt is owing the out-group Abes for their being sharp, cunning, crafty, and too clever by far. (Merton, 1968, p. 482)

The stereotype of all three Abes is identical; what varies is the affect, or the emotional tone reflected in the descriptive terms. Thus, the same stereotype evokes different emotional responses for different groups or in different people.

an explanation

Theories of Prejudice

There have been many attempts to understand individual prejudice, and I've limited this section to the more important and widely cited theories and concepts, organized around the type of explanation each proposes. First, we examine theories that focus on personality dynamics and then move on to theories that link prejudice to culture and situational factors. Finally, we look at some theories linking prejudice to competition between groups. The causes of prejudice identified in each of these perspectives are conceptually independent. They can occur separately or they can combine within the same individual and act to reinforce or negate each other.

Personality-Centered Approaches to Prejudice

Personality-centered theories tend to see prejudice as an indicator of an unhealthy personality. Prejudice helps people with emotional or personality problems to function from day to day.

Projection

One emotional function that prejudice can play is **projection:** seeing in others characteristics or feelings we can't admit we have in ourselves. People who are unable to deal with strong anger or fear or sexual desire may deny these emotions in themselves and attribute them instead to out-groups (Pettigrew, 1980, p. 825). Thus, minority groups can serve as living Rorschach ink blots, taking on the characteristics required by whatever psychodynamic issue is central for the prejudiced individual.

Projection is a psychological process not necessarily related to the objective situation of the individual. People who receive no political or economic benefit from racial or ethnic inequality may still have a strong psychological stake in maintaining the unequal status of minority groups. They may need the minority group for psychological reasons just as surely as plantation owners needed slaves for economic reasons (Levin & Levin, 1982, pp. 140–155).

The Scapegoat Hypothesis

The **scapegoat hypothesis** links prejudice to the individual's need to deal with frustration, the feelings of tension or unhappiness that result from failure to achieve a goal or other negative experiences. The unpleasant sensation of frustration can be relieved by aggression. For example, if your goal of getting to work on time is blocked by a traffic jam, your resultant frustration might be expressed by aggressively pounding your fist on your steering wheel.

How are frustration and aggression related to prejudice? Sometimes the object that caused the frustration is not available for aggression. For example, what if you lost a job because of an economic recession? How could you vent your aggression on something abstract like the economy? You have to be able to see (feel, smell, etc.) the target before you can attack it. In other situations, the source of the frustration might be too powerful to attack. If your boss unexpectedly orders you to work overtime, you might experience frustration but not direct your aggression against this powerful individual.

In circumstances where the cause of the frustration is unavailable, a process called displacement might occur, in which the frustrated individual finds a substitute target—a "scapegoat"—against which to vent hostility and aggression. Thus, instead of yelling at your boss, you might "take it out" on your spouse.

It is not uncommon, and is actually sensible in a way, to choose substitute targets that are weak and unable to respond to attacks. For members of the dominant group, minority groups are by definition less powerful and can make tempting scapegoats. Displacement to other groups is fundamentally irrational and is usually accompanied by an increase in individual prejudice. The role of prejudice in this process is rationalization: it makes the displacer seem more reasonable (at least to himself or herself).

There is a long tradition of research on this hypothesis, and the process of scapegoating has been documented many times. In a typical experiment, subjects are purposely frustrated and then offered the possibility of expressing their aggression against a minority group. Subsequently, prejudice often increases, indicating that hostility has been displaced onto the substitute target. Miller and Bugleski (1948) required 31 white men in an isolated job-training center to miss a recreational activity in order to complete a series of tedious and lengthy exams. Earlier, the men had completed a survey measuring their attitudes toward Mexicans and Japanese. After finishing the exams, the men were surveyed again and, as expected, the level of prejudice was significantly higher than before.

One implication of this theory is that the level of prejudice in a society will reflect the level of individual frustration. We would expect that "bad times" (e.g., periods of high inflation or unemployment) would cause an increase in displaced aggression and expressions of prejudice. Remember, however, that the scapegoat hypothesis is a psychological theory and individuals may displace aggressions independently of their objective condition.

The Authoritarian Personality

One of the most important contributions to the study of prejudice was made by a team of researchers led by Professor T. W. Adorno and was presented in *The Authoritarian Personality,* published in 1950. Adorno and his colleagues believed that prejudice is a component of an authoritarian personality syndrome that is developed in certain early childhood relationships with parents. Authoritarian personality tendencies develop in family situations in which discipline is harsh and parents are uncommunicative, emotionally cold, stern, and distant. The child raised in such an environment comes to see the parents, and eventually all authority figures, as dangerous and fearsome. The child is hostile and angry toward parents, but the parents are too powerful to permit expression of these feelings directly. As an adult, the individual deals with these negative emotions by displacing the hostility, more or less permanently, onto out-groups. Projection also occurs, and the out-groups are seen as hostile and threatening.

This release of negative emotions allows the individual to fabricate conventional attitudes and emotions toward parental figures, feelings that are later generalized to all authority figures. The authoritarian individual is able to express "normal" family attitudes, but *only* by splitting off the negative emotions and attaching them to out-groups. For the highly authoritarian personality, prejudice is thus a fundamental and necessary personality component. Without prejudice, the authoritarian would have to confront his or her actual feelings about parents and family.

The authoritarian personality incorporates other components besides prejudice. Another key element is *pseudopatriotism,* or support of right-wing, extremely conservative political ideas. The patriotism of the authoritarian is pseudo because it is extreme, unthinking, and highly emotional. It is a generalization of the conventionalized attachment to parental figures developed in early childhood and may be exemplified in such superpatriotic slogans as "My Country, Right or Wrong."

Limitations of Personality-Centered Approaches to Prejudice

After decades of research, it is now clear that the scapegoat hypothesis is overly simplistic. Aggression is not an automatic response to frustration, and the probability of displacement varies widely for different types of individuals. Many other variables can shape the scapegoating process. Personal threats such as divorce or illness are more likely to lead to scapegoating than communal threats such as floods or tornadoes (Feshbeck & Singer, 1957). People who are already highly prejudiced are more likely to scapegoat against minority groups (Berkowitz, 1978). Also, people are more likely to scapegoat against groups they already dislike (Berkowitz & Green, 1962).

As for the theory of the authoritarian personality, several flaws in the methodology of Adorno's group have been identified. For example, the researchers relied heavily on questionnaires (paper-and-pencil tests) to measure authoritarianism. Most of the items on the scales they used were phrased so that agreement indicated a higher level of authoritarianism. This format can cause "response set," or a tendency to agree with or endorse positive statements regardless of actual feelings. To some extent, scores on the surveys used by the researchers reflected this tendency to agree rather than authoritarianism (Bass, 1955; Jackman, 1973).

Another common criticism is that the theory measures only right-wing authoritarianism. People who are politically conservative or extremely patriotic score higher on the authoritarianism scale than extreme liberals or people who are not patriotic. This is a problem because liberals or left-wingers can also be dogmatic and close-minded in their thinking. The theory may measure only half of the full syndrome (Shils, 1954).

It is worth noting, in this regard, that Adorno and most of his associates were Austrian Jews who fled the rise of Nazism in the 1930s. In fact, the rise of Italian and German fascism stimulated the research project. Adorno and his colleagues were affected in their thinking by the racism and superpatriotism of the extreme right-wing Nazi ideology (Christie & Yahoda, 1954). Thus, this theory, like all theories, must be seen in the context of its time and the life experiences of the theorists.

Perhaps the most serious limitation of personality-centered theories of prejudice is that they do not take sufficient account of the cultural and social forces that operate on the individual. Socialization experiences, social class standing, job security, and level of education all affect scapegoating and authoritarian tendencies. These processes must be understood in the social settings in which they occur, not as disembodied psychological processes that stand alone (Simpson & Yinger, 1985, p. 74).

On the other hand, these theories do help explain some forms of prejudice. From the perspective of these theories, prejudice is "irrational." That is, prejudice is caused by personality forces and emotional conditions that are internal to the individual, not by actual contact with minority groups. Thus, these theories give us one way to understand how some people can be highly prejudiced even when they have not had any personal experience with members of the minority group.

Culture-Based Approaches to Prejudice

Unlike personality-based theories, which link prejudice to personal maladjustment, culture-based approaches see prejudice as the predictable result of growing up in a society that incorporates racist ideologies and systems of exploitation based on group membership.

The Vicious Cycle

The relationships among culture, racial or ethnic inequality, and individual prejudice were explored by Gunnar Myrdal in his 1944 analysis of American race relations, called *An American Dilemma*. Myrdal proposed that these forces can powerfully reinforce each other over time. The process he described is a **vicious cycle**: a certain condition is assumed to be true, and forces are then set in motion to create and perpetuate the original condition.

Figure 2.1 displays the vicious cycle as applied to prejudice and race relations. The dominant group uses its power to force the minority group into an (1) inferior status (e.g., slavery). Partly to motivate the construction of racial stratification and partly to justify its existence, (2) individual prejudice and ideologies of racism are invented and

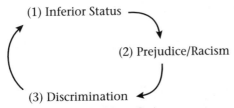

Figure 2.1 The Vicious Cycle

Source: Based on Myrdal, 1944, pp. 25–28.

accepted by the dominant group. Prejudice is reinforced by the everyday observation of the inferior status of the minority group. The fact that the minority group is in fact impoverished, enslaved, or otherwise exploited confirms and strengthens the attribution of inferiority. The belief in inferiority motivates (3) further discrimination and unequal treatment, which reinforce the inferior status, which validates the prejudice and racism, which justify further discrimination, and so on. Over not too many generations, a stable, internally reinforced system of racial inferiority becomes an integral, unremarkable, and (at least for the dominant group) accepted part of everyday life.

Culture is conservative, and the cultural legacies of prejudice and racism can long outlive the situations that created them. Thus, for future generations, prejudice will be sustained and reproduced by socialization into a racist culture. Contrary to authoritarian personality theory, this culture-based approach sees prejudice as an indication that a person is "normal" and well adjusted in an environment that happens to be racist.

Furthermore, in a society with strong racist traditions, prejudice can be a way of expressing social solidarity and connectedness with others. When family, peers, and neighbors all subscribe to prejudice, the pressure to conform can be strong, and people may join in the rejection of out-groups as a way of maintaining their standing in their in-groups.

We learn prejudice in the same way and for the same reasons that we learn any other aspect of our culture. Prejudice and racism come to us through our cultural heritage as a standardized package of attitudes, stereotypes, emotions, and knowledge. We learn which groups are "good" and which are "bad" in the same way (and from the same people) we learn table manners and religious beliefs (Pettigrew, 1971, p. 137; Simpson & Yinger, 1985, pp. 107–108).

The Development of Prejudice in Children

Evidence that prejudice is an outcome of socialization in racist environments can be found in research on the development of intergroup attitudes in children. Children become aware of group differences (e.g., black vs. white) at an early age. By ages 3 to 5, children can accurately classify people on the basis of skin color and other cues (Katz, 1976a, p. 126). Once these categories are mentally established, the child begins to learn the "proper" attitudes and stereotypes to associate with the various groups.

Prejudice may be taught in subtle ways. Parents who do not make overtly racist statements may still shape prejudice in their children by, for example, establishing rules about which playmates are permissible or by limiting other interracial interactions. Children may be permitted to overhear conversations in which prejudice is expressed or minority groups are referred to in unfavorable terms. Subsequently, the children will tend to imitate the attitudes and actions of their parents. It is often said that the racial attitudes are "caught and not taught" (Ashmore & del Boca, 1976).

Parents and other adult caregivers control the socialization process, at least in the early years. Parents control valuable resources (food, shelter, praise), and children are motivated to seek their approval and conform to their expectations. Thus, there are strong pressures on the child to learn and internalize the prejudices of the older generation, even when the instruction is subtle and indirect.

Social Distance

Research on the concept of **social distance,** or the degree of intimacy to which an individual is willing to admit persons of other groups, provides further evidence that prejudice has a cultural component. Social distance is similar to but not quite the same as prejudice. It is usually measured by a social distance scale invented by Emory Bogardus in 1926, which incorporates a total of seven degrees of social distance ranging from close kinship by marriage to exclusion from the country.

The most noteworthy result of social distance research is the demonstration that Americans rank other groups in similar ways across time and space. Table 2.2 presents the results of five administrations of the scale to large samples of Americans from 1926 to 1977 (the latest year for which national data are available). The earliest scores show that the sample expressed the least social distance against the English, the average score of 1.06 indicating virtually no sense of distance. The greatest distance was expressed against "Indians (of India)."

Inspect the results and note that, while the scores generally decrease from decade to decade (perhaps indicating a decline in prejudice over the years), the *rankings* of the various groups are generally the same in 1977 as they were in 1926. Considering the changes our society experienced in this half century (the Great Depression, wars, domestic strife, etc.), this continuity in rankings is remarkable.

Second, note the nature of the ranking. Groups with origins in Northern and Western Europe (English, Scots) are ranked highest, followed by groups from Southern and Eastern Europe (Italians, Poles), with racial minorities toward the bottom. These ethnic/racial preferences of the dominant group reflect the degree of exploitation and prejudice directed at each group over the course of U.S. history.

Table 2.2 Results of American Social Distance Rankings of Other Groups 1926–1977

1926	1946	1956	1966	1977
1. English 1.06	1. Americans (U.S. whites) 1.04	1. Americans (U.S. whites) 1.08	1. Americans (U.S. whites) 1.07	1. Americans (U.S. whites) 1.25
2. Americans (U.S. whites) 1.10	2. Canadians 1.11	2. Canadians 1.16	2. English 1.14	2. English 1.39
3. Canadians 1.13	3. English 1.13	3. English 1.23	3. Canadians 1.15	3. Canadians 1.42
4. Scots 1.13	4. Irish 1.24	4. French 1.47	4. French 1.36	4. French 1.58
5. Irish 1.30	5. Scots 1.26	5. Irish 1.56	5. Irish 1.40	5. Italians 1.65
6. French 1.32	6. French 1.31	6. Swedish 1.57	6. Swedish 1.42	6. Swedish 1.68
7. Germans 1.46	7. Norwegians 1.35	7. Scots 1.60	7. Norwegians 1.50	7. Irish 1.69
8. Swedish 1.54	8. Hollanders 1.37	8. Germans 1.61	8. Italians 1.51	8. Hollanders 1.82
9. Hollanders 1.56	9. Swedish 1.40	9. Hollanders 1.63	9. Scots 1.53	9. Scots 1.83
10. Norwegians 1.59	10. Germans 1.59	10. Norwegians 1.66	10. Germans 1.54	10. Indians (American) 1.84
11. Spanish 1.72	11. Finns 1.63	11. Finns 1.80	11. Hollanders 1.54	11. Germans 1.87
12. Finns 1.83	12. Czechs 1.76	12. Italians 1.89	12. Finns 1.67	12. Norwegians 1.93
13. Russians 1.88	13. Russians 1.83	13. Poles 2.07	13. Greeks 1.82	13. Spanish 1.98
14. Italians 1.94	14. Poles 1.84	14. Spanish 2.08	14. Spanish 1.93	14. Finns 2.00
15. Poles 2.01	15. Spanish 1.94	15. Greeks 2.09	15. Jews 1.97	15. Jews 2.01
16. Armenians 2.06	16. Italians 2.28	16. Jews 2.15	16. Poles 1.98	16. Greeks 2.02
17. Czechs 2.08	17. Armenians 2.29	17. Czechs 2.22	17. Czechs 2.02	17. Negroes 2.03
18. Indians (American) 2.38	18. Greeks 2.29	18. Armenians 2.33	18. Indians (American) 2.12	18. Poles 2.11
	19. Jews 2.32	19. Japanese Americans 2.34		

	1926		1946		1956		1966		1977	
	19. Jews	2.39					19. Japanese Americans	2.14	19. Mexican Americans	2.17
	20. Greeks	2.47	20. Indians (American)	2.45	20. Indians (American)	2.35	20. Armenians	2.18	20. Japanese Americans	2.18
	21. Mexicans	2.69	21. Chinese	2.50	21. Filipinos	2.46	21. Filipinos	2.31	21. Armenians	2.20
	22. Mexican Americans	—	22. Mexican Americans	2.52	22. Mexican Americans	2.51	22. Chinese	2.34	22. Czechs	2.23
	23. Japanese	2.80	23. Filipinos	2.76	23. Turks	2.52	23. Mexican Americans	2.37	23. Chinese	2.29
	24. Japanese Americans	—	24. Mexicans	2.89	24. Russians	2.56	24. Russians	2.38	24. Filipinos	2.31
	25. Filipinos	3.00	25. Turks	2.89	25. Chinese	2.68	25. Japanese	2.41	25. Japanese	2.38
	26. Negroes*	3.28	26. Japanese Americans	2.90	26. Japanese	2.70	26. Turks	2.48	26. Mexicans	2.40
	27. Turks	3.30	27. Koreans	3.05	27. Negroes	2.74	27. Koreans	2.51	27. Indians (of India)	2.55
	28. Chinese	3.36	28. Indians (of India)	3.43	28. Mexicans	2.79	28. Mexicans	2.56	28. Turks	2.55
	29. Koreans	3.60	29. Negroes	3.60	29. Indians (of India)	2.80	29. Negroes	2.56	29. Russians	2.57
	30. Indians (of India)	3.91	30. Japanese	3.61	30. Koreans	2.83	30. Indians (of India)	2.62	30. Koreans	2.63
Mean		2.14		2.12		2.08		1.92		1.93
Range		2.85		2.57		1.75		1.56		1.38

*The word *Negroes* is used in the original study.

Source: Smith & Dempsey, 1983, p. 588.

Evidence from social distance scale research is limited. The respondents—college students from a variety of campuses—were not representative samples of the population, and the differences in scores from group to group are sometimes very small. Still, the stability of the patterns strongly suggests that Americans view other groups through the same culturally shaped lens. A sense of social distance—a perception of some groups as "higher" or "better" than others—is part of the cultural package of intergroup prejudices we acquire from socialization into American culture. The social distance patterns illustrate the power of culture to shape individual perceptions and preferences and attest to the fundamentally racist nature of American culture.

Situational Influences

As a final point in our consideration of the cultural nature of prejudice, we should note the importance of the social situations in which attitudes are expressed and behavior occurs. We have noted previously the difference between what people *say* and what they *do*. Even intense prejudice may not translate into discriminatory behavior, and discrimination is not always accompanied by prejudice (see Table 2.1). One demonstration of this difference was provided by sociologist Robert LaPiere. In the 1930s, he escorted a Chinese couple on a tour of the United States. Even though anti-Chinese prejudice was quite high at the time, LaPiere and his companions dined in restaurants and stayed in hotels during the entire trip and experienced discrimination only once.

Six months later, LaPiere wrote to every establishment which the group had patronized and inquired about reservations. He indicated that some of his party were Chinese and asked if that would be a problem. Of those establishments that replied (about half), 92% said they would not serve Chinese and would be unable to accommodate the party.

Why the difference? Face-to-face, LaPiere's party experienced virtually no discrimination but, in the more impersonal mode of written correspondence, a great deal of prejudice was expressed. Although not a particularly sophisticated method of data gathering (for example, there was no way to tell if the correspondents were the same persons LaPiere and his party had dealt with in person), this episode exemplifies the difference between "saying" and "doing" and the importance of taking the situation into account.

In highly prejudiced communities or groups, the pressure to conform may cause relatively unprejudiced individuals to discriminate. If an ethnic or a racist joke is told in a group of friends or relatives, even a completely unprejudiced member of the group might smile or giggle to avoid offending the person who told the joke. Situations in which there are strong norms of equal and fair treatment, however, may stifle the tendency of even the most bigoted individual to discriminate. For example, if a community has vigorously enforced antidiscrimination laws, even the most prejudiced merchant might refrain from treating minority group customers unequally. Highly prejudiced individuals who do not discriminate may simply be responding to the need to "do business" (or, at least, avoid penalties) in an environment in which discrimination is not tolerated.

Limitations of Culture-Based Approaches

Stressing only the cultural causes of prejudice may overstate the extent to which everyone has a similar level of prejudice. No two people have the same socialization experiences or develop exactly the same prejudices (or any other attitude, for that matter). Differences in family structure, parenting style, school experiences, attitudes of peers, and a host of other factors influence the individual's personality development.

Furthermore, socialization is not a passive process; we are not neutral recipients of a culture that is simply forced upon us. Our individuality, intelligence, and curiosity affect our socialization experiences. Even close siblings may have very different experiences and, consequently, different levels of prejudice. Furthermore, we are not helpless creatures of our childhoods. People raised in extremely prejudicial settings may moderate their attitudes later in life (as may those raised in nonprejudicial settings).

The development of prejudice is further complicated by the fact that we also learn egalitarian norms and values as we are socialized. Americans learn norms of fairness and justice along with norms that condone unequal treatment based on group membership. Typically, people develop more than one attitude about other groups, and these multiple attitudes aren't set in concrete. They can change from time to time and from place to place, depending on the situation an individual is in and a variety of other variables.

Power/Conflict Theories

Personality-centered and culture-based theories can tell us why prejudice varies from person to person and from time to time within the same person and how prejudice is passed on from generation to generation. What they don't tell us is why and how prejudice begins in the first place. To deal with the origins of prejudice, we turn to power/conflict theories. These theories stress the idea that prejudice flows from intergroup competition and serves as a rationalization for exploitation and racial and ethnic stratification. We introduce several power/conflict theories here, and this perspective is prominent in the chapters to come.

Marxist Analysis

One of the tenets of Marxist theory is that the elites who control the means of production in a society also control the ideas and intellectual activity of the society. Ideologies and belief systems are shaped to support the dominance of the elites, and they change when new elites come into control: "The ruling ideas of each age have been the ideas of its ruling class" (Marx & Engels, 1967, p. 102).

Elite classes whose high status requires the subordination or exploitation of a minority group will develop and institutionalize ideologies to justify or "explain" the arrangement. For example, antiblack prejudice was used by slave owners in the American South to attempt to control perceptions and justify the exploitation of the slaves. The elites can use any ideology, including religion, to attempt to control the thought processes of exploited groups and delude them into accepting their situation in life. In slavery, those aspects of Christianity that stress meekness and humility and promise rewards (but only in heaven) were used to attempt to "brainwash" the slaves into obedience and to focus their attention on the next life, not on the misery and injustice of this life. The history of U.S. society provides many other instances in which prejudice was used to help sustain the control of elite classes. We consider many of these cases later in this text.

Split Labor Market Theory

Another theory agrees with the Marxist idea that prejudice and racist ideologies serve the interest of a specific class, but it identifies a different beneficiary. In **split labor market theory**, there are three actors in the economic sector of an industrial society. First are the elites, the capitalists who own the means of production. The other two groups are segments of the working class. The labor market is divided (or split) into higher priced labor and cheaper labor. It is in the economic self-interest of the capitalist class to use cheaper labor whenever possible. Recent immigrants and minority groups have often filled the role of cheaper labor.

Higher priced labor (usually consisting of members of the dominant group) will attempt to exclude cheaper labor from the marketplace when it can. Such efforts include barring minority groups from labor unions, violent attacks on minority communities, support for discriminatory laws, and efforts to exclude groups from the United States entirely. Prejudice is used by higher priced labor to arouse and mobilize opposition to the cheaper labor pool represented by the minority group. The economic nature of the competition and the economic self-interest of higher priced labor are obscured by appeals to racial or cultural unity against the "threat" represented by the minority group. From the perspective of split labor market theory, the major beneficiary of prejudice is not the capitalist class but the more powerful elements of the working class (Bonacich, 1976; Bonacich & Modell, 1980).

Both Marxist and split labor perspectives agree that prejudice begins as a side issue in the struggle to control or expand a group's share of resources. Prejudice is not a matter of childhood experiences, social distance, or personal likes and dislikes; prejudice exists because someone or some group gains by it.

Limitations of Power/Conflict Theories

The limits of power/conflict theories mirror those of the other theories we have discussed. Individuals who have no material stake in minority group subordination can still be extremely prejudiced. The sources of prejudice can be found in culture, socialization, family structure, and personality development as well as in politics and economics. Prejudice can have important psychological and social functions independent of group power relationships.

Types of Prejudice

Taken together, the diverse ideas we have considered up to this point illustrate the complexity and multicausal nature of prejudice. It seems no single theory can explain prejudice in all its forms. Furthermore, even if we could explain prejudice, we would still have to account for its link with discrimination. A theory of one will not necessarily explain the other.

We also need to recognize that prejudice exists alongside norms and values that are either neutral or actively antiprejudicial. Racism is at the core of the American value system, but so are the values of equality, fairness, and justice, and these egalitarian beliefs can inhibit the expression of prejudice or reduce its intensity.

What *do* we know so far? We can identify three different types of prejudice on the basis of their primary causes: (1) prejudice caused by personality needs, (2) prejudice learned during socialization into a racist community, and (3) prejudice that arises during intergroup competition. These forms of prejudice differ in characteristics other than their cause. For example, some types are more changeable than others. Personality-based prejudice may be less affected by the objective or external situation of the individual. It may not increase during times of intense competition, but it may not go away during good times either.

The second and third types of prejudice should be more responsive to the external situation of the individual, rising and falling in intensity as situations change and levels of threat and competition fluctuate. These forms of prejudice should be more responsive to reform efforts and easier to "unlearn."

Is Prejudice Declining?

Many people believe that racial prejudice and discrimination have declined to the point at which they are no longer serious problems in the United States (see D'Souza, 1995, for a recent statement of this position). Indeed, public opinion polls administered since the 1940s provide considerable evidence to support the notion that American prejudice has weakened (see Figure 2.2). In 1942, about 70% of respondents thought that black and white children should attend different schools; 40 years later, support for separate schools had dropped to less than 10%. In a similar pattern, support for the "right" of white people to maintain separate neighborhoods declined from 65% in 1942 to about 16% in 1994.

In a comparison over more recent years, the percentage of white respondents who said they would *not* vote for a qualified black candidate for president declined by almost 15 percentage points from 1972 to 1994. The fourth item displayed in the graph measures behavior more than attitude or opinion. It shows a decrease of about 15% in the number of white respondents who have *not* had a black guest to dinner in their homes. The overall trend is unmistakable: support for prejudiced statements and some forms of discrimination have fallen since World War II.

Of course, these polls also show that prejudice has not vanished. A percentage of the population continues to endorse highly prejudicial sentiments and opinions. Also, egalitarian behaviors, such as sharing meals, are much less common than simply agreeing with nonprejudiced statements. Remember also that the polls show only what people say they feel and think, not what they truly believe. It may be that prejudice remains strong in the United States but has become disguised or more subtle and indirect. We address this possibility later in this chapter.

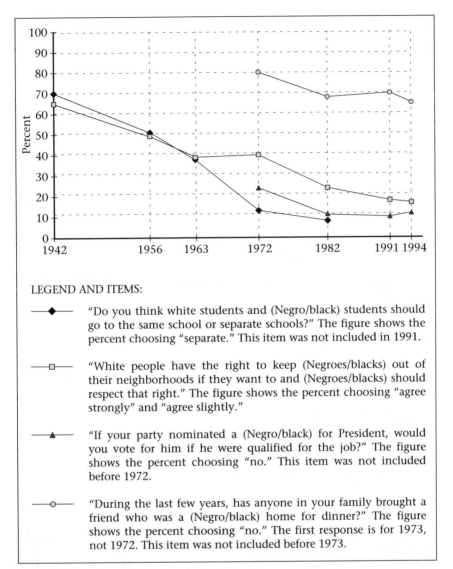

LEGEND AND ITEMS:

◆ "Do you think white students and (Negro/black) students should go to the same school or separate schools?" The figure shows the percent choosing "separate." This item was not included in 1991.

□ "White people have the right to keep (Negroes/blacks) out of their neighborhoods if they want to and (Negroes/blacks) should respect that right." The figure shows the percent choosing "agree strongly" and "agree slightly."

▲ "If your party nominated a (Negro/black) for President, would you vote for him if he were qualified for the job?" The figure shows the percent choosing "no." This item was not included before 1972.

○ "During the last few years, has anyone in your family brought a friend who was a (Negro/black) home for dinner?" The figure shows the percent choosing "no." The first response is for 1973, not 1972. This item was not included before 1973.

Figure 2.2 Declining Prejudice in the United States

Sources: 1942, 1956, 1963: Hyman & Sheatsley, 1984; Greeley & Sheatsley, 1971. 1972, 1982, 1991, and 1994 data are taken from the General Social Survey, National Opinion Research Council, 1994. Results are accurate within ±3 or 4 percentage points.

Putting aside caveats and qualifications for now, the decline in the willingness of the U.S. public to agree with prejudiced statements is dramatic and indicates a decline in blatant and overt prejudice. How can we explain these changes? What factors might be responsible? Let's consider three possible causes of the decline in overt prejudice.

Persuasion and the Mass Media

Persuasion is a form of communication that is deliberately intended to change opinions and attitudes (Farley, 1995, p. 29). It advocates a particular point of view and attempts to create agreement. The persuasive communication may be highly emotional or dry and factual, delivered face-to-face or through the mass media. The latter, particularly television, have become major forms of communication since World War II.

Persuasion is a familiar feature of our consumer-oriented society. Among the myriad messages we encounter are exhortations for racial brotherhood and an end to prejudice and racism. Conversely, we also receive messages intended to reinforce or increase stereotypical thinking.

How effective are these persuasive messages in changing prejudice? The short answer is: not very. Research shows that people are quite adept at evading messages that challenge their beliefs or values. Selective perception, the tendency to filter out disconcerting information, permits people to maintain their views even in the face of massive persuasion to the contrary. Prejudiced people tend to be unmoved by arguments for tolerance, and nonprejudiced people tend to be unpersuaded by racist messages. Persuasion tends to reinforce attitudes rather than change them, and people take from the message what they need to sustain their point of view (Ball-Rokeach, Grube, & Rokeach, 1981; Hur & Robinson, 1978; Vidmar & Rokeach, 1974).

Given the ease with which persuasion can be deflected, it seems unlikely that it can account for the decrease in overt prejudice. We must search elsewhere for an explanation.

Education

Education differs from persuasion in both goals and methods. Persuasion aims to change opinions and attitudes, whereas education is more neutral and objective. Educational arguments and interpretations are more grounded in "the facts," which are examined critically and from multiple viewpoints.

Education has frequently been singled out as the most effective cure for prejudice. Education, like travel, is said to "broaden one's perspective" and encourage a more sophisticated view of human affairs. People with higher levels of education are more likely to view others in terms of their abilities and not in terms of physical or ethnic characteristics. Some theories of assimilation regard education as one of the forces of modernization that will lead to a more rational, competency based society.

This view is supported by the fact that educational levels have increased dramatically since the 1940s, the period during which public opinion polls show an apparent decline in prejudice. Between 1950 and 1993, the percentage of the U.S. population with a high school diploma increased from 34% to more than 80%. In the same time period, the percentage of those with college degrees rose at an even faster rate, from about 6% to almost 22% (U.S. Bureau of the Census, 1994).

Many studies have found statistical correlations between an individual's level of prejudice and level of education. Figure 2.3 shows the relationships between two of the measures of prejudice used in Figure 2.2 and level of education for 1994.

Support for the more prejudiced responses declines as education increases. White respondents with less education express greater support for racially exclusive neighborhoods and are more likely to say they would not vote for a qualified black presidential candidate nominated by their party.

This correlation between increased education and decreased prejudice seems to support the common wisdom that education is the antidote to prejudice. A number of caveats and qualifications must be noted, though. Correlation is not the same thing as causation. Just

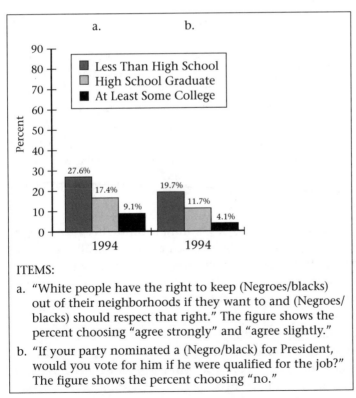

ITEMS:

a. "White people have the right to keep (Negroes/blacks) out of their neighborhoods if they want to and (Negroes/blacks) should respect that right." The figure shows the percent choosing "agree strongly" and "agree slightly."

b. "If your party nominated a (Negro/black) for President, would you vote for him if he were qualified for the job?" The figure shows the percent choosing "no."

Figure 2.3 Prejudice and Education

Source: General Social Survey, National Opinion Research Council, 1994.

because two variables change together over time or are otherwise statistically associated does not prove that one is causing the other. It is tempting to conclude that increased education is the direct cause of the apparent decline in prejudice. However, it is possible that prejudice has not so much declined as it has become more subtle and indirect, or that people are simply hiding their true feelings from the public opinion pollsters.

Prejudice is almost always measured by surveys or interviews. All we can say for sure about these research techniques is that they measure what people say they feel. These public statements might be different from how people really feel or might not record the full range of their feelings about racial and ethnic issues. People typically have many attitudes about a subject, especially one as emotionally charged as prejudice. Different situations may activate different sets of attitudes, and more tolerant responses may be evoked when responding to a scientific public opinion poll. This may be especially true for the more educated, who are more likely to be aware of the "correct" responses to items measuring prejudice and more likely to express socially acceptable opinions. The bottom line is that it is hard to determine how much of the apparent reduction in prejudice is genuine and how much is conformity to the fashionable attitudes of the day.

Research also shows that the impact of education on prejudice is subject to many of the same kinds of limitations as persuasion is. People evade unpleasant or disconcerting information in the classroom just as they can deflect persuasive messages in the media. Selective perception can nullify arguments contrary to one's point of view, and even highly educated people can sustain a racist perspective of the world. (See Selznik & Steinberg, 1969; Stember, 1961; Williams, 1964.)

Contact Between Groups

Like education, contact and increased communication between groups have often been suggested as remedies to prejudice and hostile relations. However, contact between groups is not, in and of itself, an automatic antidote for negative feelings. Contact can have a variety of outcomes; depending on the nature of the situation, it can either reduce or increase prejudice.

There is evidence, though, that certain types of intergroup contact can reduce prejudice. Research has identified four factors that are especially influential on the outcome of contact between groups: equal status, intensive interaction, noncompetitive relations, and cooperative tasks. The **equal status contact hypothesis** proposes that if all of these factors are present in a situation in which members of different groups are interacting, prejudice will decline as a result. Let's examine each of these four factors.

1. *Equal Status.* Contact will reduce prejudice only when the groups involved are equal in status. Unequal interactions are more likely to sustain or even intensify prejudice since they mirror the power differentials and inequalities of the larger society. During the time of American slavery, for example, a high volume of contact existed across racial lines in the South. Interactions were conducted in a context of massive inequality, however, and contact did not encourage (to say the least) an honest and open sharing of views. This type of contact situation reinforces rather than reduces prejudice. Only in situations in which all groups have equal resources are people likely to view one another as individuals, not as representatives of their respective groups.

2. *Intensive Interaction.* The contact has to be more than superficial. It must last for a significant length of time and the participants must be fully involved. Standing next to each other at a bus stop or eating at adjoining tables in a restaurant does not meet this criterion; people of different groups must deal with one another face-to-face and on a personal level.

3. *Noncompetitive Relations.* The contact must occur in an atmosphere free from competition between groups. Competition is likely to increase defensiveness and in-group solidarity and, as a result, prejudice. In recent years, some school systems have been desegregated in ways that enhanced rather than reduced negative feelings between groups. As a result, intergroup contact has been increased, but the minority schoolchildren are seen as "invaders" and outsiders competing for control of dominant group institutions or resources (see Farley, 1995, pp. 371–378 for a review). If contact is to have a moderating effect on attitudes, it must occur in a setting where there is nothing at stake, no real (or imagined) resource that might be allocated differently as a result of the contact.

4. *Cooperative Tasks.* Finally, intergroup contact will be most likely to reduce prejudice if it goes beyond the mere absence of competition. The most effective situations are those in which members of all groups are required to complete a task that could not be accomplished by one group alone or by individuals acting autonomously. If people are bound together by cooperative behavior across group lines, the participants are more likely to come to regard one another as individuals, not as caricatures or stereotypical representatives of their groups.

Research on the Contact Hypothesis

One persuasive and interesting illustration of the contact hypothesis is the Robbers Cave experiment, conducted in the 1950s at a summer camp for boys. The boys were divided into two groups which competed with each other in a variety of activities. Intergroup hostility and negative feelings (prejudice) increased as competition intensified. Then, the experimenters contrived a number of situations in which all of the campers were required to cooperate. For example, a plumbing emergency was fabricated that required everyone to participate in a search for a leak in the water lines. Over several such episodes, prejudices declined and friendships were eventually formed across group lines (Sherif et al., 1961).

In another classic study, Deutsch and Collins (1951) examined the antiblack prejudices of white residents of public housing projects. Their work is significant because Deutsch and Collins were able to eliminate the problem of self-selection. In other studies, participation in intergroup contact situations is voluntary and likely to appeal only to people who are not very prejudiced in the first place. Any change in prejudice might be due to the characteristics of the people involved, not to the contact situation itself. In contrast, some of the white participants in the Deutsch and Collins study were randomly assigned to live in close proximity to black families. The participants had no control over their living arrangement and thus were not self-selected for lower prejudice.

A total of four public housing projects were studied. In two of the projects, black and white families were assigned to separate buildings or areas. In the remaining two, dwelling units were assigned regardless of race. The researchers found that the white families living in the integrated projects were less prejudiced and more likely to interact with their black neighbors than those living in the segregated setting. They concluded that the higher volume of interracial contact had led to lower prejudice.

Interracial contact has been studied in a number of other contexts, including the military (both in war and peace), schools, neighborhoods, and workplaces. Conclusions similar to those in the Deutsch and Collins study are common. (See Amir, 1976; Katz & Taylor, 1988; Miller & Brewer, 1984.)

Recent Trends in Intergroup Contact

Since the 1950s, concerted attempts have been made to reduce discrimination against minority groups in virtually all American institutions. These efforts have increased structural assimilation or integration and provided opportunities for dominant and minority group members to associate with each other. Compared to the days of seg-regation, when blacks and white were separated in schools, jobs, and neighborhoods, there is certainly more contact across group lines today.

Some of this increased contact has reduced prejudice. In other in-stances, contact situations that seem "on paper" to be highly condu-cive to the reduction of prejudice have had no effect or have actually made matters worse. For example, schools and universities across the country have been officially integrated for decades, but these situa-tions often don't seem to lead to increased acceptance and the growth of friendships across group boundaries. The groups involved—whites, African Americans, Chicanos, Asians, and Native Americans—some-times organize themselves in a way that minimizes face-to-face inter-action and contact across social dividing lines. The school buildings are integrated, but actual contact across groups is much rarer.

The contact hypothesis offers a possible explanation for this pattern of separation within integration. Students are typically organized along lines that meet some, but not all, of the conditions specified ear-lier for a contact situation to result in lower prejudice. Even when stu-dents from the various racial and ethnic groups are roughly equal in status, they do not engage in very many cooperative activities that cross group lines. Classrooms themselves are typically competitive and individualistic; students compete for grades and recognition on a one-by-one basis. Cooperation among students (either within or across groups) is not required and, in fact, not particularly encouraged. The group separation and the lack of opportunities for cooperation often extend beyond the classroom into clubs, sports, and other activities.

The separation might be reduced and positive contacts increased by encouraging cooperative activities between members of different groups. One successful attempt to increase cooperation and positive contact used a cooperative learning technique called the **jigsaw method** (Aronson & Gonzalez, 1988). In this experiment, fifth-grade students were divided into groups. Researchers ensured that each group included both dominant and minority group children. A learn-ing task was assigned to them, separated into parts like the pieces of a jigsaw puzzle. Each student was responsible for learning one part of the lesson and then teaching his or her part to the other students in their groups. Everyone was tested on *all* of the pieces, not just his or her own. Each study group needed to make sure that everyone had all of the information necessary to pass the test. This goal could be achieved only through the cooperation of all members of the group.

Unlike typical classroom activities, the jigsaw method satisfies all of the characteristics for a positive contact experience: Students of equal status are engaged in a cooperative project in which mutual interdependence is essential for the success of all. As we would expect under true equal status contact, prejudice was reduced as a result of this experience. Aronson and Gonzalez point out that the students did not need to be idealistic or motivated by a commitment to racial justice for this method to work. Rather, the students were motivated by pure self-interest; without the help of every member of their group, they could not pass the tests (1988, p. 307).

Limitations of the Contact Hypothesis

Reductions in prejudice resulting from contact tend to be specific to the situation. That is, the changed attitudes in one situation (e.g., the workplace) don't necessarily generalize to other situations (e.g., neighborhoods). As we have seen, both prejudice and discrimination are situational and can be astonishingly resilient. Nonetheless, although equal status contact may not be a panacea, it does seem to reduce prejudice and discrimination (see Sigelman & Welch, 1993, for a recent study).

Prospects for Further Reductions in Overt Prejudice

Each of the three preceding explanations for the reduction in overt prejudice is based on assumptions about the causes of prejudice. All assume that prejudice fluctuates and tends to vary from situation to situation. The persuasion and education explanations make two additional key assumptions: (1) prejudice is the result of misinformation or inadequate information about other groups; and (2) prejudice causes discrimination, or, more generally, attitudes cause behaviors. If people acquire new or better information about other groups, their prejudice, followed by their rates of discrimination, will decrease.

In contrast, the equal status contact hypothesis assumes that discrimination is the cause of prejudice (or that behaviors cause attitudes). If people behave in nondiscriminatory ways, their level of prejudice will decline. These contrasting causal models are depicted in Table 2.3.

Both of these causal models are partially correct; in other words, neither causal model is complete by itself. To create a more comprehensive synthesis, we need to recognize that prejudice and discrimination (1) have multiple causes; (2) are not necessarily causes of each other, since either may occur in the absence of the other; and (3) can change as situations change. We also need to recognize the different types of prejudice: prejudice arising from personality needs; prejudice learned as a result of socialization in a racist culture (which can be called *traditional* prejudice); and prejudice arising as the result of intergroup competition. Different strategies for change are appropriate for different

Table 2.3 Two Models of the Causal Relationship
Between Prejudice and Discrimination

Model	Assumes	Proposes
Persuasion and education	Prejudice causes discrimination	New information reduces prejudice, which in turn reduces discrimination
Equal status contact hypothesis	Discrimination causes prejudice	Contact situation reduces discrimination, which in turn reduces prejudice

types of prejudice and no one strategy will work all of the time. These elements can be combined in some concluding statements.

- Neither persuasion, nor education, nor contact is likely to have much impact on personality-based prejudice. If prejudice is deeply embedded or serves as an important emotional crutch, it will not respond to information or experience. It may be impossible to eliminate this type of prejudice altogether. A more realistic goal might be to discourage its open expression. The greater the extent to which everyday social situations discourage prejudice, the more likely that even people with strong personality needs for prejudice will not express it overtly. If prejudice does not manifest itself in discrimination, negative consequences would be minimized.

- Culture-based, or "traditional," prejudice is more open to change and more responsive to persuasion, education, and contact with members of other groups. It seems likely that much of the reduction in overt prejudice over the past 50 years reflects a decline in traditional prejudice sparked in large part by antidiscrimination laws, increased intergroup contact, protests from minority groups, and, perhaps, rising levels of education.

- The key to reducing prejudice caused by group conflict is to reduce the likelihood of such clashes. The problems here are conflict and inequality, not prejudice. Group rivalries tend to be provoked by inequities in the distribution of resources and opportunities rather than by stereotypes or negative attitudes. Even powerful persuasion or extensive education cannot eliminate this type of prejudice. As long as society is stratified along racial and ethnic lines, unequal contact situations will be common and group conflicts will continue. Efforts to decrease hostile attitudes without also reducing inequality and exploitative relationships treat the symptoms instead of the disease.

A major limitation of all three approaches to reducing prejudice—persuasion, education, and intergroup contact—is that none of them speaks directly to the situation of minority groups, the fundamental problems of inequality, or the system of privilege that sustains the advantages of the dominant group. Dominant group prejudice is a problem, but it's not *the* problem. Reducing prejudice will not eliminate minority group poverty or unemployment or end institutional discrimination in schools or the criminal justice system. Remember that individual prejudice and discrimination are not the same things as ideological racism and institutional discrimination, and that any one of these variables can change independently of the others. Thus, we should not confuse the recent reductions in prejudice with the resolution of American minority group problems. Prejudice is only part of the problem and is not, in many ways, the most important part.

Unless there is a reduction in the level of racial and ethnic stratification in American society, individual prejudice will persist at some level in spite of persuasion, rising levels of education, and increased intergroup contact. The system of dominant group privilege requires rationalization and justification and thus a continuing need for prejudice. Further, the vicious cycles created in previous generations will continue to turn and minority group inequality will continue to be taken as proof of the allegations of inferiority included in traditional stereotypes. Until there is an end to racial and ethnic stratification, prejudice may weaken, but it will not entirely disappear.

Modern Racism

A number of scholars reject the idea that prejudice in the United States has declined and argue that it has simply changed forms. They have been investigating symbolic racism, or **modern racism**, a more subtle, complex, and indirect way to express negative feelings toward minority groups and opposition to change in dominant-minority relations (see Bobo, 1988; Kinder & Sears, 1981; Kluegel & Smith, 1982; McConahy, 1986; Sears, 1988).

People who are affected by modern racism have negative feelings (the affective aspect of prejudice) toward minority groups but reject the idea of genetic or biological inferiority and do not think in terms of the traditional stereotypes. Instead, their prejudicial feelings are expressed indirectly and subtly. Modern racism incorporates several assumptions: (1) there is no longer any serious or important discrimination in American society, (2) any continuing racial inequality is the fault of members of the minority group, and (3) demands for preferential treatment or affirmative action for minorities are unfair and unjustified. Modern racism tends to "blame the victim" and place the responsibility for change and improvements on the minority groups, not on the larger society.

To illustrate the difference between traditional and modern racism, consider the results of a recent public opinion survey administered to a representative sample of Americans (National Opinion Research Council, 1994). Respondents were asked to choose from among several explanations of why blacks, on the average, have "worse jobs, income, and housing than white people." Respondents could choose as many explanations as they wanted.

One explanation, consistent with traditional antiblack prejudice, attributed racial inequality to the genetic or biological inferiority of African Americans ("the differences are mainly because blacks have less in-born ability to learn"). Only 13% of the white respondents chose this explanation.

A second explanation attributed continuing racial inequality to discrimination and a third to the lack of opportunity for an education. Forty-three percent of white respondents chose the former and 51% chose the latter.

A fourth explanation, consistent with modern racism, attributes racial inequality to a lack of effort by African Americans ("the differences are because most blacks just don't have the motivation or willpower to pull themselves up out of poverty"). Fifty-two percent of the white respondents chose this explanation, the most popular of the four.

Thus, the survey found relatively little support for the traditional view of black inferiority and widespread support for the idea that racial inequality was the result of discrimination and lack of educational opportunities, views that are consistent with the analysis presented in this text. However, the single most popular explanation was that racial inequality stems from problems in the black community, not in the society as a whole. The perception seems to be that African Americans could solve their problems themselves but are not willing to do so.

What makes this view an expression of prejudice? Besides blaming the victim, it deflects attention away from centuries of oppression and the continuing patterns of inequality and discrimination in modern society. It stereotypes African Americans and encourages the expression of negative affect against them (but without invoking the traditional image of innate inferiority).

Also, researchers have consistently found that modern racism is correlated with opposition to policies and programs intended to reduce racial inequality. In the survey summarized earlier, for example, those who chose the "motivation or willpower" explanation for continuing racial inequality were the most likely to oppose school busing

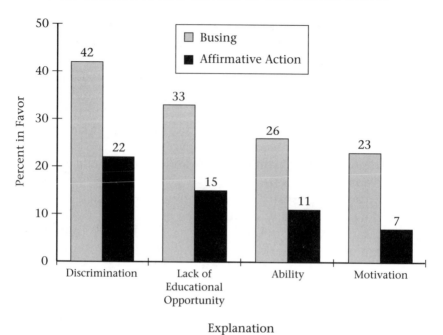

Explanation

Figure 2.4 Support for Busing and Affirmative Action by Explanation of Racial Inequality

and affirmative action programs. In fact, as Figure 2.4 shows, the "modern racists" were more opposed to these programs than the "traditional racists"! (See also Kluegel, 1990.)

Finally, a survey administered to a nationally representative sample in the fall of 1995 found that white Americans were grossly misinformed about the actual situations of black Americans. The majority of the white respondents expressed the belief that black Americans had achieved equality in jobs, income, housing, education, and a number of other areas and that discrimination and racism were, at most, minor problems (Gladwell, 1995; Morin, 1995). In reality, as we will see in chapter 5, sharp inequalities between black and white Americans, indicative of widespread discrimination and racism, persist in all the areas cited. This misperception of racial equality is quite consistent with the idea that modern racism is widespread and strong. If most whites believe that the racial problems of the past have been eliminated, they are relieved of responsibility for any inequalities that remain. The burden of addressing America's minority problems is left to the minorities.

Thus, even as traditional or overt prejudice has declined, modern racism has risen to take its place. On the one hand, the fading of traditional prejudice is a kind of progress in American race relations, the importance of which should not be understated. On the other hand, there is considerable evidence that antiblack prejudice has simply changed form rather than declined. While subtle and diffuse racism is probably preferable to the blunt and vicious variety, it should not be mistaken for the demise of prejudice.

Conclusion

Individual prejudice is complex, multifaceted, and tenacious. It may emanate from childhood experiences, family structures, parents and peer groups, or conflict between groups. Prejudice exists at the level of the individual but is sustained by communities and entire societies, perpetuated by culture, and passed on by socialization. Social science research has identified some ways to reduce prejudice (equal status contact and, perhaps, education) and has documented the decline of its traditional, overt form. Research has also shown, however, that prejudice is stubborn and has found a new form of expression (modern racism) as the old became unfashionable.

MAIN POINTS

- Theories of prejudice vary by the type of explanation they propose. Theories may seek the causes of prejudice in personality characteristics, culture, or group conflict.

- Evidence suggests that traditional prejudice in the United States has been declining.

- Declining prejudice has been attributed to persuasion and rising levels of education, but the equal contact hypothesis seems to be a more powerful explanation.

- No explanation for the reduction of prejudice speaks directly to the fundamental problems of racial and ethnic inequality. Individual prejudice will persist at some level as long as U.S. society continues to be racially and ethnically stratified.

- Modern racism combines negative feelings toward minorities with rejection of traditional stereotypes. This form of prejudice may manifest itself in "blaming the victim" or in opposition to programs designed to improve the situations of minority groups.

FOR FURTHER READING

Allport, Gordon. 1954. *The Nature of Prejudice*. Reading, MA: Addison-Wesley.

Bonacich, Edna, & Modell, John. 1980. *The Economic Basis of Ethnic Solidarity: Small Business in the Japanese American Community*. Berkeley: University of California Press.

Dovidio, John F., & Gartner, Samuel (Eds.). 1986. *Prejudice, Discrimination and Racism*. Orlando, FL: Academic Press.

Katz, Phyllis, & Taylor, Dalmas (Eds.). 1988. *Eliminating Racism: Profiles in Controversy*. New York: Plenum Press.

Kinder, Donald R., & Sears, David O. 1981. "Prejudice and Politics: Symbolic Racism Versus Racial Threats to the Good Life." *Journal of Personality and Social Psychology,* 40: 414–431.

Kluegel, James R., & Smith, Eliot R. 1982. "Whites' Beliefs About Blacks' Opportunities." *American Sociological Review,* 47: 518–532.

Levin, Jack, & Levin, William. 1982. *The Functions of Discrimination and Prejudice*. New York: Harper & Row.

Miller, Norman, & Brewer, Marilyn. (Eds.). 1984. *Groups in Contact: The Psychology of Desegregation*. Orlando, FL: Academic Press.

Pettigrew, Thomas. 1980. "Prejudice." In Stephen Thornstrom (Ed.), *Harvard Encyclopedia of Ethnic Groups* (pp. 820–829). Cambridge: Harvard University Press.

Simpson, George, & Yinger, Milton. 1985. *Racial and Cultural Minorities: An Analysis of Prejudice and Discrimination*. New York: Plenum Press.

Prior to industrialization, minority groups faced repressive control systems and attacks on their culture and social institutions. The efforts to resist domination produced bloody conflicts and some extraordinary individuals. These struggles took on new forms as industrialization began and new systems of control were created.

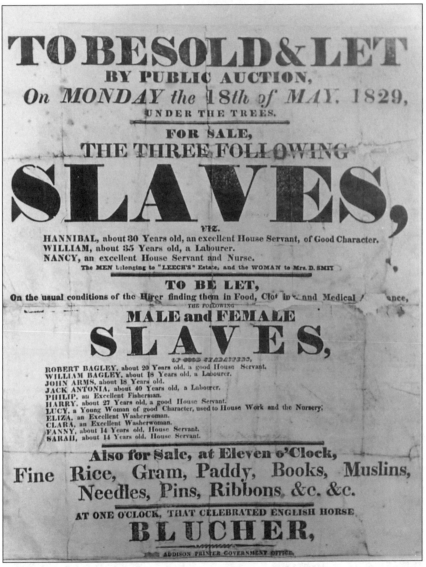

A poster for a slave auction. Note that rice and other "commodities" are also offered for sale.

Harriet Tubman helped to run the Underground Railroad, which led runaway slaves to freedom in the North.

Workers on a cotton plantation supervised by an overseer on horseback.

Chinese laborers building the Central Pacific Railroad.

The capture and death of Sitting Bull, one of countless armed conflicts between Native Americans and the U.S. Army.

Mexican-American cotton pickers at work in Texas.

The Jim Crow system of segregation pervaded all aspects of everyday life, including drinking fountains.

Immigrants arriving in New York City from Europe.

- Many african slaves ran away and joind indian tribes.

- Mexico taken by force conquord

Colonized minority - made into society by force, unwiling

CHAPTER 3

The Creation of Minority Groups in the Preindustrial Era

More discrimination, more negatively toward blacks.

W hy was slavery created in colonial America? Why were Africans enslaved but not Native Americans or Europeans? Why did Native Americans lose at least 75% of their population by the 1890s? How did the Mexican population in the Southwest become "Mexican Americans"? How did the experience of becoming a subordinated minority group vary by gender?

This chapter answers these and other questions and analyzes the creation of minority groups in the United States before the industrial revolution. We begin in the colonial times of the 1600s, when the subsistence technology (the means by which the society satisfies basic needs such as hunger and thirst) was agriculture. Several new ideas are introduced, and two themes run throughout this chapter and the remainder of the text:

1. *The nature of dominant-minority group relations at any point in time is largely a function of the characteristics of the society as a whole.* The situation of a minority group will reflect the realities of everyday social life and, particularly, the subsistence technology. Subsistence technology is like the foundation of a society, shaping and affecting every other aspect of the social structure, including dominant-minority relationships.

2. *The contact situation (the conditions under which groups first encounter each other) is the single most significant factor in the development of the relationship between dominant and minority groups.* The social, political, and economic situation at first contact has long-lasting consequences for the minority group, including the levels of inequality, discrimination, and prejudice the group will face.

With these two themes in mind, we explore two theories about the evolution of group relations. We then apply these ideas to three groups that became minorities while the United States was still agricultural: African Americans, Native Americans, and Mexican Americans.

The Contact Situation

The nature of the initial meeting between groups shapes the fate of both. We use two theories as analytical guides in understanding this crucial phase of intergroup relations.

The Noel Hypothesis

Sociologist Donald Noel developed a hypothesis that helps to explain how the contact situation shapes all subsequent relationships between dominant and minority group. His central idea is that if groups come together in a contact situation that is characterized by ethnocentrism, competition, and a differential in power, then some form of racial or ethnic stratification will result (Noel, 1968, p. 163).

Ethnocentrism is the tendency to judge other groups or lifestyles by the standards of one's own culture. It is similar to prejudice and is a common and perhaps even universal human trait. It can be illustrated by ideas about food and "good eating," both of which vary widely from culture to culture. If you cringe at the thought of eating dog, snails, raw fish, or ants, you're being ethnocentric—that is, you're letting your definitions of food affect how you view the eating habits of others.

Ethnocentrism is important because it creates social boundaries between groups. Without some degree of ethnocentrism, people would not sort themselves out along group lines, and the characteristics that differentiate "us" from "them" would not be identified.

Competition is the struggle between the groups over a scarce commodity. Simply put, the group that wins the competition becomes the dominant group, and the losers become the minority group. The competition could center on land, jobs, housing, education, or politics—or anything that is mutually desired by both groups or that one group has and the other group wants. Competition provides the eventual dominant group with the motivation to establish superiority and exploit, control, or eliminate the minority group.

A **differential in power** is the third feature of the contact situation. Power is the ability to achieve one's goals even in the face of opposition. The amount of power commanded by a group is a function of three factors. First is group size. All other things being equal, larger groups have more power. Second, the amount of discipline and leadership can make a difference, and better organized groups will gener-

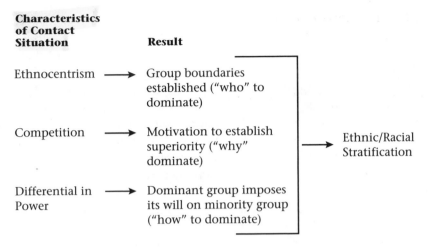

Figure 3.1 A Model of the Establishment of Minority Group Status

ally have the advantage over poorly organized groups. The third component of power is resources, or anything that can be used to help the group achieve its goals. Depending on the context, a resource could be anything from land to guns to information to money. The greater the number and variety of resources at the disposal of a group, the greater its potential ability to dominate other groups. To summarize, a larger, better organized group with more resources will generally be able to impose its will on smaller, less well-organized groups with fewer resources.

A model of the Noel hypothesis is presented in Figure 3.1. This model can be used to analyze both the creation of minority status and changes in dominant-minority structures.

The Blauner Hypothesis

Another important aspect of the contact situation was analyzed by sociologist Robert Blauner in his book *Racial Oppression in America* (1972). Blauner distinguishes between two types of initial relationships: colonization and immigration.

Colonized minority groups, such as Native Americans, African Americans, and Mexican Americans, were forced into minority status by the superior military and political power of the dominant group. At the time of their contact with the dominant group, colonized minority groups are subjected to massive inequalities and attacks on their culture. They are assigned to positions such as slavery, from which any form of assimilation is difficult and perhaps even forbidden by the dominant group. The inequality and powerlessness of colonized minority groups are perpetuated and reinforced through their highly visible racial characteristics. Typically, prejudice and racism directed at colonized groups are harsher and more persistent than that directed at immigrant groups.

In contrast, **immigrant minority groups** are, at least in part, voluntary participants in the host society. Immigrant groups have at least some control over their destination and their position in the host society. As a result, they do not occupy such markedly inferior positions as colonized groups do. They retain enough internal organization and resources to pursue their own self-interest and commonly experience more rapid acceptance and easier movement toward equality. The boundary with the dominant group is not so rigidly maintained, especially when the groups are racially similar. Acculturation and, particularly, integration are significantly more attainable for immigrant groups than for groups formed by conquest or colonization.

These differences in initial relationships have consequences that persist long after the original contact. For example, based on such measures of equality as average income, years of education, and unemployment rate, the descendants of immigrants from Europe are roughly equal with the dominant group today, whereas the descendants of colonized and conquered groups (e.g., African Americans) rank below national norms of equality.

Although Blauner's two types of minority groups lie at opposite ends of a continuum, there are intermediate positions. Enclave and middleman minorities often originate as immigrants who bring with them some resources and thus have more opportunity than colonized minority groups to carve out a place for themselves in the host society. Unlike European immigrant groups, however, many of these minorities are racially identifiable, and certain kinds of opportunities may be closed to them. For instance, citizenship was expressly forbidden to immigrants from China for most of the last hundred years. Thus, the Asian immigrant experience cannot be equated with European immigrant patterns (Blauner, 1972, p. 55). Because they combine characteristics of both the colonized and the immigrant minority group experience, we could predict that in terms of equality, enclave and middleman minority groups will occupy an intermediate status between the more assimilated white ethnic groups and the racial minorities.

Blauner's typology has proven to be an extremely useful conceptual tool for the analysis of U.S. dominant-minority relations and is used extensively in this text. In fact, when we conduct case studies of minority groups starting in chapter 5, we cover the groups in approximate order from those created by colonization to those created by im-migration. Of course, since it is difficult to objectively or precisely measure such things as the extent of colonization, the exact order of the groups is somewhat arbitrary and open to debate.

The Creation of Minority Group Status for African Americans

The first permanent British colony in North America was founded at Jamestown, Virginia, in 1607. The first Africans in British America, 20 of them, arrived 12 years later on a Dutch merchant ship. They were considered cargo, not passengers, and the master of the ship traded them to the Virginia colonists for food and water.

Britain and its colonies did not practice slavery at this time, and these first 20 Africans were almost certainly incorporated into colonial society as **indentured servants,** contract laborers who are obligated to serve a master for a term of years. Indentured servants were common throughout the colonies and this status provided a convenient way of defining these 20 newcomers, who were, after all, purchased in exchange for provisions.

The number of Africans in the British colonies grew slowly, and the position of these indentured servants remained ambiguous for several decades. On the one hand, some became free citizens and successful farmers who, like their white neighbors, purchased African and white indentured servants (Smedley, 1993, p. 99). On the other hand, by the 1640s many Africans were being brought to the colonies as servants whose indenture did not expire or, very nearly, as slaves (Franklin, 1967, pp. 72–73).

It was not until the 1660s that the first slave laws were enacted. In the century that followed, hundreds of additional laws were passed to clarify and formalize the status of Africans in colonial America. By the 1750s slavery was very clearly defined in law and in custom, and the idea that a person could own another person—not just the labor of the person, but the actual person—had been thoroughly institutionalized.

What caused slavery? Why did the colonists deliberately create this repressive system of control? Why did they enslave Africans and not other groups?

American Slavery

The Noel hypothesis helps explain why colonists chose to enslave Africans rather than Native Americans or white indentured servants. First, all three groups were the objects of ethnocentrism from the colonial elites. Africans and Native Americans were perceived as different on religious as well as racial grounds. White indentured servants, who were often Irish Catholic, criminals, or paupers, occupied a lowly status in society and were seen as different from the British Protestants who dominated colonial society.

Second, competition of some sort existed between the colonists and all three groups. The competition with Native Americans was direct and centered on control of land. Competition with indentured servants, both white and black, was more indirect; these groups had the labor that the landowners needed. A form of agricultural production called the **plantation system** had begun to emerge in the colonies. This system was based on cultivating large tracts of land. In these preindustrial times, most farm work was done by hand, not machine, and the labor-intensive technology required a large, disciplined, cheap workforce (Curtain, 1990).

Noel's third variable, differential in power, is the key factor that explains why Africans were enslaved instead of the other groups. During the first decades of colonial history, the balance of power between the colonists and Native Americans was relatively even (Lurie, 1982, pp. 131–133). The colonists were outnumbered and their muskets and cannons were only marginally more effective than the Native Americans' bows and spears. The Native American tribes were well organized and capable of resisting the colonists.

White indentured servants had the advantage of being preferred over black indentured servants (Noel, 1968, p. 168). This gave them bargaining power and the ability to negotiate better treatment. If the planters had attempted to enslave white indentured servants, this source of labor would have dwindled.

In contrast, Africans became indentured servants only by force and coercion. In Blauner's terms, they were a colonized group that did not freely choose to enter the British colonies. Thus, they had no bargaining power. As opposed to Native Americans, they had no nearby relatives, no knowledge of the countryside, and no safe havens to escape to.

The plantation owners needed human labor and lots of it, and they chose what seemed to them to be the most cost-effective solution. Table 3.1 summarizes the impact of the three factors in the Noel hypothesis on each of the three potential sources of labor in colonial America.

Paternalistic Relations

A society with a small elite class and a plantation-based economy will often develop a form of minority relations called **paternalism** (Van den Berghe, 1967; Wilson, 1973). The key features of paternalism are

Table 3.1 The Noel Hypothesis Applied to the Origins of Slavery in North America

[handwritten: competing for power, control]

Potential Sources of Labor	Three Causal Factors		
	Ethno-centrism	Competition	Differential in Power
White indentured servants	Yes	Yes	No
Native Americans	Yes	Yes	No
Black indentured servants	Yes	Yes	Yes

vast power differentials and huge inequalities between dominant and minority groups, elaborate and repressive systems of control, castelike barriers between groups, and low rates of overt conflict. We consider each of these characteristics in turn.

As slavery evolved in the colonies, the dominant group shaped the system to fit its needs. The plantation elite enacted an elaborate system of laws and customs that gave masters nearly total power over slaves. Slaves were defined as **chattel**, or personal property, rather than as persons, and were accorded no civil or political rights. Slaves could not own property, sign contracts, or bring lawsuits. The masters were given the legal authority to determine almost every aspect of a slave's life, including work schedules, living arrangements, diets, even names (Elkins, 1959; Genovese, 1974; Jordan, 1968; Stampp, 1956).

The law permitted the master to determine the type and severity of punishment for misbehavior. Slaves were forbidden by law to read or write, and marriages between slaves were not legally recognized. Masters could separate husbands from wives and parents from children. *[handwritten: slave no rights]* Slaves had little formal decision-making ability and little control of their lives or the lives of their loved ones.

Slavery was a **caste system**, or a closed stratification system. In a caste system, there is no mobility between social positions, and the social class you are born into (your ascribed status) is permanent. Slave status was for life and was passed on to any children a slave might have. Whites, no matter what they did, could not become slaves.

Interaction between whites and slaves was governed by a rigid code of etiquette. Slaves were expected to show deference and humility and visibly display their lower status in interactions with whites. These codes made it possible for blacks and whites to work together, sometimes intimately, sometimes for their entire lives, without threatening the system. Plantation and farm work required close contact between blacks and whites, and status differentials were maintained socially rather than physically.

The frequent but unequal interactions allowed the elites to maintain a "pseudotolerance," or an attitude of benevolent despotism toward their slaves. Their prejudice and racism were often expressed as a *positive* emotion of affection for their slaves (Wilson, 1973, pp. 52–55). For their part, the slaves often could not hate their owners as much as they hated the system that constrained them. The system defined slaves as property, yet they were, undeniably, human beings as well. Thus, slavery was based on a contradiction: "The master learned to treat his slaves both as property and as men and women, the slaves learned to express and affirm their humanity even while they were constrained in much of their lives to accept their status as chattel" (Parish, 1989, p. 1).

The formal powerlessness of slaves made it difficult for them to openly reject or resist the system. Open defiance could result in punishment or even death, but other forms of resistance proved to be more successful. Slaves were constantly running away. Escape was difficult, but that did not deter thousands from attempting the feat, some of them repeatedly. Many runaway slaves received help from the Underground Railroad, an informal network supported by African Americans and whites involved in **abolitionism,** the movement to end slavery. These escapes created colorful legends and heroic figures, including Frederick Douglass, Sojourner Truth, and Harriet Tubman.

Slaves also used the forms of resistance most readily available to them: sabotage, intentional carelessness, and work slowdowns. These behaviors were widespread and document the rejection of the system by its victims (Parish, 1989, p. 73).

On an everyday basis, the slaves managed their lives and families as best they could. Most were neither docile victims nor unyielding rebels. As the institution of slavery developed, a distinct African-American experience accumulated and traditions of resistance and accommodation developed side by side. Most slaves worked to create a world for themselves within the confines and restraints of the plantation system, avoiding the more vicious repressiveness of slavery as much as possible while attending to their own needs and those of their families. An African-American culture was forged in response to the realities of slavery and was manifested in folklore, music, religion, family structures, and other aspects of everyday life.

The Dimensions of Minority Status

Let's examine how some of the concepts introduced in chapter 1 can be applied to our discussion. First of all, the key concepts for understanding the creation of slavery are power and institutional discrimination. The plantation elite used their greater power to consign Africans to an inferior status. The system of racial inequality was implemented and reinforced by institutionalized discrimination. The legal and political institutions of colonial society were shaped to benefit the landowners and give them almost total control over their slaves.

As for prejudice and racism, most scholars agree that they were more the *results* of systems of racial inequality than the *causes* (Jordan, 1968, p. 80; Smedley, 1993, pp. 96–110). The colonists did not enslave Africans because they were prejudiced or because they disliked blacks or thought them inferior. The decision to enslave Africans was a response to a labor supply problem. The primary roles of prejudice and racism in the creation of minority group status are to rationalize and "explain" the system of racial or ethnic advantage (Wilson, 1973, pp. 76–78).

Prejudice and racism help to mobilize support for the creation of minority group status and to stabilize the system as it emerges. Prejudice and racism can help insulate a system like slavery from questioning and criticism and make it appear reasonable and even desirable. Thus, the intensity and popularity of Southern racism actually reached its height two hundred years *after* slavery began to emerge. During the early 1800s, the American abolitionist movement brought slavery under heavy attack and, in response, the ideology of antiblack racism was strengthened (Wilson, 1973, p. 79). The greater the opposition to a system of racial stratification, the greater the need of the beneficiaries to rationalize.

Once created, dominant group prejudice and racism become common ways of thinking about the minority group. In colonial society, antiblack beliefs and feelings became part of the culture shared by the dominant group and were passed on from generation to generation through the process of socialization. These relationships are presented graphically in Figure 3.2.

What effect did slavery have on assimilation and the culture of the slaves? There is an enormous literature on this question and many issues remain unsettled; however, some conclusions about assimilation

Figure 3.2 A Model for the Creation of Prejudice and Racism

and slavery have emerged from recent research. It is clear that Africans were forced to acculturate to the Anglo-American culture of the dominant group. The plantation elite or their overseers needed to communicate with their workforce and insisted that English be spoken. Within a generation or two, African languages died out. Some African words and language patterns survived, but to the extent that culture depends on language, Africans under slavery experienced massive acculturation. Integration was not a real possibility under slavery.

For the slaves, acculturation was clearly a coercive process. Because they were a colonized minority group and unwilling participants in the system, African Americans had little choice but to adjust as best they could to the conditions established by the plantation elite. Their traditional culture was suppressed, and their choices for adjustment to the system were sharply constrained (Blauner, 1972, p. 66). While some African cultural elements survived slavery, and a unique African-American culture emerged from this experience, African Americans had to assimilate on terms dictated by their owners (Blassingame, 1972; Genovese, 1974; Gutman, 1976).

The Creation of Minority Group Status for Native Americans

Many Americans don't realize that Native American societies were (and are) highly variable in culture, language, size, and subsistence technology. Some tribes were small, nomadic hunters and gatherers, whereas others were more developed and maintained permanent villages and gardens. Regardless of their exact nature, all of these societies were devastated by the inexorable advance of white society. Contact began in the East, and these first interactions established a pattern of conflict and defeat for Native Americans that continued until the last tribe was defeated in the late 1800s.

The centuries-long struggle caused a massive loss of population among Native Americans. It is estimated that in 1492, there were anywhere from 1 million to more than 18 million Native Americans living in what became the continental United States (Snipp, 1992, p. 354). In 1890, when the Indian Wars finally ended, the number of Native Americans had fallen to less than 250,000, a population decline of at least 75% (Wax, 1971, p. 17; see also McNickle, 1973).

Very little of this decline was due to warfare. The greatest loss was caused by the diseases that the European brought with them, and by the destruction of the food supplies on which Native American societies relied. Native Americans died by the thousands from smallpox, cholera, and other diseases (Wax, 1971, p. 17; see also Snipp, 1989).

Traditional hunting grounds and garden plots were taken over by the expanding American society, and game such as buffalo was slaughtered to the point of extinction. The result of the contact situation for Native Americans very nearly approached genocide.

Competition for Land

The Noel hypothesis, with its emphasis on group conflict and power, provides a way of distinguishing the experiences of Native Americans from those of African Americans. Whereas slavery resulted from a struggle over control of labor, competition between Native Americans and whites centered on control of land. In 1763 the British Crown attempted to regulate the conflicts over land by ruling that the various tribes were to be considered "sovereign nations with inalienable rights to their land" (McNickle, 1973). In other words, each tribe was to be treated as a nation-state, like France or Russia, and tribal lands could not simply be expropriated by the colonists. Rather, treaties had to be signed and the tribes had to be compensated for any losses.

This principle of sovereignty, which was continued after the American Revolution, is important because it established a unique relationship between the federal government and Native American tribes. The fact that the policy was ignored in practice and that treaties were regularly broken or unilaterally renegotiated by white society gives Native Americans unique legal claims against the federal government. We further examine the implications of these broken treaties in chapter 6.

In the eastern United States, the period of open conflict over land was ended by the Indian Removal Act of 1830. In this legislation, the federal government required all eastern tribes to move to new lands west of the Mississippi. In spite of widespread resistance, the policy was successfully implemented and the eastern tribes lost virtually all of their land.

In the West, the grim story of competition for land, hostility, and violence repeated itself. Wars were fought, territory was expropriated, atrocities were committed on both sides, and the Indian nations were gradually defeated. By 1890, almost all Native Americans lived on reservations controlled by the federal government. Not surprisingly, reservation land was usually undesirable and often worthless.

The 1890s mark a low point in Native American history, a time of great demoralization and sadness. The tribes had to find a way to adapt to reservation life and subordination to the federal government. Although elements of the tribal way of life survived, the tribes were impoverished and without resources and had little ability to pursue their own interests.

Native Americans, like African Americans, had become a colonized minority group and the reservations, like the plantations, were paternalistic systems. Native Americans were controlled by an elaborate federal bureaucracy and everyday life on the reservations was dominated by a government-appointed Indian agent, who controlled rations, the judicial system, schools, housing, and health services. The agent was answerable to his distant superiors in Washington, not to the local tribes (Wax, 1971).

The Dimensions of Minority Status

During the centuries of struggle and conflict, a particular set of prejudices and stereotypes for Native Americans emerged in the dominant culture. These stereotypes were quite different from those that developed for African Americans, who were stereotyped as lazy, irresponsible, and having a childlike need for supervision. Note how this image helped to justify the subordinate, highly controlled status of the slave. Native Americans, in contrast, were stereotyped as bloodthirsty, ferocious, and cruel. This stereotype of savagery helped to justify the near extermination of Native Americans. Thus, the nature and content of stereotypes reflect the contact situation, as do so many other aspects of minority group status.

In part because of their long history of conflict with U.S. society, Native Americans have been less interested in assimilation than other minority groups. Individual Native Americans have, of course, moved into the larger society, but the separate tribes have pursued pluralism and even separatism, even though they have generally lacked the power to make much progress toward these goals. Quite to the contrary, Native Americans were often subjected to a policy of forced Americanization consistent with Blauner's analysis of colonized minority groups.

After conquest, federal authorities frequently suppressed Native American religions and languages and bypassed the traditional political institutions. Native Americans were forced to adopt white values regarding land ownership and property in general. Once the reservation system was in operation, Indian children were required to attend boarding schools that were sometimes hundreds of miles away from parents and kin, where they were required to speak English, convert to Christianity, and become educated in the ways of Western civilization.

A law passed in 1887 called the Dawes Act illustrates this policy of forced acculturation. The goal of the law was to transform Native Americans into farmers by dividing Indian land among the families of each tribe. The intent was to give each family the means to survive like their white neighbors, in other words, to impose the Anglo cultural patterns of private property and farming on Native Americans.

Although the law seems benevolent in intent, it was flawed by a gross lack of understanding of Native American cultures and, in many ways, was a direct attack on those cultures. Most Native American tribes were unfamiliar with farming and little was done to prepare the tribes for the transition. More important, Native Americans had little or no concept of land as private property, and it was relatively easy for land speculators and others to separate Indian families from the land allocated to them. Some 140 million acres were allocated to the tribes in 1887. By the 1930s nearly 90 million of those acres had been lost. Most of the remaining land was desert or otherwise nonproductive (Wax, 1971, p. 55).

The Creation of Minority Group Status for Mexican Americans

In the early 1800s, the Southwest was sparsely settled and its economy was based on farming and herding. Most people lived in villages and small towns or on ranches and farms. Social and political life was organized around family and the Catholic church and tended to be dominated by wealthy landowners (Cortes, 1980).

Regional Variations in Domination

Some of the first effects of U.S. expansion to the West were felt in Texas, which in the 1820s was a part of the nation of Mexico. Texas was not heavily defended and the farmland of east Texas was a tempting resource for cotton-growing interests in the American South. Mexico reluctantly agreed to permit immigration, and by 1835 Anglo Americans outnumbered Mexicans 6 to 1. The attempts by the Mexican government to control the immigrants were clumsy and ineffective and eventually precipitated a successful revolution. In newly independent Texas, relations between Mexicans and Anglos remained relatively cordial and competition was muted by the abundance of land and opportunity. As the Anglo population increased, however, competition and open conflict also increased (Alvarez, 1973, p. 922).

The United States annexed Texas in 1846, provoking full-scale war with Mexico. The war ended in 1848, with the United States acquiring much of what is now the Southwest. Additional territory was purchased from Mexico in 1853. Without moving an inch, the Mexican population of the Southwest had become a conquered people and a minority group.

Following the war, relations in Texas between Mexicans (or *Tejanos*) and Anglos continued to sour. The political and legal rights of the *Tejanos* were often ignored in the hunger for land. Increasingly impoverished and powerless, they had few resources with which to resist

Anglo-American domination. Land increasingly came under Anglo control, a process reinforced by widespread violence and lynchings (Moquin & Van Doren, 1971, p. 253).

As the subordinate status of Mexican Americans in Texas was being solidified, contacts between Anglos and Mexicans in California increased. The gold rush of 1849 spurred a massive population movement from the East. Early relations with *Californios* (native Mexicans in the state) had been relatively cordial, but the rapid growth of an Anglo majority after statehood in 1850 stimulated conflict and soured relationships. Eventually *Californios,* like *Tejanos,* lost their land and their political power. Laws were passed encouraging Anglos to settle on land traditionally held by *Californios.* By the mid-1850s, a massive transfer of land to Anglo-American hands had taken place in California.

Prejudice and racism played a major role in these developments. The Mexican heritage was suppressed and eliminated from public life, and Anglo Americans used violence and discrimination to exploit *Californios* and control the new wealth generated by gold mining (Mirande, 1985, pp. 20–21).

Only in New Mexico did Mexican Americans retain some political power and economic clout, mostly because of the relatively large size of the group and their skill in mobilizing for political activity. New Mexico did not become a state until 1912 and Mexican Americans played a prominent role in territorial affairs. More than a third of the seats at the 1910 state constitutional convention were held by Mexican Americans, who managed to include a number of important provisions in the final document, among them a ban on segregated schools (Cortes, 1980, p. 706).

Thus, the contact situation for Mexican Americans was highly variable by region. Although some areas were affected more rapidly and more completely than others, the ultimate result of all of these contact situations was the creation of minority group status.

Competition for Land and Labor

Ethnocentrism, the first factor in the Noel hypothesis, was present from the very first contact. Many Anglo migrants to the Southwest brought antiblack and anti-Indian prejudices with them. In fact, many of the settlers who moved into Texas came directly from the South in search of new lands for the cultivation of cotton. They readily transferred their prejudiced views to at least the poorer Mexicans, who were stereotyped as lazy and shiftless (McLemore, 1973, p. 664). The visibility of group boundaries was reinforced by physical and religious differences. Mexicans were a mixture of Spanish and Native American heritage, and physical differences with Caucasian Americans provided a convenient way of marking group membership.

Also, the vast majority of Mexicans were Roman Catholic, whereas the vast majority of Anglo Americans were Protestant.

Competition for land began with the first contact between the groups. However, for many years the population density was low in the Southwest and the competition did not immediately or always erupt into violent domination and expropriation. Nonetheless, the loss of land and power for Mexican Americans was inexorable but variable in speed.

Unlike Native Americans, the labor as well as the land of Mexicans was coveted. In ranches, farms, mining, and railroad construction, Mexican Americans became a vital source of inexpensive labor. During times of high demand, their numbers were supplemented by workers from Mexico. When times got hard, these workers were forced back south of the border. Thus began a pattern of labor flow that continues to the present day.

Like the other colonized groups we have discussed, Mexican Americans were subjected to a coercive brand of assimilation. Their culture was attacked and, in institution after institution, Mexican heritage and the Spanish language were suppressed. By the mid-1850s in California, for example, Spanish was forbidden in public school instruction (Moore, 1970, p. 19).

Forced acculturation was part of the overall process by which the dominance of Anglo Americans was established. In their subservient positions, Mexican Americans, like slaves, were forced to acculturate in order to survive. Unlike African Americans, however, Mexican Americans maintained close ties with their homeland. Constant movement across the border with Mexico kept the Spanish language and the Mexican heritage alive in the Southwest. Nonetheless, 19th-century Mexican Americans fit Blauner's category of a colonized minority group.

Gender and Colonization

The creation of minority status often affected men and women differently. Conquest and domination disrupted and destroyed innumerable social and cultural patterns. On occasion, women gained in status and power, but always at the expense of impoverishment and loss of autonomy for the group as whole.

African Americans

Slavery provides a clear example of how the creation of minority status may affect men and women differently. In chapter 1, I pointed out that minority women are doubly oppressed by their gender and their race. For black slave women, a third constraint was added: "Black in a white society, slave in a free society, women in a society ruled by men, female slaves had the least formal power and were perhaps the most vulnerable group of antebellum America" (White, 1985, p. 15).

Given their status, slave women had little in common with white women of the antebellum South. The race/gender roles of the day idealized Southern white women and placed them on a pedestal. A romanticized conception of femininity was inconsistent with the roles that women slaves were required to play. Besides domestic chores, female slaves also worked in the fields and did their share of the hardest, most physically demanding, least "feminine" work. Reflecting their vulnerability and powerlessness, slave women were sometimes used to breed more slaves to sell. They were also raped and sexually abused by the males of the dominant group (Blassingame, 1972, p. 83).

Most often, slave women worked in sex-segregated groups. They attended the births and cared for the children of both races, cooked and cleaned, wove cloth and sewed clothes, and did the laundry. They tended to work longer hours than the men, doing housework and other chores long after the men retired (White, 1985, p. 122).

The group-oriented, cooperative nature of their tasks gave female slaves an opportunity to develop same-sex bonds and relationships. They used their networks and interpersonal bonds to resist the system. For instance, slave women sometimes induced abortions rather than bring more children into bondage. Because they usually controlled the role of midwife, they could disguise the abortions as miscarriages (White, 1985, pp. 125–126). The networks of relationships among female slaves also provided mutual aid and support, solace, and companionship (Andersen, 1993, pp. 164–165).

Slave women shaped a world different from that of male slaves and vastly different from that of white women. In this world, their experiences were controlled not only by their race and their slave status but also by their gender.

Native Americans

The initial consequences of contact were variable for Native American women. In some situations their status and power relative to men actually increased at first, whereas in other situations they lost status. The women of the Navajo tribe (located mainly in what is now Arizona and New Mexico) were traditionally responsible for herd animals and livestock. When the Spanish introduced sheep and goats into the region, the importance of herding increased, and the power and status of women grew with it.

Women of the Great Plains tribes, however, were responsible for gardening while the men hunted. Contact with European cultures brought the horse, and the productivity of the male hunters increased significantly. Males became even more dominant and women suffered a loss of status and power (Evans, 1989, pp. 12–18).

Mexican Americans

The roles of Mexican-American women were organized around family and domestic responsibilities. In the Southwest, most Mexican Americans lived in small rural communities in extended family structures dominated by males. In this traditional setting, women devoted their energies to child-rearing and household tasks. As Mexican Americans were reduced to a landless labor force, women along with men suffered the economic devastation that accompanied military conquest. The kinds of jobs available to the men (mining, seasonal farm work, railroad construction) often required them to be away from home for extended periods of time, and women had to take over their traditional tasks. The decision-making power of Mexican-American women increased and they were often forced to work outside the household in order for the family to survive economically (Becerra, 1988, pp. 146–151).

Conclusion

Native Americans, Africans, and Mexicans, in their separate fates, were involuntary players in the growth and development of U.S. economic and political power. None of these groups had much choice in their respective fates; all three were overpowered and relegated to a subordinate status. Many views of assimilation (like the melting pot) have little relevance for these situations. These colonized groups were coercively acculturated in the context of paternalistic relations in an agrarian economy. Meaningful integration or structural assimilation was not a real possibility, especially for blacks and Native Americans. The experience of subordination varied by gender, but the differences always manifested themselves in the context of conquest and colonization.

MAIN POINTS

- Minority-dominant relations are shaped by the characteristics of society as a whole, particularly by subsistence technology. The contact situation is the single most important factor in the development of minority-dominant relations.

- The Noel hypothesis and the Blauner hypothesis provide a useful conceptual framework for analyzing the creation of minority group status and changes in that status over time.

- Slavery in colonial America was created to solve a labor supply problem in the plantation-based economy. Competition with Native Americans centered on control of the land. Competition with Mexican Americans was over both land and labor. All three groups were colonized and subjected to forced acculturation.

- Conquest and colonization affected men and women differently. Minority women have been doubly oppressed by their gender as well as by their minority group status.

FOR FURTHER READING

Acuna, Rodolfo. 1988. *Occupied America* (3rd ed.). New York: Harper & Row.

Blassingame, John. 1972. *The Slave Community: Plantation Life in the Antebellum South.* New York: Oxford University Press.

Brown, Dee. 1970. *Bury My Heart at Wounded Knee.* New York: Holt, Rinehart & Winston.

Genovese, Eugene. 1974. *Roll, Jordan, Roll.* New York: Pantheon Books.

Geschwender, James A. 1978. *Racial Stratification in America.* Dubuque, IA: Wm. C. Brown Publishers.

Gutman, Herbert G. 1976. *The Black Family in Slavery and Freedom.* New York: Vintage Books.

Nabakov, Peter. (Ed.). 1991. *Native American Testimony.* New York: Penguin Books.

Wilson, William J. 1973. *Power, Racism, and Privilege: Race Relations in Theoretical and Sociohistorical Perspectives.* New York: The Free Press.

CHAPTER 4

Industrialization and Dominant-Minority Relations

hy did so many people leave Europe in the 19th century? Why did they immigrate to the United States? Why did American slavery end and what replaced it? Why did black Southerners begin to move out of the South early in this century? The answer to all of these questions is the industrial revolution, a process that transformed both U.S. society and U.S. minority groups.

One theme stated at the beginning of chapter 3 was that the subsistence technology of a society shapes dominant-minority group relations. A corollary of this theme, explored in this chapter, is that *dominant-minority relations change as the subsistence technology changes*. Beginning in Europe in the 1700s, a profound change in subsistence technology began with the industrial revolution. Industrial technology quickly became more productive than the labor-intensive agrarian technology, and industrialization eventually came to affect every aspect of social life around the globe. The industrial revolution changed the nature of work, altered the family institution, lowered birth and death rates, and created new minority groups and profoundly changed the situations of others.

The key innovations associated with the industrial revolution were the application of machine power to production and the harnessing of inanimate sources of energy, such as steam and coal, to fuel the machines (Lenski, Nolan, & Lenski, 1995). As machines replaced humans and animals, work became many times more productive, the economy grew, and the volume and variety of goods produced increased dramatically.

In an industrial economy, the close, paternalistic control of minority groups found in agrarian societies became less feasible. The older system of control required mostly unskilled labor and bound minority group members to specific owners and land. An industrial economy, in contrast, requires a workforce that is geographically and socially mobile, skilled, and literate. Furthermore, with industrialization comes urbanization, and paternalistic control is difficult to maintain in a city (Yans-McLaughlin, 1990).

Thus, as industrialization progresses, agrarian paternalism tends to give way to a new system of group relations called the **rigid competitive system**. Under this new system, minority group members compete for jobs and other valued commodities with dominant group members, especially the lower-class segments of the dominant group. As competition increases, the threatened members of the dominant group become more hostile, and attacks on the minority groups increase. Defensive structures are created to minimize or eliminate minority group encroachment on jobs, housing, or other valuable goods or services (Van den Berghe, 1967; Wilson, 1973).

Paternalistic systems such as slavery required the minority group to be an active, if involuntary, participant. In rigid competitive systems, the dominant group seeks to preserve its advantage by handicapping the minority group's ability to compete effectively or, in some cases, by removing the minority group from competition altogether. For example, in a rigid competitive system, the dominant group might eliminate the political power of a minority group by depriving them of the right to vote.

The industrial revolution took place over the course of more than a century and its effects on dominant-minority relations were continual but gradual. In this chapter, we begin with two minority group situations that have their origin in the early phases of industrialization: immigration from Europe and Asia between the 1820s and 1920s and changes in black-white relations following the Civil War. Each of these situations is tracked into the 20th century. Then, the discussion is brought into the modern era by examining the later stages of industrialization and their implications for dominant-minority relations. This final discussion introduces some new concepts and establishes some important groundwork for the chapters to come.

Immigrant Minority Groups

As industrialization began in Europe, agriculture was modernized and the need for human labor in rural areas declined. The peasant class found it increasingly difficult to live as their ancestors had. At the same time, the rural population began to grow. In response to these pressures, peasants began to migrate toward urban areas, where factories were being built and opportunities for employment were available. The urban job supply turned out to be unreliable, however, and not everyone could find work. Many responded to opportunities available in the New World, especially in the United States. As industrialization took hold in Europe, the population movement to the cities and to North America grew to become the largest in human history. Between the 1820s and the 1920s, about 40 million people immigrated to the United States.

Old and New Immigrants

The first wave of immigrants to the United States came from the British Isles, where industrialization began, and especially from Ireland, where the dislocations of industrialization were compounded by famine and starvation. Between 1820 and 1880, immigration from other parts of Northern and Western Europe was also substantial. This time period is often called the **Old Immigration**.

Later, as industrialization spread east and south, the immigrants started to come from Eastern and Southern Europe. This second period, beginning in the 1880s and continuing into the 1920s, is called the **New Immigration**. Both waves of immigration are indicated in Figure 4.1. Note that the New Immigration was much more voluminous than the Old.

Of course, not all immigrants were motivated by the economic changes wrought by industrialization. Some were escaping political repression and others sought religious freedom. For example, Jews from Eastern Europe and Russia were the victims of intense persecution beginning in the 1880s and fled their homes in fear for their lives (Howe, 1976; Sklare, 1971).

All of these immigrant groups became minority groups in America, at least for a time. Many were the victims of vast economic, political, or social changes in their country of origin, and their victimization often continued when they arrived in the United States.

Push and Pull: Why the United States?

What drew the immigrants to the United States? The choice sometimes hinged on matters as simple as the cost of the fare, but a more general explanation is related to comparative levels of development. When industrialization began in Europe, the United States was still a frontier society with an abundance of fertile land. Throughout the 1800s, American society was expanding into and conquering new territory. Once the threat of Indians and Mexicans was dealt with, land was cheap or free, and plentiful.

The continuing westward movement of population within the United States also created opportunities. Industrialization began in the East, but many native-born American workers declined the strenuous,

Immig.   From 90's: Southern/rural to over 1/2 second
urban/north.

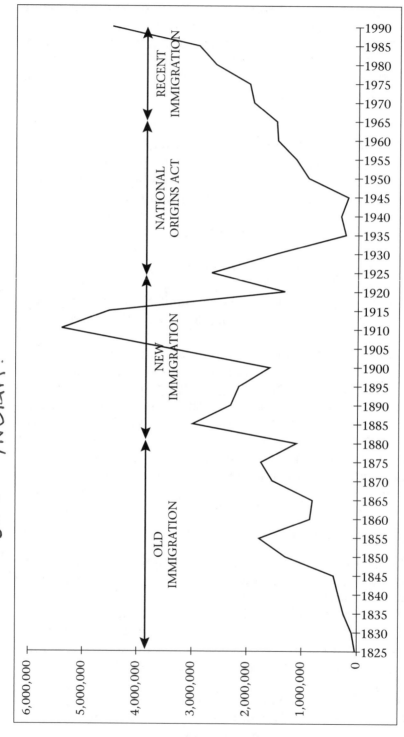

Figure 4.1 Immigration to the United States, 1820–1990 (5-year totals)

Source: U.S. Immigration and Naturalization Service, 1993.

low-paying jobs created by the process and moved west instead. These openings in the job market were subsequently filled by European immigrants (Higham, 1975, p. 23). Thus, as industrialization caused population movement out of Europe, the combination of industrialization and the frontier society in the United States created opportunities for the immigrants. These **push and pull** factors underlie the massive transfer of population from the Old World to the New.

Adaptation to U.S. Society

The immigrant groups from Europe varied in their rate of assimilation and in the reactions of American society to their arrival. Many of the differences between groups can be accounted for in terms of contact situations, competition, power resources, and the characteristics of the immigrants themselves.

Some immigrant groups were able to take advantage of the cheap frontier land, and they tended to acculturate and integrate with less difficulty. For example, many Germans and Scandinavians settled on frontier farmland. They moved into areas where there was less competition for land (once Indians and Mexicans were eliminated) and economic success. Also, they lowered their social visibility by dispersing themselves across the vast expanses of the central plains.

Applying the Noel hypothesis, we see that the level of ethnocentrism directed against these groups was relatively low. Germans and Scandinavians were racially and religiously similar to the dominant group. Because they dispersed themselves across areas of low population density, contact and competition with dominant group members were low. Although these groups still were targets of prejudice and rejection, their assimilation, compared with many other groups, was relatively swift.

In contrast, peasant immigrant groups typically lacked the resources to move to the frontier. These groups, first the Irish and later the Italians, Poles, and a host of others, settled largely in the cities of the industrializing Northeast. They differed from the dominant group in language and religion and came from cultures that did not have strong democratic traditions. Some, like Italians and Jews, were even seen as a separate race (Higham, 1963).

Many native-born Americans viewed the peasant immigrants as threats to Anglo-American cultural and racial purity. The immigrants competed directly with dominant group members for jobs and living space in the cities, and, especially after the 1880s, pressure to close the national doors and end these perceived threats was considerable and, as we will see, ultimately successful.

Immigrants From Asia

Between 1820 and 1920, Asian immigrants came mainly from China and, later, Japan. These immigrants were motivated by the same forces that inspired immigration from Europe: the disruption of traditional social relations directly or indirectly caused by industrialization and the appearance of new opportunities in other parts of the globe (Chan, 1990).

Much of China had been colonized by the rapidly industrializing nations of Europe and experienced great political and economic turmoil throughout the 19th century. In addition, the population was growing and land was scarce. These disruptions and discontents spurred the population movement out of China. Chinese immigrants were drawn to the United States by the California gold rush of 1849 and other opportunities created by the development of the West (Chan, 1990; Lyman, 1974; Tsai, 1986).

Applying the Noel hypothesis, ethnocentrism against the Chinese was based on racial and cultural differences. Competition centered on the gold mines and other jobs. At first, competition was muted because the West Coast economy was growing, jobs were abundant, and the number of Chinese was low. In fact, Chinese laborers were widely praised for their industriousness and tirelessness (Tsai, 1986, p. 17).

After the 1860s, however, the economic boom slowed and jobs became more scarce. Migration from the East continued, competition increased, and an anti-Chinese campaign of harassment, discrimination, and violence began (Tsai, 1986). The Chinese were a small group—there were only about 100,000 in the entire country in 1870—and, by law, they were not permitted to become citizens. Hence, they controlled few power resources with which to defend themselves, and they were forced out of the mainstream economy. The Chinese reacted by forming Chinatowns, separate subcommunities based on small businesses such as laundries (Lyman, 1974, p. 77). The campaign against the Chinese experienced its ultimate triumph with the passage of the Chinese Exclusion Act of 1882, which banned virtually all immigration from China.

Consistent with the predictions of split labor market theory (see chapter 2), the primary antagonists of Chinese immigrants were workers and organized labor. Other social classes, such as factory owners, might actually have benefited from the continued supply of cheaper labor created by immigration from China. Conflicts such as the anti-Chinese campaign can be especially intense because they confound racial and ethnic antagonisms with disputes between different social classes.

After the 1880s, immigration from Japan began. The Japanese immigrants were also mostly young men displaced from traditional agricultural pursuits by the industrial revolution and other changes. They came to the West Coast in pursuit of economic opportunities and soon became the victims of an anti-Japanese campaign similar to that which had been directed at the Chinese. By the 1920s they, too, were dwelling in separate communities that depended on small, family-run businesses for economic survival (Kitano, 1980, p. 563).

Intergroup Conflict and the Campaign Against Immigrants

The Chinese Exclusion Act of 1882 was an early victory for the restrictionists, who wanted to limit or eliminate immigration. The movement for restriction fluctuated in strength with the business cycle, the volume of immigration, and a host of other variables. The dominant group was rarely completely unified on the issue. Two of the chief protagonists in this drama were the native-born American working class on one hand, and industrialists (large employers, factory and mine owners, etc.) on the other. These groups often found their interests diametrically opposed. The working class began to band together in trade unions and other organizations to improve working conditions and to increase wages and job security, demands that the industrialists typically resisted.

European immigrants, as well as immigrants from Asia, were involved in this ongoing conflict in a number of ways. For one thing, the industrialists sometimes used immigrants as strike breakers. Many immigrants came from impoverished backgrounds and were willing to work for wages below what native-born workers considered fair. Needless to say, these episodes inflamed resentment against the immigrants, sometimes to fever pitch.

The antagonism between the working class and immigrants from Europe was tempered by two facts: many American workers were themselves immigrants or the children of immigrants, and immigrants supplied much of the leadership for the early union movement. In the late 19th and early 20th centuries, the most prominent leaders of the labor movement were Irish, German, and Jewish first- and second-generation immigrants (Higham, 1975, p. 24).

The industrialists did not fail to notice the dependence of the labor movement on immigrant leadership. To many of them, it appeared that the union movement was a creation of politically radical immigrants. Although some industrialists saw unrestricted immigration as providing an endless supply of cheap labor, others were alarmed and wanted to restrict immigration in order to weaken the union movement. Thus, the interests of labor and capital sometimes overlapped and sometimes split. In this volatile atmosphere, a third force, consisting of racists and **nativists** (people opposed to the entry of any group that was not Protestant and white) and extremist groups such as the Ku Klux Klan, was added to the shifting anti-immigrant coalition of workers and industrialists (Higham, 1963).

The strength of the restrictionists waxed and waned. Consistent with the Noel hypothesis, they were strongest during hard times, when the threat of competition seemed most serious. Their ultimate victory came with the passage of the National Origins Act in 1924, which drastically reduced immigration overall and banned immigration from Asia. As a reflection of American prejudices of the era, a quota system was established that greatly favored immigrants from Northern and Western Europe as opposed to those from Southern and Eastern Europe. As can be seen in Figure 4.1, the act had a marked and immediate effect on the volume of immigration. By the time the Great Depression took hold of the American economy, immigration had dropped to the lowest levels in a century. The National Origins Act remained in effect until the mid-1960s.

The Assimilation of Immigrants

According to the "classical" model of assimilation, industrialization and modernization ensure the eventual Americanization of immigrants. Immigrants are "huddled masses," uprooted from their traditional social anchors in the old country. In this view, the host society is open to all and neutral in its distribution of rewards and opportunities. Different groups assimilate at different speeds largely as a function of the resources and cultural characteristics that they bring with them. Crucial among these are education and familiarity with English.

Implicit in this view is **human capital theory**. This theory views status attainment, or the level of success achieved by an individual in society, as a result of educational level, personal values and skills, and other individual characteristics and abilities. Education is seen as an investment in human capital, not unlike the investment a business might make in machinery or new technology. The greater the investment in a person's human capital, the higher the probability of success. For example, Blau and Duncan (1967), in their pioneering statement of this perspective, found that for people from elite social classes, success is not so much a result of being born into an affluent family as it is a result of the superior education that affluence makes possible.

The human capital view of individual mobility is based on the assumption that American society is largely open and fair. Success is a direct result of individual effort and the wise investment of personal resources. People who fail haven't tried hard enough, haven't made the right kinds of educational investments, or have values or habits that limit their ability to compete.

Another important characteristic of the classical view is that it sees assimilation as a linear, step-by-step process marked by generations. The first generation—the actual immigrants—settled in ethnic neighborhoods (Little Italy, Chinatown, etc.) and made only a limited movement toward acculturation and integration. Many of them had to leave their neighborhood to find work and thereby acquired some familiarity with the larger society. Nonetheless, the first generation lived and died largely within the context of the old country, re-created within the new.

The second generation, or the children of the immigrants, were born in the United States but in households and neighborhoods that were ethnic, not American. They learned the old language first and were socialized in the old ways. When they entered the public schools, however, they were socialized into Anglo-American culture. Very often, the world they learned about at school conflicted with the world they inhabited at home.

For example, old country values often expected children to subordinate their self-interest to the interests of the family as a whole. Marriages were arranged or at least heavily influenced by the parents. These expectations conflicted sharply with American ideas about individualism and romantic love. Differences of this sort often caused painful conflict between the more ethnic first generation and their more Americanized children.

As the second generation progressed toward adulthood and entered the mainstream economy, they tended to move out of the old neighborhood. They were much more acculturated than their parents, spoke fluent English, and enjoyed a wider range of occupational choices and opportunities. They sometimes were limited by discrimination, but they were upwardly mobile and left the ethnic subcommunity behind.

The third generation, or the grandchildren of the immigrants, were typically born and raised in nonethnic settings. English was their first and often their only language, and their values were thoroughly American. Ethnicity for this generation was a relatively minor part of their daily realities and their self-images. They completed the assimilation process and were both acculturated and integrated.

Table 4.1 Some Comparisons Between Italians and WASPs

		Generation		
	WASPs[1]	First	Second	Third and Fourth
Percent with some college	42.4	19.0	19.4	41.7
Average years of education	12.6	9.0	11.1	13.4
Percentage				
White collar	34.7	20.0	22.5	28.8
Blue collar	37.9	65.0	53.9	39.0
Average occupational prestige	42.5	34.3	36.8	42.5
Percentage of "unmixed" Italian males marrying non-Italian females		21.9	51.4	67.3

1. WASPs were not separated by generation and some of the differences between groups may be the result of factors such as age. That is, the older WASPs may have had levels of education more comparable to first-generation Italian Americans than to WASPs as a whole.

Source: Adapted from Alba, 1985, tables 5-3, 5-4, and 6-2. The data are originally from the NORC General Social Surveys, 1975–1980, and the Current Population Survey, 1979.

Some data on Italian immigrants and their descendants illustrate the generational process. Table 4.1 shows that the educational and occupational characteristics of Italian Americans converges with those of the white Anglo-Saxon Protestants (WASPs) as the generations progress. The percentage of respondents "with at least some college" shows a gap of more than 20 points between the Italians of the first and second generations and WASPs. Italians of the third and fourth generations, though, are virtually identical to WASPs on this measure of integration in the secondary sector. The other differences in integration in the public sector shrink in a similar fashion from generation to generation. The last comparison in Table 4.1 measures marital assimilation. It displays the percentage of males of "unmixed" or 100% Italian heritage who married females outside the Italian community. Note that this type of integration also increases by generation.

These data are quite consistent with the classical view of assimilation by generation. The problem with the classical view is not so much that it is wrong but that it describes only one of many possible immigration experiences. The patterns of acculturation before integration and a linear progression across the generations from ethnic to American describe the experiences of European immigrants far more accurately than they describe those from Asia. Within the European group, the model fits Northern and Western Europeans more than it fits immigrants from Ireland and from Southern and Eastern Europe.

One other problem with the classical view is that it treats the adjustment and status attainment of immigrants as an individual matter. Scholars have demonstrated that immigration to the United States was, in large measure, a group phenomenon. For example, immigrants often followed chains established and maintained by others. The chains and networks supplied money for passage, family news, and job offers and were held together by the ties of kinship, culture, and a sense of common peoplehood (Bodnar, 1985; Tilly, 1990).

Here's how chain immigration worked: an immigrant, upon arrival in the United States, would send his or her address back to the home village. Before long, another immigrant from the village, perhaps a brother or other relative, would arrive at the residence of the original immigrant, who would provide a place to sleep and an orientation to the new society. As time passed, others would arrive from the village. The compatriots would tend to settle in close proximity to each other, in the same building or block. Soon, entire neighborhoods were filled with people from a certain village or province. In these ethnic enclaves, the old language was spoken and the old ways observed. Businesses were started, churches or synagogues founded, families were begun, and mutual aid societies and other organizations were formed. There was safety in numbers and comfort and security in a familiar, if transplanted, set of traditions and customs.

For some groups—victims of rejection such as the Jews and Chinese—these ethnic neighborhoods became the dominant structure of their lives. Rather than undergoing a linear, generation-by-generation assimilation process, these groups built separate enclaves, largely independent of the larger society. Quite contrary to the classical view, it was the networks and resources developed in the enclaves that made it possible for members of the group to eventually succeed in the larger society (Morawska, 1990).

The classical model also tends to de-emphasize the variations in the speed of assimilation from group to group. One factor that affected the rate of assimilation was the extent to which the group desired to be Americanized. Some groups were very committed to Americanization. Eastern European Jews, for example, fled their homelands in fear for their lives and planned to make America their home from the beginning, even in the face of discrimination and rejection.

Other immigrants had no intention of becoming American. These **sojourners,** or "birds of passage," intended to return once they had accumulated enough capital to be successful in their homeland. A large percentage of Italian immigrants were sojourners. While almost 4 million Italians arrived between 1899 and 1924, some 2.1 million departed during the same interval (Nelli, 1980, p. 547).

For other groups, assimilation was very much affected by social class variables. The huge majority of the post-1880s European immigrants were laborers who entered the society at the bottom of the economic ladder and stayed on or near that level for the next half century (Bodnar, 1985; Morawska, 1990). Many of these groups did not acculturate to middle-class American culture but to an urban working-class, blue-collar set of lifestyles and values. Even today, ethnicity for many groups remains interconnected with social class factors, and a familiar stereotype of white ethnics is the hard hat construction worker.

Immigrants came to the United States because of the opportunities available in an expanding, industrializing economy. The levels of success they enjoyed were not simple matters of values, skills, or investments in education. Although these things were important (for some groups more than others), immigrants were also, at various times, the victims of discrimination and were excluded from the institutions of the larger society and exploited for their labor. These processes of discrimination and acceptance, exclusion and inclusion, and Americanization and exploitation affected different groups in different ways.

Gender and Immigration

The great bulk of the literature on immigration concerns the experience in general or is focused specifically on male immigrants. The experiences of female immigrants have been much less recorded and, hence, are less accessible. Many immigrant women came from cultures with strong patriarchal traditions in which they had little access to leadership roles, education, and high-prestige occupations. Like slave women, the voice of immigrant women is muted. However, the research that has been done documents the fact that immigrant women played multiple roles in addition to wife and mother both during immigration and during the process of adjusting to U.S. society (Seller, 1987, p. 198).

It was common for the males to immigrate first and send for the women only after the men had secured lodging, a job, and some security. In some cases, though, women were prominent among the first wave of immigrants. For example, a high percentage of Irish immigrants were young single women seeking jobs. Many were employed in domestic work, a role that permitted them to live "respectably" in a family setting (Blessing, 1980).

The economic situation of immigrant families was typically precarious, so it was common for women of all ages to work for wages. The type and location of the work varied from group to group. Whereas Irish women were concentrated in domestic work and in factories and mills, this was rare for Italian women. Italian culture strictly prohibited contact between single women and men (Alba, 1985, p. 53). Thus, acceptable work situations for Italian women usually involved work that could be done at home: doing laundry, taking in boarders, and doing piecework for the garment industry. Italian women who did work outside the home were very likely to work alongside other immigrant women.

Eastern European Jewish women represent still another pattern. Most came with their husbands and children in intact family units and few held jobs outside the family. When they did, it was typically in the garment industry or in family-run shops (Steinberg, 1981, p. 161).

Chinese women immigrants were unique in that they were scarce. Chinese immigrants were overwhelmingly male sojourners, and the Chinese Exclusion Act of 1882 prevented the men from sending for the women. The result was a grossly unbalanced sex ratio. Early in this century, Chinese men outnumbered Chinese women by about 250 to 1 (Lai, 1980, p. 223). The scarcity of females made it difficult to create a stable family life and delayed the appearance of a second generation until the 1920s (Chan, 1990, p. 66).

It was common for immigrant women to place highest priority on family needs and to take jobs only as these duties permitted (Evans, 1989). More closely connected to home and family than the men, immigrant women were less likely to learn to read or speak English or otherwise acculturate and were significantly more influential in preserving the heritage of their groups.

It was more common for younger, single, second-generation women to seek employment outside the home. They found opportunities in the industrial sector and in clerical and sales work, occupations that were quickly stereotyped as women's work. Women were seen as working only to supplement the family budget, and this assumption was used to justify a lower wage scale, about half of what men earned (Evans, 1989, p. 135). These patterns of discrimination motivated many women, immigrants and others, to join the labor movement.

African Americans: From Slavery to Segregation

Industrialization not only stimulated immigration to the United States, it was also responsible, in a way, for the end of slavery. The Northern states began to industrialize early in the 1800s, while the South remained primarily agricultural. This economic diversity was one underlying cause of the regional conflict that led to the Civil War. The more industrialized North had more resources than the South and, in a bloody war of attrition, defeated the Confederacy and brought an end to slavery.

The system of race relations that emerged in the South after the Civil War was similar in some ways to the rigid competitive systems of group relations that sought to limit the threats represented by Asian and European immigrants. For Southern blacks, however, the system was far more elaborate and inescapable. The greater oppressiveness was a function of the long history of inferior status and powerlessness for black Americans and, in part, was a result of the particular needs of Southern agriculture. The greater rigidity was also made possible by the greater social visibility of racial, as opposed to cultural, differences.

Following the end of the Civil War in 1865, the federal government enforced racial freedom in the defeated Southern states, and the period of **Reconstruction** was a brief respite in the long history of oppression of African Americans. Black Southerners voted and were elected to high political offices. Schools for the former slaves were opened, land and houses were purchased, and businesses were started. The era was short, however, and began to end when the federal government demobilized its army of occupation and turned its attention to other matters. By the 1880s black Southerners were being rapidly pushed into a new system of exploitation and inequality.

Slavery had left black Southerners impoverished, largely uneducated, and with few power resources. When Reconstruction ended and new threats of racial oppression appeared, they found it difficult to defend their group interests. Furthermore, after centuries of slavery, prejudice and racism were thoroughly ingrained in Southern culture, and whites were predisposed to see racial inequality and exploitation of African Americans as normal and inevitable.

De Jure Segregation

The system of race relations that replaced slavery in the South was **de jure segregation**, sometimes referred to as the Jim Crow system. Segregation means that groups are physically and socially separated, with the minority group consigned to an inferior position. The phrase *de jure* ("by law") means that the system is sanctioned by the legal code;

the inferior status of blacks was actually mandated or required by state and local laws. For example, Southern cities had laws requiring blacks to ride in the back of the bus. If a black person refused to comply with this seating arrangement, he or she was breaking a law, not just a custom, and could be arrested.

De jure segregation came to encompass all aspects of Southern life. Neighborhoods, jobs, stores, restaurants, and parks were all eventually segregated. When movie theaters, sports stadiums, and interstate buses appeared in the South, they, too, were quickly segregated.

In a vicious cycle, the logic of segregation took on a life of its own. The more African Americans were excluded, the greater their objective poverty and powerlessness became. The more inferior their status, the easier it was to mandate even more inequality. High levels of inequality reinforced racial prejudice and made it easy to use racism to justify still more separation. The system kept turning on itself, finding new social niches to segregate and reinforcing the inequality that was its starting point. At the height of the Jim Crow era, separate bibles were used in courtrooms and even interracial games of checkers and dominoes were banned (Woodward, 1974, p. 118).

What caused this massive separation of the races? Once again, the Noel hypothesis provides a useful conceptual framework. Segregation flowed from the social, economic, and political realities of the post–Civil War South, where the plantation elite remained the dominant class and cotton remained the primary crop. The landowners still needed a workforce to farm the land, and they turned to a system of **sharecropping**, or tenant farming (Geschwender, 1978, p. 158; Wilson, 1973, p. 99). Sharecroppers would work the land in return for a share of the profit when the crop was taken to market. The landowner would supply a place to live and food and clothing on credit and deduct these debts from the tenant's share of the profits. The accounts were kept by the landowner and, because they lacked political and civil rights, black sharecroppers found it difficult to keep an unscrupulous landowner honest. The landowner could claim that he was still owed money and the sharecroppers could be bound to the land until their "debts" was paid off (Geschwender, 1978, p. 163).

Segregation and sharecropping also protected the white Southern working class from direct competition. As the South began to industrialize, white workers were able to monopolize the better paying jobs, while black Southerners remained a rural peasantry, excluded from education and participation in the process of modernization. This pattern of "separate development" for the black and white communities was reinforced by still more laws that limited the options and life courses available to black Southerners.

A final force behind the creation of de jure segregation was more political than economic. As the 19th century drew to a close, a wave of agrarian radicalism known as populism spread across the country. This antielitist movement attempted to unite poor Southerners of both races against the traditional elite classes.

The elites were frightened by the possibility of a loss of power and used racial hatred to split whites and blacks. To prevent future threats, southern states deprived blacks of the right to vote (Woodward, 1974). By the early part of this century, the political power of the Southern black community was virtually nonexistent. For example, as late as 1896, there were more than 100,000 registered black voters in Louisiana. In 1898, the state adopted a new constitution which contained provisions making it very difficult for blacks to vote, and by 1900, only about 5,000 blacks were still registered. Similar declines took place throughout the South, and black political powerlessness was a reality by 1905 (Franklin, 1967).

De jure segregation was approved by the U.S. Supreme Court in the case of *Plessy v. Ferguson* in 1896. The Court found that it was constitutional for states to provide separate facilities (schools, parks, etc.) for blacks as long as the separate facilities were fully equal. The southern states paid very close attention to the parts of the decision that approved separation but ignored the part about equality.

Under de jure segregation, as under slavery, the subordination of the black community was reinforced and supplemented by an elaborate system of racial etiquette. Everyday interactions between blacks and whites were guided by rigid codes. Whites were addressed as "Mister" or "Ma'am" while blacks were called by their first names. In the presence of whites, blacks were expected to be humble and deferential, remove their hats, cast their eyes down, and give way on narrow sidewalks. If an African American had reason to call on anyone in the white community, he or she was expected to go to the back door.

Anyone who ignored these expectations ran the risk of reprisal and even death by lynching. During the decades in which the Jim Crow system was being imposed, lynchings averaged almost one every other day in the South (Franklin, 1967, pp. 439–440). The bulk of this violence was racial and was intended to reinforce the system of racial advantage or to punish transgressors. Various organizations such as the Ku Klux Klan engaged in terrorism against the black community and anyone else who failed to conform to the dictates of the system.

As the system of racial advantage formed and solidified, levels of prejudice and racism increased (Wilson, 1973, p. 101). The new system needed justification and rationalization just as slavery had, and antiblack prejudice and racism developed into an especially negative brand of rejection and exclusion in the South.

Migration North

Resistance to the coming of Jim Crow in the Southern black community was ineffective. The power differentials were still too large and racial hatred and violence too virulent for African Americans in the South to have much impact on the course of events. As was the case under slavery, overt resistance risked massive reprisals.

However, de jure segregation differed from slavery in one important way: Black Southerners were no longer tied to a specific master or plantation and had personal freedom of movement. At the turn of the century, a massive movement of population northward began. Slowly at first, African Americans began to move out of the South and from rural areas to cities (Table 4.2). By doing so, African Americans moved from areas of great resistance to racial change to areas of lower resistance. In the northern cities, for example, it was far easier to register and to vote. Black political power began to grow and eventually provided many of the crucial resources that fueled the civil rights movement of the 1950s and 1960s.

When African-American migrants arrived in the industrializing cities of the North, they found more opportunity and a better life. They also found rejection and discrimination by labor unions, industrialists, and hostile immigrant groups. Compared with the European immigrant groups before them, the barriers to integration were significantly stronger for African Americans because of the permanent nature of the racial differences.

Sociologist Stanley Lieberson (1980) has attempted to explain why immigrants from Southern and Eastern Europe rose faster than African Americans from the South. In his view, the timing of the arrival of these groups in the northern cities is crucial. By the time African Americans began to appear in sizable numbers, the immigrants had been in place for generations. Industrialists used African Americans as

Table 4.2 Population Characteristics of African Americans

	Regional Distribution (%)				Urban Distribution (%)		
	South	North-east	North Central	West	U.S.	South	Non-South
1890	90	4	6	<1	20	15	62
1920	85	7	8	<1	34	25	85
1940	77	11	11	1	50	36	89
1960	60	16	20	8	73	58	95

Sources: Geschwender, 1978, p. 173; U.S. Bureau of the Census, 1977, p. 30.

they had used immigrants, as strike breakers and scabs. Immigrants and large segments of the working class saw black Southerners as a threat and sought to exclude them from unions and from access to better paying jobs.

According to Lieberson, Southern blacks actually *aided* the upward mobility of European immigrants. Whites became less concerned about the immigrants as their alarm over the presence of blacks increased. The greater antipathy for blacks made the immigrants less undesirable and hastened their admittance to the institutions of the larger society. As the white immigrants and their descendants rose, American cities began to develop a concentration of low-income blacks who were economically vulnerable and politically weak (Wilson, 1987, p. 34).

Excluded from the mainstream of American life by segregation and discrimination, African Americans, like many immigrant groups, constructed a separate subsociety and subculture around family, the neighborhood, church, schools, businesses, and organizations of all types. A black middle class emerged based on leadership roles in the church, education, and business. Black colleges and universities were constructed, and organizations such as the National Association for the Advancement of Colored People (NAACP) were created to protest the plight of African Americans and work for equality. However, Jim Crow was a formidable opponent and there were few improvements in the situation of black Americans, North or South, prior to the 1950s.

Gender and Race

For African American men and women alike, the changes wrought by industrialization and the population movement to the North created new possibilities and new roles. However, as the group continued to be exploited and excluded in both the North and the South, black women continued to be among the most vulnerable groups.

As sharecropping and segregation began to shape race relations in the South, women often turned to work in the fields or to domestic work in order to help their families survive. One former slave woman noted that women "do double duty, a man's share in the field and a woman's part at home" (Evans, 1989, p. 121). During the bleak decades following the end of Reconstruction, Southern black families, and black women in particular, lived "close to the bone" (Evans, 1989, p. 121).

In the cities and in the northern neighborhoods, African-American women played roles that sometimes paralleled the roles of immigrant women. Discrimination and racism created constant problems of unemployment for the men, and families often relied on the income supplied by the women to make ends meet. It was comparatively easy for women to find work, but only in low-paying, less desirable areas such as domestic work. In both the South and the North, African-American women worked outside the home in larger proportion than white women. For example, in 1900, 41% of black women were employed, compared with only 16% of white women (Staples, 1988, p. 307). The move north increased employment opportunities, but black women found themselves in the lowest paying and least desirable jobs.

To illustrate, as late as 1930, 90% of employed black women worked in just two types of jobs: agriculture and domestic or personal service (Steinberg, 1981, pp. 206–207). Since the inception of segregation, African-American women have had consistently higher unemployment rates and lower incomes than black men and white women have had (Almquist, 1979, p. 437). These gaps persist to the present day.

Late Industrialization and Minority Groups

Industrialization continued through the 20th century and continued to shape the larger society and dominant-minority relations. The United States in the 1990s bears little resemblance to the society it was a century ago. The population has more than tripled in size and has urbanized even more rapidly than it grew. As the society grew in size and complexity, new organizational forms (bureaucracies, corporations, multinational businesses) and new technologies (nuclear power, computers) came to dominate everyday life. Levels of education rose and the public schools produced one of the most literate populations and best trained workforces in the history of the world.

Minority groups also grew in size, and most became even more urbanized than the general population. Minority group members have come to participate in an increasing array of occupations, and their average levels of education have risen. In spite of these real improvements, however, virtually all U.S. minority groups continue to face serious problems of poverty, unemployment, discrimination, and exclusion. In this section we outline the important features of a "late industrial" society and examine some of its implications for minority groups. We note some of the ways in which the process of industrialization has aided minority groups and address some of the remaining barriers to full participation in the larger society.

Urbanization

We have already noted that urbanization made close, paternalistic controls of minority groups irrelevant. For example, the racial etiquette required by Southern de jure segregation, such as blacks deferring to whites on crowded sidewalks, tends to disappear in the crowded chaos of an urban rush hour. Besides weakening dominant group controls, urbanization also created the potential for minority groups to mobilize and organize large numbers of people. As stated in chapter 1, the sheer size of a group is one source of power. Without the freedom to organize, however, size means little, and urbanization increased *both* the concentrations of population and the freedom to organize.

Occupational Specialization

Industrialization increased occupational specialization and the number of different jobs available in the workforce. The growing needs of the urban population increased the variety of jobs available in the production, transport, and sale of goods and services. Occupational specialization was also stimulated by the very nature of industrial production. Complex manufacturing processes could be performed more efficiently if they were broken down into the narrower component tasks. It was easier and more efficient to train the workforce in the simpler, specialized jobs. Assembly lines were invented and work was subdivided. The sheer number of different occupations grew, and the division of labor became increasingly complex.

The complexity of the industrial job structure and the growing number of different tasks made it difficult to maintain rigid, castelike divisions of labor between dominant and minority groups. Rigid competitive forms of group relations, such as Jim Crow segregation, became less viable as the job market became more complex and changeable. Simple, clear rules about which groups can do which jobs disappeared. As the more repressive systems of control weakened, job opportunities for minority group members sometimes increased. But, as the relationships between group membership and position in the job market became more blurred, conflict between groups increased. For example, African Americans moving from the South to the urban North often found themselves in competition for jobs with white ethnic groups, labor unions, and elements of the dominant group.

Bureaucracy

As industrialization continued, privately owned corporations and businesses came to have workforces numbering in the hundreds of thousands. Huge factories employing thousands of workers became common. To coordinate the efforts of these huge workforces, bureaucracy became the dominant form of organization in the economy and, indeed, throughout the society. Bureaucracies are large-scale, impersonal, formal organizations that are run "by the book." They are governed by rules and regulations (i.e., red tape) and are "rational" in that they attempt to find the most efficient way of accomplishing their tasks. Although bureaucracies frequently fail to attain the ideal of fully rational efficiency, there is a tendency to recruit, reward, and promote employees based on competence and performance (Gerth & Mills, 1946).

The stress on rationality and objectivity can counteract the more blatant forms of racism and increase the array of opportunities available to members of minority groups. Although they are often nullified by other forces (see Blumer, 1965), these antiprejudicial tendencies do not exist at all or are much weaker in preindustrial economies.

The history of the concept of race illustrates the effect of rationality and scientific ways of thinking. Today, the great majority of the scientific community regards race as a biological triviality, a conclusion based on decades of research. This scientific finding undermined and contributed to the destruction of systems of privilege based solely on race (e.g., segregated school systems) and individual perceptual systems (e.g., traditional prejudice) based on the assumption that race was a crucial personal characteristic.

Growth of White-Collar Jobs and the Service Sector

Industrialization changed the composition of the labor force. As work became more complex and specialized, the need to coordinate and regulate the production process increased and, as a result, bureaucracies and other organizations grew larger still. Within these organizations, white-collar occupations—those that coordinate, manage, and deal with the flow of paperwork—continued to expand. As industrialization progressed, mechanization and automation began to reduce the number of manual or blue-collar workers, and white-collar occupations became the dominant sector of the job market in the United States.

The changing nature of the workforce can be explained by looking at the proportional representation of three different types of jobs:

- **Extractive (or primary) occupations** are those that produce raw materials, such as food and agricultural products, minerals, and lumber. The jobs in this sector are generally low paid and often involve unskilled manual labor.
- **Manufacturing (or secondary) occupations** transform raw materials into finished products ready for sale in the marketplace. These blue-collar jobs also involve manual labor, but these jobs often require higher levels of skill and are more highly rewarded. Examples of occupations in this sector would include the assembly-line jobs that transform steel, rubber, plastic, and other materials into finished automobiles.

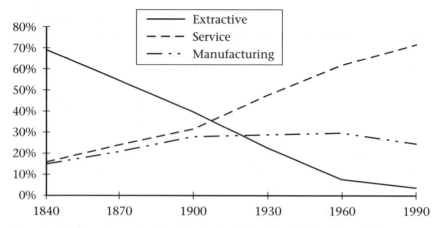

Figure 4.2 The Changing American Labor Force: The Distribution of Jobs, 1940–1990 (Percentages)

Source: Adapted from Lenski, Nolan, and Lenski, 1995, p. 281. Reprinted by permission.

- **Service (or tertiary) occupations** don't produce "things" but, rather, provide services. As urbanization increased and self-sufficiency decreased, opportunities for work in this sector grew. Examples of tertiary occupations would include police officer, clerk, waiter, teacher, nurse, and cab driver.

The course of industrialization is traced in the changing structure of the labor market depicted in Figure 4.2. In 1840, when industrialization was only beginning in the United States, most of the workforce was in the extractive sector, with agriculture being the dominant occupation. As industrialization progressed, the manufacturing or secondary sector grew, reaching a peak after World War II. Today, the large majority of jobs are in the service, or tertiary, sector.

The service sector includes a highly varied array of occupations. At the lower end are low-paying jobs with few, if any, benefits or chances for advancement (e.g., washing dishes in a restaurant). At the upper end are high-prestige, lucrative positions such as Supreme Court justice and star entertainers and athletes.

The changing structure of the job market helps to clarify the nature of intergroup competition and the sources of wealth and power in the society. Job growth, especially since the 1930s, has been in the service sector. Compared to jobs in the manufacturing sector, service jobs have different entry requirements and are often less well paid. We would expect the economic situation of minority groups to reflect these fundamental changes.

One concept that describes the recent evolution of the American job market is **deindustrialization,** a shift from manufacturing to the service sector and to information processing. The U.S. economy has lost millions of unionized, high-paying manufacturing jobs over the past several decades, and the downward trend (see Figure 4.2) will continue. The industrial jobs that sustained so many generations of American workers have moved to other nations with cheaper workforces or have been eliminated by robots or other automated manufacturing processes.

The new jobs created in the service sector are either high-paying technical, professional, or administrative jobs with demanding entry requirements (e.g., physician or nurse) or low-paid, low-skilled jobs with few benefits and little security (e.g., receptionist, nurse's aide). Thus, job growth in the United States has been either in areas in which educationally deprived minority group members find it difficult to compete or in areas that offer little compensation, upward mobility, or security.

The Growing Importance of Education

Education has become an increasingly important prerequisite for employability. A high school degree—or more often a college degree—has become the minimum entry-level requirement for an increasing percentage of jobs. However, opportunities for high-quality education are not distributed equally across the population. For much of this century, some minority groups, including African Americans and Mexican Americans, have been systematically excluded from the schools of the dominant society and are today less likely to have the educational backgrounds needed to compete for better jobs. Access to education is a key issue for almost all U.S. minority groups and the average educational levels of these groups have been rising since World War II. Still, minority children are much more likely to attend segregated, underfunded, deteriorated schools and to receive inferior educations.

The Split Labor Market

The changing composition of the labor force and increasing importance of educational credentials has created a split labor market in the U.S. economy. The labor market is divided into two segments or types of jobs. The **primary labor market** includes jobs usually located in large, bureaucratic organizations. These positions offer higher pay, security, opportunities for advancement, health and retirement benefits, and other amenities. Entry requirements often include college degrees, even when the work could be competently performed by people with fewer years of schooling.

In the **secondary labor market**, sometimes called the competitive market, are low-paid, low-skilled, insecure jobs. Many of these jobs are in the service sector. They do not represent a career and offer little opportunity for promotion or upward mobility. Very often, they do not offer health or retirement benefits, are part time, seasonal, or temporary, and have high rates of turnover.

Many American minority groups are concentrated in the secondary job market. Their position is maintained not so much by direct or obvious discrimination based on race, ethnicity, religion, or gender, but rather by the educational and other credentials required to enter the primary sector. The differential distribution of educational opportunities, in the past as well as in the present, effectively protects workers in the primary sector from competition from minority groups.

Globalization

During the 20th century, the United States became an economic, political, and military world power with interests around the globe. These worldwide ties have created new minority groups through population movement and changed the status of others. Immigration to this country has been considerable for the past three decades. The American economy is one of the most productive in the world, and jobs, even those in the low-paid secondary sector, are the primary goals for millions of newcomers. For other immigrants, this country continues to play its historic role as a refuge from political and religious persecution.

Many of the wars, conflicts, and other disputes in which the United States has been involved have had consequences for American minority groups. For instance, both Puerto Ricans and Cuban Americans became U.S. minority groups as the result of processes set in motion during the Spanish-American War of 1898. The mobilization of the economy for both World War I and World War II created new job opportunities for many minority groups, including African Americans and Mexican Americans. After the Korean War, international ties were forged between the United States and South Korea, which led to increased immigration from Korea. More recent entanglements in Southeast Asia led to the immigration of Vietnamese, Cambodian, and other Asian groups.

Dominant-minority relations in the United States have been increasingly played out on an international stage as the world has effectively "shrunk" in size and become more interconnected by international organizations such as the United Nations, by ties of trade and commerce, and by modern means of transportation and communication. In a world in which two-thirds of the population is nonwhite and many important nations (such as China, India, and Nigeria) represent peoples of color, the treatment of racial minorities by the U.S. dominant group has come under increased scrutiny. It is difficult to preach principles of fairness, equality, and justice—which the United States claims as its own—when domestic realities suggest an embarrassing failure to fully implement these standards. Part of the pressure for the United States to end blatant systems of discrimination such as de jure segregation came from the desire to maintain a leading position in the world.

The Shift From Rigid to Fluid Competitive Relationships

The changes outlined in the previous section are so fundamental and profound that they are often described in terms of a shift in subsistence technology: from an industrial society, based on manufacturing, to a postindustrial society, based on information processing and computer-related or other new technologies.

As the subsistence technology has evolved and changed, so have American dominant-minority relations. The rigid competitive systems like Jim Crow, associated with earlier phases of industrialization, have given way to **fluid competitive systems** of group relations. In fluid competitive relations, there are no formal or legal barriers to competition (as in Jim Crow laws). Both geographic and social mobility are greater and the limitations imposed by minority group status are less restrictive and burdensome. Rigid caste systems of stratification, in which group membership determines opportunities and adult statuses and jobs, are replaced by more open class systems, in which there is a weaker relationship between group membership and wealth, prestige, and power. Because fluid competitive systems are more open and the position of the minority group is less fixed, the fear of competition from minority groups becomes more widespread for the dominant group, and intergroup conflict increases. Table 4.3 compares the characteristics of the three systems of group relations.

Compared to previous systems, the fluid competitive system is closer to the American ideal of an open, fair system of stratification in which effort and competence are rewarded, and race, ethnicity, gender, religion, and other "birthmarks" are irrelevant. However, as we will see in the following chapters, race and ethnicity continue to affect life chances and limit opportunities for minority group members even in fluid competitive systems. People continue to identify themselves with particular groups (ethnocentrism), and competition for resources continues to play out along group lines. Even though the American stratification system is more open than it has been in the past, racial and ethnic inequality remain primary realities of everyday life.

Table 4.3 Characteristics of Three Systems of Group Relationships

| | Paternalistic | Competitive | |
		Rigid	Fluid
Subsistence Technology	Agrarian	Early industrial	Advanced industrial
Stratification	*Caste.* Group determines status.	*Mixed.* Elements of caste and class. Group determines status.	*Variable.* Class more important. Group strongly affects status but inequality varies within groups.
Division of Labor	*By group.* Simple division of labor.	*Mostly by group.* Some sharing of jobs by different groups.	*Group moderately related to job.* Complex specialization. Great variation within groups.
Contact Be- tween Groups	*High rates, but contact unequal.*	*Lower rates of contact, mostly unequal and often conflictual.*	*Higher rates of contact and highest rates of equal status contact;* conflict common
Power Differential	*Maximum.* Minority groups have little ability to pursue self- interest.	*Less.* Minority groups have some ability to pursue self- interest.	*Least.* Minority groups have more ability to pursue self- interest.

Source: Based on Farley, 1995, p. 81.

Modern Institutional Discrimination

Virtually all American minority groups lag behind national averages in income, employment, and other measures of equality. These in-equalities persist in spite of dramatic declines in overt prejudice (see chapter 2), the dismantling of de jure segregation, and the introduction of numerous laws designed to ensure that all people are treated without regard to race, gender, or ethnicity. Shouldn't there be less minority group inequality?

As we saw in chapter 2, many Americans attribute the persisting patterns of inequality to the minority groups' lack of willpower or motivation to get ahead. In the remaining chapters of this text, how-ever, I argue that the major barrier facing minority groups in late industrial, post–Jim Crow America is a more subtle but still powerful form of discrimination: **modern institutional discrimination.**

As you recall from chapter 1, institutional discrimination is built into the everyday operation of the social structure of society. The routine procedures and policies of institutions and organizations are arranged so that minority group members are automatically put at a disadvantage. In the Jim Crow era in the South, African Americans were deprived of the right to vote by overt institutional discrimination and could acquire little in the way of power.

The forms of institutional discrimination that persist in the present are more subtle and less overt than those that defined the Jim Crow system. In fact, they are often unintentional or unconscious and exist more in the results for minority groups than in the intentions or prejudices of dominant group members. Modern institutional discrimination is not necessarily linked to prejudice, and the decisionmakers who implement it may think of themselves as behaving rationally and in the best interests of the organization.

When employers make hiring decisions based solely on educational criteria, they may be putting minority group members at a disadvantage. When banks use strictly economic criteria to deny money for home mortgages or home improvement loans in certain "run-down" neighborhoods, they may be handicapping the efforts of minority groups to cope with the results of the blatant, legal housing segregation of the past. When businesspeople decide to reduce their overhead by moving their operations away from center cities, they may be reducing the ability of America's highly urbanized minority groups to earn a living and educate their children. When educators rely solely on tests of ability, which have been developed from white, middle-class experiences, to decide who will be placed in college preparatory courses, they may be limiting the ability of minority group children to compete for jobs in the primary sector.

Any and all of these decisions can and do have devastating consequences for minority individuals, even though decisionmakers may be entirely unaware of the discriminatory effects. Employers, bankers, and educators do not have to be personally prejudiced in order for their actions to have negative consequences for minority groups. Modern institutional discrimination helps to perpetuate systems of inequality that are just as pervasive and stifling as those of the past.

To illustrate, consider the effects of **past-in-present institutional discrimination**, which involves practices in the present that have discriminatory consequences because of some pattern of discrimination or exclusion in the past (Feagin & Feagin, 1986, p. 32). One form of this discrimination is found in workforces organized around the principle of seniority. In these systems, which are quite common, workers who have been on the job longer have higher incomes, more privileges, and other benefits such as longer vacations. The "old-timers" often have more job security and are designated in official, written policy as the last to be fired or laid off in the event of hard times. The privileges of seniority may be thought of by workers and employers alike as just rewards for long years of service, familiarity with the job, and so forth.

These practices may be perfectly reasonable, neutral, and fair. Personnel policies based on seniority, however, can have discriminatory results in the present because, in the past, members of minority groups were excluded from specific occupations by racist labor unions, discriminatory employers, or both. As a result, minority group workers may have fewer years of experience than dominant group workers and may be the first to go when layoffs are necessary. The adage "last hired, first fired" describes the situation of minority group employees who are more vulnerable not because of some overtly racist policy, but because of the routine operation of the seemingly neutral principle of seniority.

It is much more difficult to identify, measure, and eliminate this more subtle form of institutional discrimination. Some of the most bitter disputes in recent dominant-minority relations have concerned public policy and law in this area. Among the most controversial programs is affirmative action, an umbrella term for a variety of programs which, among other goals, attempt to ameliorate the legacy of past discrimination. In cases such as New *York City v. Sheet Metal Workers Union (1986)*, *Fire Fighters Local Union No. 1784 v. Stotts* (1984), and *United Steelworkers of America v. Weber* (1979), the Supreme Court has generally found that programs designed to favor minority employees as a strategy for overcoming overt discrimination in the past are constitutional. Virtually all of these decisions, though, were based on narrow margins (e.g., votes of 5 to 4) and featured acrimonious and bitter debates. More recently, in the case of *Adarand Constructors v. Pena*, decided in June of 1995, the Court narrowed the grounds on which such past grievances could be redressed. The impact of this decision, once more based on a 5 to 4 vote, is uncertain, but many observers thought that affirmative action programs had been dealt a serious blow.

Controversy and confusion continue to surround affirmative action. On the one hand, in July of 1995, President Bill Clinton endorsed affirmative action and pledged to continue these programs (Carney, 1995, p. 35). On the other hand, the state of California may terminate all such programs, and many politicians are calling for similar action nationwide. Affirmative action appears to be very much in danger. If it is ended, one of the few tools available to combat modern institutional discrimination would be eliminated (see Steinberg, 1995).

The Implications for Women

The trends identified in this chapter have affected women in general and minority women in particular. For the past several decades, women have been entering the labor force in large numbers, but they have been concentrated in a limited array of occupations. In 1990 almost 60% of all women were in the labor force, as compared to 76% of all men. Furthermore, between 1960 and 1990, the participation in the workforce of married women with children nearly tripled. Most of these "new workers" held gender-segregated jobs with other women, jobs heavily concentrated in the low-paid service sector. As late as 1990, almost 50% of employed women worked in sales, in clerical jobs, or in other service work (Andersen, 1993, pp. 114–116).

Women can be considered a minority group in several ways. Many female workers face barriers to equality that are similar to those faced by minority group members, including segregation in low-paying service jobs and lack of seniority due to previous discrimination and exclusion. The issues faced by women as a group, however, are different and include sexual harassment and issues relating to maternity leave and child care.

Female members of minority groups face a double disadvantage; the problems and inequalities attached to their minority group membership are confounded with those faced by women as a group. The issues they face as women (and mothers and wives) are overlaid on the barriers of racial and ethnic prejudice and discrimination. Minority women are often the poorest, most vulnerable, and exploited groups in U.S. society (Ortiz, 1994).

Conclusion

This chapter has focused on the continuing industrial revolution and its impact on contemporary dominant-minority relations. For the most part, changes in the situations of American minority groups have been presented as the results of fundamental changes in the economic structure of the larger society. However, changes in dominant-minority relations don't "just happen" as society modernizes. The minority groups themselves and their allies have been largely responsible for the positive improvements in dominant-minority relations since the mid-20th century. While the *opportunity* to pursue favorable change was the result of broad structural changes in American society, the *realization* of these opportunities came from the efforts of the many who gave their time, their voices, their resources, and sometimes their lives in pursuit of racial justice in America. Since World War II, African Americans have often been in the vanguard of protest activity, and we turn to them in the next chapter.

MAIN POINTS

- Industrialization was the underlying cause of immigration to the United States and of the shift in black-white relations from slavery to segregation. In the early phases of industrialization, paternalistic group relations were replaced by rigid competitive relations.

- Industrialization continued into the 20th century and the United States has become a mature industrial society or, perhaps, a postindustrial society.

- The more recent phases of industrialization have caused a shift from rigid to fluid competitive group relations.

- Modern institutional discrimination is a major factor accounting for the continuing inequality between minority and dominant groups.

- Industrialization affected women in much the same ways as it affected minority groups. The positive changes that have occurred in dominant-minority relations were largely the results of the actions taken by the minority groups themselves and their allies.

FOR FURTHER READING

Bluestone, Barry, & Harrison, Bennet. 1982. *The Deindustrialization of America.* New York: Basic Books.

Feagin, Joe R., & Feagin, Clairece Booher. 1986. *Discrimination American Style: Institutional Racism and Sexism.* Malabar, FL: Robert E. Krieger Publishing Company.

Geschwender, James A. 1978. *Racial Stratification in America.* Dubuque, IA: Wm. C. Brown Publishers.

Handlin, Oscar. 1951. *The Uprooted.* New York: Grosset & Dunlap.

Van den Berghe, Pierre. 1967. *Race and Racism: A Comparative Perspective.* New York: John Wiley & Sons.

Wilson, William J. 1973. *Power, Racism, and Privilege: Race Relations in Theoretical and Sociohistorical Perspectives.* New York: The Free Press.

Woodward, C. Vann. 1974. *The Strange Career of Jim Crow* (3rd ed.). New York: Oxford University Press.

Yans-McLaughlin, Virginia. (Ed.). 1990. *Immigration Reconsidered: History, Sociology, and Politics.* New York: Oxford University Press.

CHAPTER 5

African Americans

From Segregation to Modern Institutional Discrimination and Racism

At the end of the 19th century, African Americans were a Southern rural peasantry, largely unskilled and uneducated. Following the Civil War, they were forced into the sharecropping system of agriculture and barred from the better paying industrial and manufacturing jobs in the urban areas. The system of de jure segregation disenfranchised them and stripped them of the legal and civil rights they had briefly enjoyed during Reconstruction. The huge majority of African Americans had few political rights, few occupational choices, and few vehicles for expressing their views, grievances, and concerns.

Today, as the 20th century draws to a close, African Americans are highly urbanized, dispersed throughout the United States, and represented in virtually every occupational grouping. Poverty, racism, discrimination, and prejudice still are major obstacles, but African Americans are visible at the highest levels of the society. Some of the best known, most successful and respected people in the world are African Americans: Martin Luther King, Jr., Malcolm X, Michael Jordan, Shirley Chisholm, Jesse Jackson, Toni Morrison, Maya Angelou, Muhammad Ali, Barbara Jordan, and General Colin Powell, to name just a few.

How did these changes come about and what do they signify? What problems are obscured by the glittering success stories mentioned above? Is there support for the view held by so many white Americans that the barriers to racial equality have been eliminated?

To understand the trajectories of change that lead to the present, we must deal with the watershed events in black-white relations: the end of de jure segregation, the triumphs (and the limitations) of the civil rights movement of the 1950s and 1960s, the urban riots and Black Power movement of the 1960s, and the continuing racial divisions within U.S. society since the 1970s. Behind these changes lie the powerful pressures of industrialization and modernization, the shift from rigid to fluid competitive group relations, changing distributions of power, declining levels of overt prejudice, and new ideas about assimilation and pluralism. In less abstract terms, the changes in black-white relations in the 20th century were the direct result of protest, resistance, and the concerted actions of thousands of individuals, black and white.

The End of De Jure Segregation

As stressed in chapter 4, relations between minority and dominant groups change as a result of changes in the larger society, especially transformations in subsistence technology. As industrialization and urbanization progressed, a series of social, political, economic, and legal processes was set in motion that ultimately destroyed Jim Crow segregation. No single date or specific event marks the end of de jure segregation. The system ended as it had begun—gradually and in a series of discrete episodes and incidents.

As the 20th century progressed, the agricultural economy of the South was eventually modernized and mechanized. Agricultural work became less labor intensive, and the need to maintain a large, powerless workforce declined (Geschwender, 1978, pp. 175–177). As machines displaced people in the rural economy, black Southerners moved to the North and to urban areas, where it was easier to register to vote and pursue other avenues for improving the situation of their group. The weight of the growing black vote began to be felt in the 1930s and was large enough to make a difference in local, state, and even national politics by the 1940s.

Wartime Developments

An opportunity for the exertion of the slowly growing political strength of African Americans occurred during the early days of World War II. In 1941 race relations in the United States were still in the rigid competitive phase and racial discrimination was widespread, even in the industries crucial to the nation's defense. That year a group of African Americans, led by labor leader A. Philip Randolph, head of the Brotherhood of Sleeping Car Porters, threatened to march on Washington to protest the discriminatory treatment.

Recognizing the need to mobilize all segments of the population for the world war, and recognizing the rising power of the northern African-American community, President Franklin D. Roosevelt headed off Randolph's march on Washington by signing an executive order banning discrimination in defense-related industries (Geschwender, 1978, pp. 199–200). This executive order was significant in two ways. First, the signing meant that a group of black Americans not only had their grievances heard at the highest level of the society, but they also succeeded in getting what they wanted. Second, the federal government made an unprecedented commitment to fair employment rights for black Americans. This alliance between the federal government and African Americans was tentative but it foreshadowed some of the dynamics of racial change that took place in the 1950s and 1960s.

The Postwar Period

The nation entered a period of prosperity after the war, and African Americans continued to accumulate political and economic power. During prosperous times, the intensity of intergroup competition is often muted by a decline in the dominant group's resistance to change and sense of threat. When the economic "pie" is expanding, the "slices" claimed by minority groups can increase without threatening the size of anyone else's portions, and the prejudice that is generated during intergroup competition is held in check.

Also, some of the economic prosperity found its way into African-American communities throughout the nation and further increased their pool of economic and political resources. Independent, African-American–controlled organizations and institutions, such as churches and colleges, had been created in response to Jim Crow segregation. During this period of economic growth, these groups grew in size and power. The increasingly elaborate infrastructure of the black community provided material resources, leadership, and the "people power" to lead the fight against segregation and discrimination.

By the late 1940s, the African-American community began to have an active role in national politics. In 1948, for example, President Harry Truman recognized that he could not be reelected without the support of African-American voters, and as a result the Democratic party adopted a civil rights plank in its party platform (Wilson, 1973, p. 123). These increases in freedom and strength were used to fuel a variety of efforts that sped the demise of Jim Crow segregation.

The Civil Rights Movement

The civil rights movement was a multifaceted campaign to end legalized segregation and ameliorate the massive inequalities faced by black Americans. The campaign lasted for more than a decade and included lawsuits and courtroom battles as well as protest marches and demonstrations.

Brown v. Board of Education of Topeka

Undoubtedly, the single most powerful blow to de jure segregation was delivered by the U.S. Supreme Court in the decision of *Brown v. Board of*

Education of Topeka in 1954. In this decision, the Court reversed the *Plessy v. Ferguson* decision of 1896 and ruled that racially separate facilities are inherently unequal and, therefore, unconstitutional.

The landmark *Brown* decision didn't "just happen," though. It was the culmination of decades of planning and effort by the National Association for the Advancement of Colored People (NAACP) and individuals such as Thurgood Marshall, the NAACP's chief counsel, who was later appointed to the Supreme Court in 1967. The NAACP had been founded in 1909 by a coalition of white liberals and African Americans and had early on developed a strategy of "legalism" for attacking Jim Crow. The basic idea behind this strategy was to find instances in which the civil rights of a black American had been violated and then to bring suit against the relevant governmental agency. The NAACP's lawsuits were intended to extend far beyond the specific case being argued. The goal was to persuade the courts to declare segregation unconstitutional not only in the specific instance being tried but in all similar cases.

The *Brown* decision was the triumphant outcome of this strategy. The principle established by *Brown* was assimilationist: it ordered the educational institution of the dominant group to be opened up, freely and equally, to all. The significance of the Supreme Court's decision was not that Linda Brown, the child in whose name the case was argued, would attend a different school, or even that the school system of Topeka, Kansas, would be integrated. Instead, the significance lay in the rejection of the *principle* of de jure segregation in the South and, by implication, throughout the nation. The *Brown* decision dealt a crippling blow to Jim Crow segregation.

The blow was not fatal, however. The southern states responded to the *Brown* decision by stalling and mounting campaigns of massive resistance. Jim Crow laws remained on the books for years. White Southerners actively defended the system of racial privilege and attempted to forestall change through violence and intimidation. Racist and terrorist groups like the Ku Klux Klan (which had been largely dormant since the 1920s) appeared, and white politicians and other leaders competed with one another to express the most adamant statements of racist resistance (Wilson, 1973, p. 128).

Nonviolent Direct Action and Protest

Considerable effort and years of struggle would be required to actualize the intent of the *Brown* decision and overcome Southern defiance and resistance. The central force in this struggle was a protest movement, the beginning of which is often traced to events occurring in Montgomery, Alabama, on December 1, 1955. On that day, Rosa

Parks, a seamstress and NAACP member, rode the city bus home from work. As the bus filled up, she was ordered to surrender her seat to a white passenger. When she refused, the police were called, and Rosa Parks was jailed for violating a local segregation ordinance.

The black community of Montgomery protested the arrest and began a boycott of the city buses. African Americans created car pools, shared taxis, and walked (in some cases, for miles) to and from work. They stayed off the buses until victory was achieved and the city was ordered to desegregate its buses. The Montgomery boycott was led by the Reverend Martin Luther King, Jr., the new minister of a local Baptist church.

From these beginnings sprang the protest movement that eventually defeated de jure segregation. For the next decade, the movement used a variety of means to challenge and change the racist system that had exploited and oppressed African Americans for so many decades. The central tactics involved **nonviolent direct action**, a variety of techniques by which the movement confronted the system of de jure segregation head-on; not in the courtroom or in the state legislature, but directly in the streets (King, 1958, 1963, 1968). Nonviolent protest was intended to confront the forces of evil rather than the people who happened to be doing evil, and it attempted to win the friendship and support of its enemies rather than defeat or humiliate them. Above all, nonviolent protest required courage and discipline; it was not a method for cowards (King, 1958, pp. 83–84).

The movement used different tactics for different situations. Segregated restaurants and lunch counters were targeted for sit-ins, in which black customers would request service, and when service was denied ("We don't serve Colored here"), they would firmly and politely refuse to leave. Freedom Rides involving integrated groups of travelers were used to test the desegregation of Southern buses and bus terminals. The systematic disenfranchisement of African Americans in the South was countered by voter registration drives and educational programs. Other forms of segregation were met with marches, prayer meetings, and a variety of other forms of protest.

The high point for the movement came in August of 1963 when the March on Washington was organized to dramatize continuing American segregation and racism and to rally support for the civil rights movement. Some 250,000 people, black and white, attended and heard Dr. King's famous "I Have a Dream" speech.

The March on Washington was widely reported in the mass media and served to crystallize much of the sentiment for racial equality in America. It also provoked attitudes and actions resistant to racial equality. Just weeks after the march, a black church in Birmingham,

Alabama, was bombed, taking the lives of four little girls. It would take more than protests and marches to finally extirpate de jure segregation, and the necessary tools were finally provided by the U.S. Congress. (See Killian, 1975; King, 1958, 1963, 1968; Morris, 1984, for more information on the civil rights movement.)

Landmark Legislation

The successes of the protest movement, combined with changing public opinion and the legal principles established by the Supreme Court, coalesced in the mid-1960s to stimulate the passage of two laws that, together, ended de jure segregation. In 1964 the U.S. Congress passed the Civil Rights Act banning discrimination on the grounds of race, color, religion, national origin, or gender. The law applied to publicly owned facilities such as parks and municipal swimming pools, businesses, and other facilities open to the public, and any programs that received federal aid.

Congress followed up with the Voting Rights Act in 1965, which required that the same standards be used in registering *all* citizens in federal, state, and local elections. The act banned literacy tests and other practices that had been used to prevent blacks from registering to vote. This law gave the franchise back to black Southerners and laid the groundwork for increasing black political power.

The Success and Limitations of the Civil Rights Movement

Why did the civil rights movement succeed? A comprehensive list of reasons would be legion and far beyond the scope of this text. We can, however, cite some of the most important factors, especially those consistent with the general points about dominant-minority relations that have been made in previous chapters.

1. Rigid competitive systems of minority group control like de jure segregation were incompatible with the evolving structure of U.S. society. Although the Jim Crow system wasn't automatically "doomed" by modernization, it was weakened by the continuing industrialization and urbanization of the society as a whole, and the South in particular.
2. The civil rights movement was assimilationist and embraced the dominant code of American values and beliefs (e.g., liberty, equality, and freedom). The movement demanded nothing more for African Americans than the civil, legal, and political rights available to whites as an American birthright. Thus, the goals of the movement could be seen as legitimate and nonthreatening by many in the white community.

3. Because of the "legitimacy" of its goals, the movement could form alliances with other groups (white liberals, Jews, college students, and others) and create favorable public opinion and goodwill in the society as a whole. The support of others was crucial to the success of the movement because black Southerners had few resources of their own, other than their numbers and their courage. By mobilizing the resources of other, more powerful groups, black Southerners forged alliances and created support that was brought to bear on their opposition.

4. The mass media, particularly TV, was generally sympathetic in its coverage of the nonviolent protests. The public at large was able to witness black Americans being refused some simple service or opportunity (e.g., the right to eat at a public lunch counter, register to vote, or attend a public university). Americans of all groups and classes were outraged at the brutality of some Southern police departments and groups like the Ku Klux Klan. Through the media, the movement reinforced the moral consensus that rejected "old-fashioned" racial prejudice and Jim Crow segregation. The blatantly repressive systems of the past could not be sustained in the new climate of opinion, and, eventually, federal legislation eliminated legal segregation in Southern institutions.

The civil rights movement in the South achieved its goal of ending de jure segregation. However, the movement found it difficult to survive the demise of its primary enemy. The confrontational tactics that had been so effective against de jure segregation proved less effective when attention turned to the actual distribution of jobs, wealth, political power, and other valued goods and services.

Developments Outside the South

Outside the South, the allocation of opportunity and resources had always been the central concern of the African-American community. Although the blatantly racist Jim Crow system was largely limited to the South, African Americans in other regions also faced widespread discrimination and exclusion.

De Facto Segregation

Racial discrimination outside the South was less overt but still pervasive, especially in housing, education, and employment. This pattern is often called **de facto segregation**, which is segregation resulting from the apparently voluntary choices of dominant and minority groups alike. Theoretically, no person, law, or specific group is responsible for de facto segregation; it "just happens" as people and groups make choices about where to live and work.

The distinction between de facto and de jure segregation is misleading: the de facto variety of segregation is often the de jure variety in thin disguise. While cities and states outside the South may not have had actual Jim Crow laws, de facto segregation was often the direct result of intentionally racist decisions made by governmental and quasi-governmental agencies such as real estate boards, school boards, and zoning boards.

Regardless of the actual responsibility for these patterns, African-American communities outside the South faced more poverty, higher unemployment, and lower quality housing and schools than did white communities. There was, however, no clear or visible equivalent of Jim Crow to attack or to blame for these patterns of inequality. In the 1960s the African-American community outside the South expressed its frustration over the slow pace of change in two ways: urban unrest and a movement for change, which rose to prominence as the civil rights movement faded.

Urban Unrest

In the mid-1960s the frustration and anger of urban black communities erupted into a series of violent uprisings. The riots began in the summer of 1965 in Watts, a neighborhood in Los Angeles, and over the next four years virtually every large black urban community experienced similar outbursts. Racial violence was hardly a new phenomenon in America. Race riots occurred as early as the Civil War, and various time periods have seen racial violence of considerable magnitude.

The riots of the 1960s were different, however. Most race riots in the past involved attacks by whites against blacks, often including the invasion and destruction of African-American neighborhoods. The urban unrest of the 1960s centered on attacks by blacks against the symbols of their oppression and frustration: white-owned businesses and the police, who were seen as an army of occupation and whose excessive use of force was often the immediate precipitator of riots (Conot, 1967; National Advisory Commission, 1968).

The Black Power Movement

The riots were an unmistakable sign that the problems of race relations had not been resolved by ending Jim Crow segregation. Outside the South, the problems were different and called for different solutions. As the civil rights movement was celebrating its victory in the South, a new protest movement became prominent. The **Black Power movement** was a loose coalition of organizations and spokespersons that encompassed a variety of ideas and views, many of which differed sharply from those of the civil rights movement. Some of the central ideas included racial pride ("Black is beautiful" was an important slogan of the day), interest in African heritages, and black nationalism.

One theme sharply separating the Black Power movement from the assimilationist, coalition-building civil rights movement was the idea that the destiny of African Americans should be determined only by members of the group. Most adherents of the Black Power movement felt that white racism and institutional discrimination, forces buried deep in the core of American culture and society, were the causes of racial inequality in America. Thus, if African Americans were ever to be truly empowered, they would have to liberate themselves and do it on their own terms. Some black power advocates rejected the goal of assimilation into white society, arguing that integration would require blacks to become part of the very system that had, for centuries, oppressed and excluded them and other poor peoples of color. Many organizations in the movement restricted membership to blacks only. Local black power groups worked to increase African-American control over schools, police, welfare programs, and other public services that operated in black neighborhoods.

In the 1960s the Nation of Islam, popularly known as the Black Muslims, became the best known organization within the Black Power movement. The Black Muslims expressed the themes of the movement in angry, impatient, and outspoken tones. They denounced the hypocrisy, greed, and racism of American society and advocated staunch resistance and racial separation. And the Muslims did more than talk. Pursuing their goal of self-determination, they worked to create a separate, independent black economic and social enclave within the United States. They opened businesses and stores in black neighborhoods and tried to deal only with other Muslim-owned firms. Their goal was to develop the black community economically and supply jobs and capital for expansion solely by using their own resources (Essien-Udom, 1962; Lincoln, 1961; Malcolm X, 1964; Wolfenstein, 1993).

It may be useful to stress the distinction made by the Nation of Islam and other black power groups between racial *separation* and racial *segregation*. The former is a process of empowerment whereby the strength of the group increases as it becomes more autonomous and self-controlled. The latter is a system of inequality in which the black community is powerless and controlled by the dominant group. Thus, the black power groups were working to find ways in which African Americans could develop their own resources and deal with the dominant group from a more powerful position.

The most prominent spokesperson for the Black Muslims was Malcolm X. Born Malcolm Little, he converted to Islam and joined the Nation of Islam while serving a prison term. He articulated the themes of black power with eloquence and charisma and became a well-known but threatening figure to the white community. After a dispute with Elijah Muhammad, the leader of the Nation of Islam, Malcolm X founded his own organization in which he continued to express and develop the ideas of black nationalism until his assassination in 1965.

Malcolm X and other black power leaders advocated autonomy and independence and a pluralistic direction for the black protest movement. They saw the black community as a colonized, exploited population in need not of integration, but of liberation from the un-yielding racial oppression of white America.

Protest, Power, and Pluralism

By the end of the 1960s, the riots had ended and the most militant and dramatic manifestations of the Black Power movement had faded. In many cases, the anger of black power activists had been countered by the violence of the police and other agencies, and many of the most powerful spokespersons of the movement were dead; others were in jail or in exile. The nation's commitment to racial change wavered and weakened as other concerns, such as the Vietnam War, competed for attention. Richard M. Nixon was elected president in 1968 and made no pretense of being an ally of the black protest movement. The pressure from the federal government for racial equality was reduced. The boiling turmoil of the mid-1960s faded but the idea of black power had been thoroughly entrenched in the black community.

In some part, the pluralistic themes of black power were a reaction to the failure of assimilation and integration in the 1950s and 1960s. Laws had been passed, court decisions had been widely publicized, promises and pledges had been made by presidents, congressmen, ministers, and other leaders. For many black Americans, though, little changed. The problems of their parents and grandparents continued to constrain and limit their lives and, as far into the future as they could see, the lives of their children. The pluralistic black power ideology was, in part, a response to the failure to go beyond the repeal of Jim Crow laws and to fully implement the promises of integration and equality.

Black nationalism was and remains more than simply a reaction to a failed dream. It was also a different way of defining what it means to be black in America. In the context of black-white relations in the 1960s, the Black Power movement served a variety of purposes. First, black power, along with the civil rights movement, helped to carve out a new identity for African Americans. The cultural stereotypes of African Americans had stressed laziness, irresponsibility, and inferiority. This image needed to be refuted, rejected, and buried. The black protest movements supplied a view of African Americans emphasizing power, assertiveness, seriousness of purpose, intelligence, and courage.

Second, black power served as a new rallying cry for solidarity and unified action. Following the success of the civil rights movement, these new themes and ideas helped to focus attention on "unfinished business": the black-white inequalities that remained in U.S. society.

Finally, the ideology provided an analysis of the problems of American race relations in the 1960s. The civil rights movement had, of course, analyzed race relations in terms of integration, equality of opportunity, and an end to exclusion. After the demise of Jim Crow, that analysis became less relevant. A new language was needed to describe and analyze the continuation of racial inequality. Black power argued that the continuing problems of U.S. race relations were structural and institutional, not individual or legal. To take the next steps toward actualizing racial equality and justice would require a fundamental and far-reaching restructuring of society. White Americans, the beneficiaries of the system, would not support such restructuring. The necessary energy and commitment must come from black Americans pursuing their own self-interest.

The nationalistic and pluralistic demands of the Black Power movement evoked defensiveness and a sense of threat in white society. By questioning the value of assimilation and celebrating a separate African heritage, equal in legitimacy with white European heritages, the Black Power movement questioned the legitimacy and worth of Anglo-American values. Moreover, many black power spokespersons condemned Anglo-American values fiercely and openly, and implicated them in the creation and maintenance of a centuries-long system of racial repression. Today, 30 years after the success of the civil rights movement, assertive and critical demands by the black community are still perceived as a threat.

Gender and Black Protest

Both the civil rights movement and the Black Power movement tended to be male-dominated. African-American women were often viewed as supporters of men rather than equal partners in liberation. Although African-American women were heavily involved in the struggle, they were often denied leadership roles or decision-making positions in favor of men. In fact, the women in one organization, the Student Non-Violent Coordinating Committee (SNCC), wrote position papers to protest their relegation to lowly clerical positions and the frequent references to them as "girls" (Andersen, 1993, p. 284).

The Nation of Islam emphasized female subservience, imposing a strict code of behavior and dress for women and separating the sexes in many temple and community activities. Thus, the battle against racism and the battle against sexism were separate struggles, with separate and often contradictory agendas.

Because African-American women were already deeply involved in community and church work, they often used their organizational skills and energy to further the cause of black liberation. In the view of many, African-American women were the backbone of the movement, even if they were often relegated to less glamorous but vital organizational work (Evans, 1979).

The importance of the role played by women can be illustrated by Fannie Lou Hamer of Mississippi, an African-American woman who became a prominent leader in the black liberation movement. Born in 1917 to parents who were sharecroppers, Hamer's life was so circumscribed that, until she attended her first rally at the beginning of the civil rights movement, she was unaware that blacks *could*—even theoretically—register and vote. She volunteered to register the very next day and became an activist in the movement. As a result, Hamer lost her job, was evicted from her house, and was jailed and beaten on a number of occasions. She devoted herself entirely to the civil rights movement and founded the Freedom party, which successfully challenged the racially segregated Democratic party and the all-white political structure of the state of Mississippi (Evans, 1989; Hamer, 1967).

Black-White Relations Since the 1960s

By the 1970s the basic outlines of present-day black-white relations had been established. Further reductions in racial inequality have been slow and, in many areas, the progress of the African-American community has stagnated or actually reversed. The remaining problems are enormous, deep-rooted, and inextricably mixed with the structure and functioning of modern U.S. society. As was the case in earlier eras, racism and racial inequality today cannot be addressed apart from an understanding of the trends of change in the larger society. This section considers the separation that characterizes U.S. race relations and then applies many of the concepts developed in previous chapters to assess contemporary black-white relations.

Continuing Separation

More than 25 years ago, a presidential commission charged with investigating black urban unrest warned that the United States was "moving towards two societies, one black, one white, separate and unequal" (National Advisory Commission, 1968). Although one might quibble with the commission's use of the phrase *moving towards* and the suggestion that U.S. society was at one time racially unified, the warning still seems prophetic. Without denying that progress *has* been made, most African Americans and white Americans continue to live in worlds that are indeed separate and unequal.

Huge areas of the dominant society continue to be "off-limits" to blacks. Racial exclusivity—of neighborhoods, schools, organizations, and a host of other social locations—is supported by many whites. This hostility is countered by blacks in areas and organizations under their control. To illustrate, in the mid-1980s two black youths were murdered for encroaching on "white" territory in Howard Beach and Bensonhurst, two New York City neighborhoods (Hacker, 1992, pp. 193–195). Also, efforts to desegregate schools have been met with staunch resistance and even violence (Lukas, 1985). In an echo of the racism of Jim Crow segregation, in 1994 a national chain of restaurants was successfully sued for discrimination against African-American customers (Labaton, 1994).

In black communities, feelings of frustration and anger continue to run deep. The unrest and discontent have been manifested in riots, although more sporadically in the present than in the 1960s. For example, Miami has been the site of three major riots since 1980, all precipitated by actions involving the police.

In 1992 the acquittal of the policemen accused of beating Rodney King in Los Angeles caused the eruption of violence in several cities. The worst disturbance occurred in the Watts section of Los Angeles, where 58 people lost their lives and millions of dollars of property damage was done (Wilkens, 1992). In some ways, the riots that followed the King verdict were different from the urban unrest of the 1960s. The more recent riots were multiracial and involved Hispanics as well as blacks. In fact, most of the fatalities were from these two groups. Also, many of the businesses that were looted and burned were owned by Korean Americans, and many of the attacks were against whites directly, as in the beating of truck driver Reginald Denny.

In other ways, the riots shared many similarities. Both were spontaneous and expressed diffuse but bitter discontent with the racial status quo. Both signaled continuing racial inequality, urban poverty, and despair, and the reality of separate nations, unequal and hostile. (See Gooding-Williams, 1993.)

Urbanization and Increasing Class Differentiation

As the repressive force of de jure segregation receded and black Americans moved out of the rural South, social class inequality within the black population increased. Since the 1960s, the black middle class has grown, but so has black poverty.

The Black Middle Class

A small black middle class had been in existence prior to the Civil War (Frazier, 1957). The civil rights movement and various laws (e.g., equal opportunity and affirmative action programs) designed to combat institutional discrimination and expand the access of minority group members to jobs and education increased the range of opportunities open to the black middle class (Wilson, 1980). As openness and tolerance increased in the larger society, this more affluent segment grew in size. There is considerable debate, however, regarding the significance of this development. One of the livelier arguments concerns the relative importance of race and class in shaping the lives of black Americans and other minority groups. Race, one position argues, is no longer the primary controlling influence in the lives of black Americans, and blacks and whites at the same social class level or with the same credentials have the same opportunities (Wilson, 1980). The playing field is level, and what matters is competence and willingness to work hard, not skin color.

The opposite position holds that the success of the black middle class has been overstated and that race is still the dominant factor controlling the distribution of jobs, wealth, and opportunity (Willie, 1989). For example, research has shown that, compared with the white middle class, the black middle class is more dependent on two incomes to sustain its standard of living. On the average, black middle-class families are more likely to be first-generation middle class, have living standards lower than those of white middle-class families, and be in greater danger of dropping out of the middle class. Black college graduates have higher unemployment rates than white college graduates and, when employed, report continuing, if more subtle, discrimination and prejudice (Hill, 1981; Landry, 1987).

A recent national survey found that middle-class blacks lag far behind middle-class whites in economic resources other than income. Taking all forms of wealth into account (savings, stocks, real estate, etc.), one estimate is that for every dollar possessed by middle-income whites, middle-income African Americans have 15 cents (Merida, 1995, p. A23). Not only is their economic position marginal, middle-class blacks commonly report they are unable to escape the narrow straitjacket of race. No matter what their level of success, occupation, or professional accomplishments, race continues to be seen as their primary defining characteristic in the eyes of the larger society (Cose, 1993).

There is also concern that greater class differentiation may decrease solidarity and cohesion within the black community. There is greater income variation among black Americans than ever before. The urban poor are at one extreme and some of wealthiest, most recognized figures in the world—millionaires, celebrities, business moguls, politicians, and sports and movie stars—are at the other. There is concern that the more affluent segment of the black community will disassociate itself from the plight of the less fortunate and move away from the urban neighborhoods, taking with them their affluence, their articulateness, and their leadership skills. If this trend materializes, it would reinforce the class division and further seal the fate of impoverished African Americans, who are largely concentrated in urban areas.

Urban Poverty

African Americans have become an urban minority group in recent decades, and the fate of the group is inextricably bound to the fate of America's cities. The issues of black-white relations cannot be successfully addressed without addressing urban issues and vice versa.

As the U.S. economy matured, automation and mechanization eliminated many of the manual labor jobs that had sustained city dwellers in earlier decades (Kasarda, 1989). The manufacturing, or secondary, segment of the labor force stopped growing whereas the service sector continued to expand. The jobs available to urban minority groups in the service sector, however, often pay low wages and offer no benefits, no security, and no links to more rewarding occupations.

As we saw in chapter 4, educational requirements for jobs in the urban service sector have increased. The upgraded requirements are an example of past-in-present institutional discrimination. They constitute a powerful handicap for colonized groups, such as African Americans, that have been excluded from educational opportunities for centuries.

Further, many blue-collar jobs that might have provided opportunities for impoverished urban minority groups have migrated away from the cities. Industrialists have been moving their businesses to areas where labor is cheaper, unions have less power, and taxes are lower. This movement to the suburbs, to the Sunbelt, and "offshore" has been devastating for the inner city. Poor transportation systems, lack of car ownership, and lack of affordable housing outside the center city have all combined to keep the urban poor confined to center-city ghetto neighborhoods, distant from opportunities for jobs and economic improvement (Kasarda, 1989; Massey & Denton, 1993).

The cities themselves have been victimized by the movement of jobs. As the jobs migrate, so do more affluent segments of the population. Middle-class Americans have been moving to suburbs and to the Sunbelt for decades now, leaving behind cities that are less and less able to generate the tax revenues necessary to fund schools, police forces, sewage systems, job training programs, or thousands of other programs. In addition, the infrastructure (streets, sewage systems, water pipes, subways) of most Northern and Midwestern cities is more than a century old and crumbling. The cost of rebuilding is staggering and increasingly beyond the means of the city to finance.

These industrial and economic forces affect all poor urbanites, not just minority groups or blacks in particular. The dilemma facing many African Americans is, in some part, not simply racism or discrimination; it is caused by the impersonal forces of evolving industrialization and social class structures. However, when immutable racial stigmas and centuries of prejudice are added to these economic and urban developments, the forces limiting and constraining African Americans become extremely formidable.

For the past 30 years, the African-American poor have been increasingly concentrated in narrowly delimited urban areas ("the ghetto") in which the scourge of poverty has been compounded and reinforced by a host of other problems, including joblessness, high rates of school dropout, crime, drug use, teenage pregnancy, and welfare dependency. These isolated neighborhoods are fertile grounds for the development of "oppositional cultures," which reject or invert the values of the larger society and may be most evident in "black English," music, fashion, and other forms of popular culture. These cultures can further limit one's ability to compete in school or in the primary labor market. An urban **underclass**, barred from the mainstream economy and consisting largely of poor African Americans and other minority groups of color, is quickly becoming a permanent feature of the American landscape (Kasarda, 1989; Lawson, 1992; Massey & Denton, 1993; Wilson, 1987, 1992).

Consider the parallels and contrasts between the plights of the present urban underclass and black Southerners under de jure segregation:

- In both cases, a large segment of the African-American population was cut off from opportunities for success and growth.
- In the earlier era, African Americans were isolated in the rural areas; now, they are isolated in urban areas.
- Escape from segregation was limited primarily by political and legal restrictions and blatant racial prejudice; escape in the present is limited by economic and educational deficits and a more subtle and amorphous prejudice.

The result is the same: many African Americans remain a colonized minority group, isolated, marginalized, and burdened with a legacy of powerlessness and poverty.

The Family Institution and the Culture of Poverty

The nature of the African-American family institution has been a continuing source of concern and controversy. On the one hand, some analysts see the black family as structurally weak, a cause of continuing poverty and a variety of other problems. No doubt the most famous study in this tradition was the Moynihan Report (1965), which focused on the higher rates of divorce, separation, desertion, and illegitimacy among African-American families and the fact that black families were far more likely to be female-headed than white families. Moynihan concluded that the fundamental barrier facing black Americans was a family structure which he saw as crumbling, a condition that would perpetuate the cycle of poverty entrapping black Americans (Moynihan, 1965, p. iii). Today, most of the differences between black and white family institutions identified by Moynihan are even more pronounced. Figure 5.1 compares the percentage of households headed by females (black and white) with the percentage of households headed by married couples.

The line of analysis implicit in the Moynihan Report locates the problem of urban poverty (and a host of other problems) in the characteristics of the black community. Family structure is the cause of the

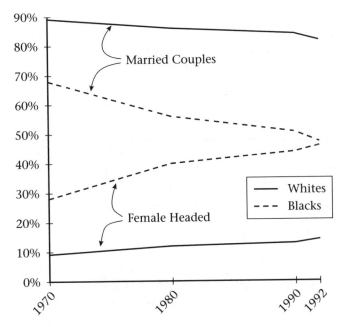

Figure 5.1 Percent of Households Female-headed and with Married Couples, by Race

Source: U.S. Bureau of the Census, 1993, p. 56.

problem and, therefore, needs to be "fixed." This argument is consistent with the **culture of poverty theory**, which argues that poverty is perpetuated by the particular characteristics of the poor. Specifically, poverty is said to encourage fatalism (the sense that one's destiny is beyond one's control) and an orientation to the present rather than the future. The desire for instant gratification is a central trait of the culture of poverty, as opposed to the ability to defer gratification, which is thought to be essential for middle-class success. Other characteristics of the culture of poverty include alcoholism, violence, authoritarianism, and high rates of family desertion by males (Lewis, 1959, 1965, 1966).

The culture of poverty theory leads to the conclusion that the problem of urban poverty would be resolved if female-headed family structures and other cultural characteristics correlated with poverty could be changed. Note that this approach is consistent with traditional assimilationist theory: the poor are seen as having "bad" or inappropriate values. If they could be equipped with "good" (i.e., white, middle class) values, the problem would be resolved.

An opposed perspective, more consistent with the concepts and theories that underlie this text, sees the matriarchal structure of the black family as the *result*, not the cause, of urban poverty, and as a *reflection* of racial discrimination and the scarcity of jobs for urban black males. In impoverished black urban neighborhoods, the supply of men able to support a family is reduced by high rates of unemployment, incarceration, and violence, conditions created by the concentration of urban poverty and the growth of the "underclass" (Massey & Denton, 1993; Wilson, 1987). Thus, the burden of child-raising tends to fall on females, and female-headed households are more common than in more advantaged neighborhoods.

Female-headed African-American families tend to be poor not because of any structural weakness but because of the lower wages accorded to women in general and to minority women in particular (see Table 5.1). The poverty reflects the interaction of sexism and racism rather than a weak or pathological family structure. Sociologist John Farley concludes:

> Black . . . female-householder families experience a double disadvantage in income—the low wages and high unemployment rates associated with minority group status *and* the low wages of women. Significantly, neither of these has anything to do with the effects of one-parent, female-headed families per se. (1995, p. 80; emphasis in original)

This view traces the cause of black urban poverty to the complex forces of past and present institutional discrimination, American racism and prejudice, the precarious position of black women in the la-

Table 5.1 Median Income by Race and Sex, 1980–1991

Whites	1991	1985	1980
Males	$30,953	$25,693	$19,720
Females	$21,555	$16,842	$11,703
Percent of white males	69.6	64.2	59.4
Blacks	**1991**	**1985**	**1980**
Males	$22,628	$17,971	$13,875
Percent of white males	73.1	70.0	70.4
Females	$19,134	$14,590	$10,915
Percent of white males	61.8	56.8	55.4

Source: U.S. Bureau of the Census, 1993, p. 465.

bor force, and continuing urbanization and industrialization. The black family is not in need of "fixing," and the attitudes and values of the urban underclass are more the results of impoverishment and hopelessness than the causes. The solution to black urban poverty lies in fundamental changes in the urban-industrial economy and sweeping alterations in the distribution of resources and opportunities.

Prejudice and Discrimination

In chapter 2, we discussed modern racism, the more subtle form of prejudice that seems to dominate contemporary race relations. Although the traditional, more overt forms of prejudice have not disappeared, contemporary expressions of prejudice seem more amorphous and indirect. A parallel process of evolution from blunt and overt forms to more subtle and covert forms has occurred in patterns of discrimination. The clarity of Jim Crow has yielded to the ambiguity of modern institutional discrimination, which may be unintended, unconscious, and unaccompanied by any overt feelings of prejudice.

The dilemmas of the African-American urban poor present a clear example of institutional discrimination. As long as American businesses and financial and political institutions continue to operate as they do, jobs will continue to migrate, cities will continue to go bankrupt, and urban poverty will continue to sustain itself decade after decade. The individual politicians, bankers, industrialists, and others who perpetuate and benefit from this system are not necessarily prejudiced and may not even be aware of these minority group issues. Yet their decisions can and do have profound effects on the perpetuation of racial inequality in America.

Acculturation

African cultures and languages were largely eradicated under slavery. Cultural domination continued after the Civil War but through a different structural arrangement. Under de jure segregation, intergroup contact diminished and the structural gap between blacks and whites widened (Woodward, 1971, p. 118). The African-American community had somewhat more autonomy but few resources to define itself and develop a distinct culture.

The centuries of cultural domination and separate development have created a unique black experience in America. African Americans share language, religion, values, and norms with the dominant society but have developed distinct variations on the general themes. Cultural differences may be most visible in the areas of music (e.g., rap), linguistic patterns, and cuisine.

The acculturation process may have been slowed, perhaps even reversed, by the Black Power movement. Beginning in the 1960s, there has been an increased interest in African culture and history and a more visible celebration of the unique African-American experiences and the innumerable contributions of African Americans to the larger society.

Secondary Structural Assimilation

Recall from chapter 1 that structural assimilation can be separated into two subprocesses. One subprocess is secondary structural assimilation, which refers to integration in more public areas such as neighborhoods, schools, political institutions, and jobs. Each of these areas is addressed below, followed by a discussion of the second subprocess, primary structural assimilation, or integration in intimate associations such as friends, kinfolk, and spouses.

Residential Integration

Black and white Americans are only slightly more likely to be neighbors today than they were 30 years ago, and typically they live in separate areas even when they share a similar income level (Massey & Denton, 1993; O'Hare et al. 1991, p. 9; O'Hare & Usdansky, 1992). A recent study concluded that the modest declines in racial housing segregation of the 1970s continued in the 1980s but represented only small steps toward an integrated society (Farley & Frey, 1994). As illustrated in Table 5.2, African Americans are heavily concentrated in urban areas and especially in center city areas, whereas whites are more dispersed and more suburban.

Residential segregation is maintained by a variety of discriminatory practices. Realtors practice racial steering by guiding clients to same-

Table 5.2 Residential Patterns by Race (in percentages)

	Blacks			Whites
	1970	1980	1990	1990
Percent living in:				
Central city	58.2	57.7	56.7	26.2
Suburbs	16.1	23.3	27.0	50.2
Nonmetropolitan areas	25.7	18.9	16.3	23.6

Source: O'Hare et al., 1991, p. 9.

race housing areas, and banks are much more likely to refuse home mortgages to black applicants than to white applicants and to "redline" (deny home improvement loans) for houses in minority group neighborhoods (Massey & Denton, 1993, pp. 83–114). "White flight" away from integrated areas also contributes to residential segregation as whites flee from even minimal neighborhood integration. These practices are supplemented, at least occasionally, by harassment of and violence against African Americans moving into majority white neighborhoods

School Integration

In 1954, the year of the landmark *Brown* school desegregation decision, the majority of black Americans lived in states operating segregated school systems. These Jim Crow schools were greatly underfunded and had less qualified teachers, shorter school years, and inadequate physical facilities. Today, ironically, the South leads the nation in school integration. Still, most black children throughout the nation attend schools with a black majority, and one third attend schools that are 90–100% minority (Pinkney, 1993, p. 65). The pressure from the federal government to integrate the schools eased considerably in the 1980s and the levels of racial school integration have not changed much since then.

Underlying and complicating the difficulty of school integration is the widespread residential segregation mentioned previously (Rivkin, 1994). The challenges for integration are especially evident in those metropolitan areas, such as Washington, D.C., that consist of a largely black inner city surrounded by largely white rings of suburbs. Even with busing, political boundaries would have to be crossed before the school systems could be substantially integrated. Without a renewed commitment to integration, American schools will remain segregated for years to come.

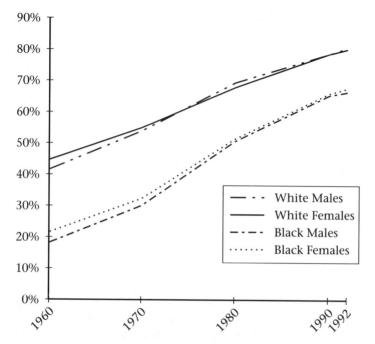

Figure 5.2 *Percentage of Persons 25 Years of Age and Over Completing High School*

Source: U.S. Bureau of the Census, 1993, p. 153

In terms of the *quantity* of education, the gap between whites and blacks has generally decreased over the century. Figure 5.2 displays the rate of high school graduation by race and sex. The racial gap has diminished since 1960 but is still quite noticeable.

Some of the remaining racial gap in education is due to social class factors. For example, African Americans are more likely to drop out of high school but, when the effects of social class background are taken into account, differences in dropout rates between blacks and whites nearly disappear (O'Hare et al., 1991, p. 21).

At the college level, African Americans are only about half as likely (11% vs. 20%) to earn a college degree as white students. Racial differences become even greater for more advanced degrees. These trends do not "bode well for the entrance of more African Americans into the higher paying, higher status occupations" (O'Hare et al., 1991, p. 21).

Political Power

Increases in African-American political power have been greater, perhaps, than in any other institutional area. With the dismantling of Jim Crow segregation, the number of blacks registered to vote has increased and the black vote has become a prominent factor in politics at all levels. High levels of residential concentration virtually guarantee some political representation for the black community, and most larger American cities, including Los Angeles, Chicago, Atlanta, New York, and Washington, D.C., have elected black mayors. The number of black elected officials at all levels of government has increased from virtually zero at the turn of the century to almost 7,500 in 1992 (O'Hare, 1992, p. 34).

However, African-American political power has not been fully mobilized, and actual turnout on election day has generally been lower than national norms. In presidential elections since 1972, between 60% and 65% of eligible white voters have voted. The comparable percentages for black voters range from 48% to 54% (U.S. Bureau of the Census, 1992, p. 269). It should be noted, though, that the black vote figured prominently in the elections of John F. Kennedy in 1960, Jimmy Carter in 1976, and Bill Clinton in 1992, and that a number of African Americans, most notably Jesse Jackson and General Colin Powell, have played prominent roles in presidential politics in recent years.

Jobs and Income

Integration in the job market and racial equality in income follow the trends established in other areas of social life: The situation of black Americans has improved since the end of de jure segregation but has stopped well short of equality. Figure 5.3 shows the differences in occupation by race. White males are twice as likely to be employed in the managerial and professional areas, whereas black males are much more concentrated in semiskilled labor and service work. Reflecting the evolution of industrialization, both black and white males are much less likely to be employed in agriculture than previous generations were. Considering that as recently as the 1930s the huge majority of black males worked in agriculture or as unskilled laborers (Steinberg, 1981, pp. 206–207), the 1990 occupational distribution represents a rapid and significant upgrading.

A similar improvement has occurred for black females. In the 1930s, about 90% of employed black women worked in agriculture or in domestic service (Steinberg, 1981, pp. 206–207). In 1990 the percentage of African-American women in these categories has dropped to less than 30%, and the majority of the group are in the two highest ranked occupational categories. Differences between black and white females are less dramatic than differences between black and white males, perhaps because women in general are less likely to be represented in higher level jobs (O'Hare, 1992, p. 24).

Unemployment rates have been at least twice as high for blacks as for whites since the 1940s. These rates vary by sex and age, and black

Men

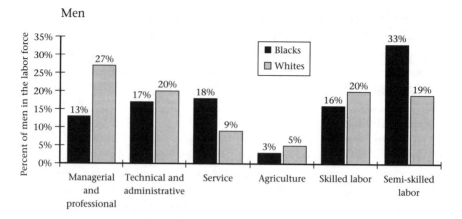

Women

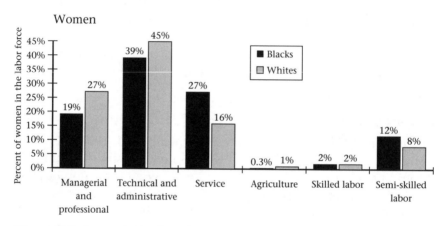

Figure 5.3 Occupation by Race and Sex, 1990
Source: O'Hare et al., 1991, p. 25

males frequently have higher unemployment rates than black females, whereas among white Americans, females always have a higher
unemployment rate. Black teenagers are especially vulnerable to unemployment. In 1986 the official unemployment rate for black teenagers ages 16–19 was almost 40%. In that same year, the rate for white
teenagers in the same age group was about 15% (U.S. Bureau of the
Census, 1988, p. 368). In 1992 the unemployment rate for black male
teenagers had risen to 42% and, for black female teenagers, to 37%.
The rates for white teenagers were 18% for males and 16% for females
(U.S. Bureau of the Census, 1993, p. 401).

The reasons for greater unemployment among blacks are various
and complex. As we have seen, lower levels of education and concentration in the job-poor center cities play a part. So, too, does lower seniority and the concentration of blacks in positions that are more
likely to become obsolete in a developing economy. At the core of

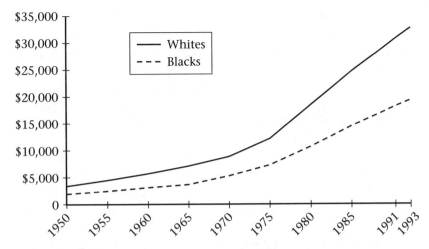

Figure 5.4 Median Family Income by Race, 1950–1991 (in current dollars)
Source: U.S. Bureau of the Census, 1972, p. 440, 1993, p. 457; Witt & Kalish, 1995, p. 3.

these patterns of unemployment and disadvantage, however, is discrimination, both individual and institutional, and the continuing presence of prejudice and racism.

The differences in education and jobs are reflected in a persistent racial income gap. In 1950 black median family income was about 54% of white median family income. By 1970 black median family income had risen to 60% of white median family income but then stabilized at that figure. Figure 5.4 displays data on median family income since 1950. The distribution of income is affected by sex as well as race, with black females continuing to be one of the lowest paid groups in the society.

Finally, poverty affects black Americans at much higher rates than white Americans. Table 5.3 indicates the percentage of white and black Americans living below the federally established, "official" poverty level in 1980 and 1992. Consistent with these statistics is the fact that in 1991 nearly half of black Americans received some form of welfare, more than triple the rate for white Americans.

Table 5.3 Poverty by Race: Percentage of Families Below Poverty Level

	1980	1992
White Americans	6.9%	8.8%
Black Americans	27.9%	30.4%

Source: U.S. Bureau of the Census, 1993, p. 46.

Primary Structural Assimilation

Given the centuries of racism and prejudice and the continuing separation of the races in housing, schools, and other areas, it should not surprise us to find that friendship and marriage choices across racial lines remain relatively uncommon. Contact in the more public areas of society, such as the workplace or school, is certainly more common today, but interpersonal ties beyond acquaintanceship are much rarer (see Figure 2.2 on the frequency of interracial dinner guests).

Along the same lines, interracial marriages are increasing in number but still make up a tiny percentage of all marriages. In 1970 there were 65,000 black-white married couples. This represented about one tenth of 1% of all married couples. The number of black-white married couples tripled to 211,000 in 1990 and by 1992 had risen to 246,000. In neither year did the number of interracial marriages approach even one half of 1% (.50%) of all married couples (U.S. Bureau of the Census, 1993, p. 54).

Conclusion

In part, the contemporary situation of African Americans is perhaps what might be expected for a group so recently "released" from exclusion and subordination. In terms of health, wealth, and quality of life, the average situation of African Americans is vastly improved compared to the beginning of the century. The overall picture of racial progress, however, is perhaps more "different" than "better." A large percentage of the African-American population has traded rural peasantry for urban poverty and faces an array of formidable and deep-rooted problems.

The situation of black Americans is intimately intermixed with the plight of our cities and the changing nature of the labor force. It is the consequence of nearly 400 years of prejudice, racism, and discrimination, but it also reflects social forces such as urbanization and industrialization and the growth and development of American society.

In acknowledging the challenges that remain, we should not downplay the real improvements in the lives of black Americans. However, the success of the few obscures a tangle of problems for the many. The problems seem to be growing worse as America moves into the postindustrial era. Poverty, unemployment, a failing educational system, residential segregation, racism, discrimination, and prejudice continue to be the inescapable reality of millions of black Americans. In many black neighborhoods, these problems are compounded by crime, drugs, violence, poor health care, malnutrition, and a host of other factors.

Given this gloomy situation, it should not be surprising to find significant strength in pluralistic, nationalistic thinking as well as resentment and anger in the black community. Black nationalism and black power remain powerful ideas, as evidenced by the Million Man March held in the fall of 1995. Hundreds of thousands (perhaps even a million) of African-American males gathered for yet another march on Washington and a day of celebration, speeches, prayer, and song. The march did not promote a specific political program or provide an action agenda for participants to follow when they returned to their home communities. Yet the themes of self-help, pride in race, autonomy, and the need to take responsibility for one's community were unmistakably and strongly stated.

Finally, the situation of the black community as the 20th century draws to a close might be characterized as structural pluralism under conditions of great inequality. The former characterization testifies to the failure of assimilation and the latter to the continuing effects, in the present, of a colonized origin. The problems that remain are less visible (or, perhaps, just better hidden from the average middle-class white American) than those of previous eras. Responsibility is more diffused and the moral certainties of opposition to slavery or to Jim Crow are long gone. Urban poverty, institutional discrimination, and modern racism are less dramatic and more difficult to measure than an overseer's whip, a lynch mob, or a sign that says Whites Only. They are, however, no less real or deadly in their consequences.

MAIN POINTS

- During the 20th century, black-white relations changed from a rigid competitive system (de jure segregation) to a fluid competitive system. Propelling this evolution were new economic and political conditions, changing laws and legal precedents, and the civil rights movement.

- Outside the South, frustration and anger over racial discrimination were expressed in urban riots in the 1960s. The Black Power movement addressed the massive problems of racial inequality remaining after the victories of the civil rights movement in the South.

- Black-white relations since the 1960s have been characterized by continuing inequality, separation, and hostility, along with substantial improvements in status for some African Americans.

- African Americans are largely acculturated, but centuries of separate development have created a unique black experience in American society.

- The secondary structural assimilation of African Americans is low. Evidence of racial inequalities in housing, schooling, politics, jobs, income, unemployment, and poverty is massive. Likewise, primary structural assimilation is low.

FOR FURTHER READING

Carmichael, Stokely, & Hamilton, Charles V. 1967. *Black Power: The Politics of Liberation in America*. New York: Vintage Books.

Hacker, Andrew. 1992. *Two Nations: Black and White, Separate, Hostile, and Unequal*. New York: Charles Scribner's Sons.

King, Martin Luther, Jr. 1958. *Stride Toward Freedom: The Montgomery Story*. New York: Harper.

———. 1963. *Why We Can't Wait*. New York: Mentor.

———. 1968. *Where Do We Go From Here: Chaos or Community?* New York: Harper & Row.

Malcolm X. 1964. *The Autobiography of Malcolm X*. New York: Grove Press.

Massey, Douglas, & Denton, Nancy. 1993. *American Apartheid*. Cambridge: Harvard University Press.

Morris, Aldon D. 1984. *The Origins of the Civil Rights Movement*. New York: Free Press.

Steinberg, Steven. 1995. *Turning Back*. Boston: Beacon Press.

CHAPTER 6

Native Americans

*From Conquest to Tribal Survival
in Industrial Society*

The contact period between Native Americans and Anglo Americans began at Jamestown in 1607 and lasted nearly 300 years. The conflicts that commenced in colonial times spread across the continent as American society expanded west, with each newly encountered tribe conquered and subordinated in turn. By the 1890s, the long, lethal contact period had ended and the surviving Native American tribes had become minority groups.

Land was at the heart of the competition. Once the tribes had been defeated and the land had come under white control, conflict cooled. Unlike other minority groups, Native Americans retained little, not even labor power, that was coveted by the white community.

By the beginning of the 20th century, Native Americans were living on isolated, rural reservations remote from the cities. At a time when rigid competitive systems controlled African Americans, European immigrants, and Mexican Americans, a decidedly paternalistic system of group relationships was constructed for Native Americans. As the situations of other minority groups were transformed by industrialization and urbanization, Native Americans continued to subsist at the fringes of development and change, marginalized, relatively powerless, and isolated. Compared with other minority groups, their links with the larger society were weaker, and the tribes were less affected by economic and social evolution.

How has the situation of Native Americans changed over the course of the 20th century? How does their status compare to that of other minority groups? What are the prospects for future improvements in quality of life? Does the fact that their minority status grew out of military conquest still affect their relationships with the larger society? Can traditional Native American cultures survive in the midst of an industrialized, rapidly changing society?

Native American Cultures

The dynamics of Native American and Anglo-American relationships have been shaped by the vast differences between the two groups in culture, values, and lifestyle. These differences have often hampered communication in the past and continue to do so in the present. A complete analysis of Native American cultures is well beyond the scope of this text, but the past experiences and present goals of the group cannot be appreciated without some understanding of their views of the world. Although there were and are hundreds of different tribes in what is now the United States, each with its own language and heritage, some widely shared cultural characteristics lie within this diversity.

Perhaps the most obvious difference between Native American culture and Western culture is in their respective conceptions of the relationship between human beings, the natural world, and the earth itself. In the Native American view, the universe is as one. Humans are simply a part of a larger reality, no different or more important than other animals, plants, trees, and the earth itself. Native Americans attempt to live in harmony with the natural world and the land, not "improve" it, or use it for their own selfish purposes.

These views differ sharply from Western concepts of land development, commercial farming, and bending the natural world to the service of humans. The concept of private property was not highly developed in Native American cultures and, from the Anglo-American perspective, was most notably absent in conceptions of land ownership. The land simply existed and the notion of owning, selling, or buying it was foreign to Native Americans. In the words of Tecumseh, a chief of the Shawnee, a man could no more sell the land than the "sea or the air he breathed" (Josephy, 1968, p. 283).

Native American cultures and societies are also more oriented to groups (e.g., the extended family, clan, or tribe) than to individuals. Self-interest is subordinated to the interest of the group, and child-rearing practices strongly encourage group loyalty. Cooperative, group activities are stressed over those of a competitive, individualistic nature. Children are expected to contribute to the welfare of the group as soon as they are old enough (Locust, 1990, p. 231).

Many Native American tribes were organized around egalitarian values that stressed the dignity and worth of every man, woman, and child. Virtually all tribes had a division of labor based on gender, and women's work was valued. Women often occupied far more important positions in tribal society than was typical for women in Anglo-American society. In many of the Native American societies that practiced gardening, women controlled the land. In other tribes, women wielded considerable power and held the most important political and religious offices. Among the Iroquois, for example, a council of older women appointed the chief of the tribe and made decisions about when to wage war (Amott & Matthaei, 1991, pp. 34–35).

These differences in values, when compounded by the power differentials that emerged, often placed Native Americans at a disadvantage when dealing with the dominant group. The Native American conception of land ownership and their lack of experience with deeds, titles, contracts, and other Western legal concepts often made it difficult for them to defend their resources from Anglo Americans. At other times, cultural differences led to the disruption of traditional practices, which in turn further weakened Native American societies. For instance, Christian missionaries and governmental representatives tried to reverse the traditional Native American division of labor in which women were responsible for the gardening. In the Western view, farm work of any kind was properly done only by males. Also, female tribal leaders were usually ignored by the military and political representatives of the dominant society, who imposed Western notions of patriarchy and male leadership on the tribes (Amott & Matthaei, 1991, p. 39).

Comparing Minority Groups

This chapter analyzes the development of relations between Native Americans and the dominant society over the course of the 20th century. To further the discussion, I compare and contrast Native Americans with other minority groups when appropriate. By comparing experiences, we can test the explanatory power of our concepts and theories. No two minority groups have had the exact same experiences, and the ideas that guide our analysis should help us understand the differences and similarities between these experiences. We begin by comparing Native Americans with African Americans.

At the turn of this century, both Native and African Americans had been conquered and colonized, but not in the same ways and not for the same purposes. Differences in their respective contact situations shaped subsequent differences in their relationships with the dominant group and their place in the larger society. At the beginning of the 20th century, the most visible enemy of African Americans was the rigid competitive system of de jure segregation in the South.

Native Americans faced the reservation system, rural isolation, and a series of threats to their traditional cultures and lifestyles. They had a different set of problems, different resources at their disposal, and different goals in mind. In contrast to African Americans and other groups, Native Americans were more interested in preserving their own institutions and heritage than in access to dominant group institutions. The differences in goals reflect the different histories of the groups and their relationships with the dominant group, the different circumstances surrounding their colonization and conquest, the type of competition with the dominant group, and the size of the power differential.

Developments After the 1890s

By 1890 the strength of the Indian nations had been depleted, and they lacked the means for further armed resistance. Politically, Native Americans were left with few resources. The huge majority were not citizens, and most tribes had little cultural basis for an understanding of representative democracy as practiced in the larger society. Even if they had been included in the political process, Native Americans were a small group, and they did not have the size and the resources to attract the interest of politicians or to sustain protest activity. The political weight of the group was further minimized by the fact that they were scattered throughout the western two thirds of the country and separated from one another by cultural and linguistic differences as well as by geographic distance.

In 1900 Native Americans were among the most impoverished groups in the society. The land they retained was generally of poor quality and they continued to lose their better land to the dominant group until the 1930s. Traditional food sources, such as buffalo and other game, had been destroyed and traditional hunting grounds and gardening plots had been lost to white farmers and ranchers. The tribes had few means of satisfying even their most basic needs. Many became totally dependent on the government for food, shelter, clothing, and other necessities.

Prospects for improvement seemed slim. Indians not only had lost their resource base, but they were also distant from the sites of industrialization and modernization and had few of the skills (literacy, familiarity with Western work habits and routines) that would enable them to compete for a place in the rapidly urbanizing and industrializing labor force of the turn of the century. Off the reservations, they were limited by racial prejudice and the strong intolerances of the era. On the reservations, they were subjected to policies designed to either maintain their powerlessness and poverty or force them to become Americanized. The future of Native Americans was in serious jeopardy, and their destructive relations with white society continued in peace as they had in war.

Reservation Life

The reservations to which the defeated Indian nations were assigned were paternalistic social systems run by agencies of the federal government, not by the tribes. In particular, the **Bureau of Indian Affairs** (BIA), an agency of the U.S. Department of the Interior, had primary responsibility for the administration of the reservations. The BIA and its local Indian superintendent controlled virtually all aspects of everyday life, including the reservation budget, the criminal justice system, and the schools, and even determined tribal membership.

The BIA executed its duties with little regard for and virtually no input from the tribes. The BIA superintendent of the reservations usually ignored traditional leadership and political institutions and dominated local Indian affairs (Spicer, 1980, p. 117). The food supply and communications with the world outside the reservation were controlled by the superintendent. This control was used to reward tribal members who cooperated and to punish those who did not.

Coercive Acculturation

Like the immigrants from Europe who were arriving in the United States at about this time, Native Americans on the reservations were subjected to a policy of coercive acculturation, or forced Americanization. Their culture was attacked, their languages and religions forbidden, and their institutions circumvented and undermined. The centerpiece of U.S. Indian policy was the Dawes Allotment Act of 1887, the deeply flawed attempt to transform Native Americans into independent farmers and impose Western notions of private property and land ownership on the tribes (see chapter 3). By allotting land to families and individuals, the legislation sought to destroy the broader kinship, clan, and tribal social structures and replace them with more Western practices promoting individualism and a strong profit motive (Cornell, 1988, p. 80). It was relatively easy for land developers, farmers, and other members of the dominant group to acquire the land that had been allotted to Native Americans. By the 1930s, 90 million acres of the original 140 million acres had been lost. Most of the land that remained in Native American hands was desert, highly eroded, or otherwise useless (Wax, 1971, p. 55).

In another parallel to the experiences of European immigrants, education was used as a major vehicle for forced acculturation. Whenever possible, the BIA sent Indian children to boarding schools distant from family and kin. In the schools, the children were intentionally separated from their native cultures and communal ties. Tribal languages, dress, and religion were all forbidden, and if native cultures were mentioned at all, they were attacked, ridiculed, and denigrated. Children of different tribes were mixed together as roommates to speed the acquisition of English. When school was not in session, children were often boarded with local white families, usually as unpaid domestic helpers or farmhands, and prevented from visiting their families and revitalizing their tribal ties (Hoxie, 1984; Spicer, 1980; Wax, 1971).

Native Americans were virtually powerless to change the reservation system or avoid the brunt of the campaign for assimilation. Nonetheless, they resented and resisted coerced Americanization, and many languages and cultural elements survived the early reservation period, although often in altered form. For example, Christian missionaries had been quite active among Native Americans for centuries. By the 1930s, the great majority of Indians were affiliated with one Christian faith or another. At the same time, traditional tribal religions continued to be active, and many new religions, some combining Christian and traditional elements, had appeared (Spicer, 1980, p. 118).

The Ghost Dance

Perhaps the most significant effort to resist forced Americanization and preserve the traditional ways of life occurred in 1890, just as armed hostilities were ending. A Paiute named Wovoka had a vision in which the Great Spirit promised that if the tribes performed a certain dance, white society would disappear, all Indian ancestors would be restored to life, and the world would be re-created. Wovoka's message spread from tribe to tribe and produced the Ghost Dance movement, which was especially popular among the Sioux of the upper Midwest. Once a powerful military force, the Sioux had only recently been defeated and forced onto reservations. They took up the dance with great intensity, and the BIA superintendent was afraid that hostilities would resume. In December of 1890, he ordered the Sioux to stop dancing and had the tribal leaders arrested.

Some Sioux feared more massive repression and a band of 350 fled to a corner of the reservation, near a creek named Wounded Knee. They were intercepted by the cavalry and ordered to disarm. In the tense atmosphere, a shot was fired and the cavalry opened fire, killing at least 200 men, women, and children (some estimate deaths as high as 300). The cavalry suffered 25 dead and about 40 wounded. This was the last military engagement of the Indian Wars and, to this day, the confrontation at Wounded Knee Creek retains a strong symbolic significance for Native Americans.

The Indian Reorganization Act

By the 1930s, the failure of the reservation system and the policy of forced assimilation was obvious to all who cared to observe. The quality of life for Native Americans had not improved, and there was little economic development and few job opportunities on the reservations. Health care and housing were woefully inadequate and education levels lagged far below national standards.

The plight of Native Americans eventually found a sympathetic ear in the administration of Franklin Delano Roosevelt, who was elected president in 1932. President Roosevelt appointed John Collier, who was sympathetic with and knowledgeable about Native Americans, as commissioner of the Bureau of Indian Affairs. He served in his post for more than a decade and was instrumental in securing the passage of the **Indian Reorganization Act (IRA)** in 1934.

This landmark legislation contained a number of significant provisions for Native Americans and broke sharply with the federal policies of the past. In particular, it rescinded the Dawes Allotment Act and the policy of individualizing tribal lands. It also provided means by which the tribes could expand their land holdings. Many of the mechanisms of coercive Americanization in the school system and elsewhere were dismantled. Financial aid was made available for the economic development of the reservations. In perhaps the most significant departure from earlier policy, the IRA proposed an increase in Native American self-governance and an end to the paternalistic role of the BIA and other federal agencies in reservation life.

Although sympathetic to Native Americans, the IRA had its limits and shortcomings. Many of its intentions were never realized and the law itself stopped well short of the complete pluralism desired by many tribes. The empowerment of the tribes generally took place on the dominant group's terms and in conformity with the central values and practices of the larger society. For example, the proposed increase in the decision-making power of the tribes was contingent on their adoption of Anglo political forms, including secret ballots, majority rule, and written constitutions. These were alien concepts to the numerous tribes that selected leaders by procedures other than popular election (e.g., leaders might be selected by councils of elders) or which made decisions by open discussion and consensus building (i.e., decisions required the agreement of *everyone* with a voice in the process, not a simple majority). The incorporation of these Western forms illustrates the basically assimilationist intent of the IRA.

The IRA had variable effects on Native American tribes, particularly Native American women. In tribes that were male dominated, the IRA gave women new rights to participate in elections, run for office, and hold leadership roles. In other cases, new political structures replaced traditional forms, some of which—like the Iroquois mentioned earlier in this chapter—had accorded women considerable power.

Although the political effects were variable, the programs funded by the IRA provided opportunities for women to receive education and

training for the first time on many reservations. Many of these opportunities were oriented to domestic tasks and other traditionally Western female roles, but some prepared Native American women for jobs
outside of the family and off the reservation, such as clerical work and
nursing (Evans, 1989, pp. 208–209).

In summary, the Indian Reorganization Act of 1934 was bolder and
more sympathetic to Native Americans in intent than in execution.
On the one hand, many tribes were suspicious of the IRA, and by
1948 fewer than a hundred tribes had voted to accept its provisions.
On the other hand, some tribes prospered (at least comparatively
speaking) under the IRA. One impoverished, landless group of Chero-
kee in Oklahoma acquired land, equipment, and expert advice
through the IRA and, between 1937 and 1949, developed a prosperous, largely debt-free farming community (Debo, 1970, pp. 294–300).

It is interesting to note that a sympathetic change in federal policy
toward Native Americans predates changes in the situations of other
minority groups by several decades. The IRA became policy 20 years
before the *Brown v. Board of Education of Topeka* school desegregation
decision, at a time when de jure segregation was very much intact
and anti-Asian and anti-Mexican prejudices were widespread and
strong. What factors might account for this timing? The answer can
be found, at least partially, in terms of power differentials and intergroup competition or, more accurately, the lack of competition.

By the 1930s, the tribes had lost almost all of their better land. The
very impoverishment and powerlessness of Native Americans made
policy changes seem trivial and reduced possible opposition. Native
Americans were a small group, surviving on the fringes of the larger
society. At a time when the idea of racial reform in other areas generated fierce resistance, a less repressive relationship with Native Americans could be established without threatening the system of privilege
or arousing much of a defensive reaction. Simply put, change could
take place, even in a time of racial repression and intolerance, because
most tribes of Native Americans had little left worth expropriating.

Termination and Other Recent Federal Policies

The IRA's stress on the legitimacy of tribal identity seemed "un-American" to many in the larger society. There was constant pressure on the
federal government to return to an individualistic policy that encouraged (or required) Americanization. Some whites viewed the tribal
structures and communal property-holding patterns as relics of an earlier era and as impediments to modernization and development. Not so
incidentally, some elements of the dominant society still coveted the
remaining Indian lands and resources, which could be more easily exploited if property ownership were more individualistic and capitalistic.

In 1953 the assimilationist forces won a victory when Congress passed a resolution calling for an end to the reservation system and to the special relationships between the tribes and the federal government. The proposed policy, called **termination**, was intended to get the federal government "out of the Indian business." It rejected the IRA and proposed a return to the system of private land ownership imposed on the tribes by the Dawes Act. The tribes were horrified at the notion of termination and opposed the policy strongly and vociferously. Under this policy, all special relationships, including treaty obligations, between the federal government and the tribes would end. Tribes would no longer exist as legally recognized entities and tribal lands and other resources would be placed in private hands (Josephy, 1968, pp. 260–261).

About a hundred tribes, most of them small, were terminated. In virtually all cases, the termination process was administered hastily. Fraud, misuse of funds, and other injustices were common. The Menominee of Wisconsin and the Klamath on the West Coast were the two largest tribes to be terminated. Both suffered devastating economic losses and precipitous declines in quality of life. Neither tribe had the business or tax base needed to finance the services formerly provided by the federal government (e.g., health care and schooling), and they were forced to sell land, timber, and other scarce resources to maintain a minimal quality of life. Many poor Native American families turned to local and state agencies, which placed severe strain on welfare budgets. The experience of the Menominee was so disastrous that, at the request of the tribe, reservation status was restored in 1973 (Deloria, 1969, pp. 60–82; McNickle, 1973, pp. 103–110; Raymer, 1974).

The termination policy aroused so much opposition from Native Americans and was such an obvious disaster that the pressure to push tribes to termination faded in the late 1950s. The policy was disavowed by the administration of President John F. Kennedy in the 1960s, although it was not formally repealed until 1975. Since the 1960s, federal Indian policy has generally followed in the tradition set by the IRA: termination and forced assimilation continue to be officially rejected and, within limits, the tribes have been granted more freedom to find their own way, at their own pace, of relating to the larger society.

Several federal programs and laws have benefited the tribes during recent decades, including the antipoverty campaign launched in the 1960s, even though the campaign was not aimed specifically at Indians. In 1970 President Richard Nixon affirmed the government's commitment to fulfilling treaty obligations and the right of the tribes to self-determination. The Indian Self-Determination and Education Assistance Act, passed in 1975, increased aid to reservation schools and

Native American students and expanded the control of the tribes over the administration of the reservations.

One interesting accommodation between tribal and U.S. institutions occurred in the state of Washington in 1994. Two Indian males had been convicted of armed robbery, but instead of sending them to prison, the judge followed the recommendation of the tribal court and permitted the men to be exiled to remote islands off the coast of Alaska (Conner, 1994, p. A19). Although this experiment failed and the youths were eventually sent to prison, it is one of the few occasions in which traditional tribal practices have been granted legitimacy in a U.S. court of law and in which there has been cooperation between tribal and societal agencies.

In general, however, the BIA continues to administer and supervise much of the everyday business of the reservations amid complaints of inefficiency, paternalism, and corruption. The quality of life on the reservations continues to lag behind national standards. We assess these present-day patterns later in the chapter.

Urban Indians

One result of the lack of jobs and slow economic development of the reservations has been a continuous migration to the cities, a movement encouraged by urban relocation programs established by the government in the 1950s. Centers for Native Americans were established in many cities, and various services (e.g., job training, English instruction) were offered to assist Native Americans in adjusting to the urban environment.

Figure 6.1 shows the rate of this movement to the city. About half of all Native Americans are now urbanized and, since 1950, Indians have urbanized faster than the general population. Nevertheless, Native Americans are still the least urbanized minority group. The population as a whole is about 75% urbanized and, as we saw in chapter 5, African Americans are almost 84% urban.

As with African Americans, Native Americans arrived in the cities after the mainstream economy had begun to de-emphasize blue-collar or manufacturing jobs. Because of their relatively low average levels of educational attainment and their racial and cultural differences, Native Americans in the city tended to encounter the same travails of urban poverty experienced by African Americans and other minority groups of color, including high rates of unemployment and inadequate health care, education, and housing.

Native Americans living in the city are, on the average, better off than those living on reservations, where unemployment can reach 80% or even 90%. But the improvement is relative. Income figures for urban Indians are comparable to those for African Americans and are

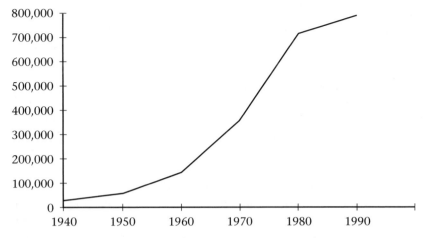

Figure 6.1 Urbanization of Native Americans, Number Living in Metropolitan Areas

Source: U.S. Bureau of the Census, 1990.

well below those for whites. Their unemployment rate runs about twice the national average (Cornell, 1988, p. 132). Thus, moving to the city often trades rural poverty for the urban variety with little net improvement in life chances.

Native Americans will probably remain more rural than other minority groups for years to come. In spite of the poverty and lack of opportunities for schooling and jobs, the reservation offers some advantages in services and lifestyle. On the reservation, there may be opportunities for political participation and leadership roles that are not available in the cities, where Indians make up a tiny minority. Reservations may also offer closeness to kinfolk, friends, religious services, and tribal celebrations (Snipp, 1989, p. 84). Negative experiences in urban areas will probably sustain a continuing return to the reservations.

Although the economic benefits of urbanization have been slim, other advantages have accrued from life in the city. Urban Indians have been one of the sources of strength and manpower for a movement of protest that began early in the 20th century. As with other minority groups, Native Americans have been actively involved in the pursuit of their own self-interest. We turn to this protest movement in the next section.

Protest and Resistance

In one sense, a Native American resistance movement began upon first contact with European civilization. As this century began and BIA-administered reservations and coercive Americanization came to dominate tribal life, new forms of protest and activism appeared. The modern movement was tiny at first and, with few exceptions, achieved a measure of success only in recent decades. In fact, the Native American protest movement in the past was not so much unsuccessful as simply ignored. The goals of the protest movement have focused on protecting Native American resources and the rights and privileges granted them by treaty, striking a balance between integration and pluralism, and forming a relationship with the dominant group that would permit a broader array of life chances without sacrificing Indian identity and heritage.

In the 1960s and 1970s, Native Americans benefited from the declining levels of traditional, blatant prejudice and racism in the society as a whole, as did African Americans and other minority groups. The media began to present Indians in a more favorable, less stereotypical way. Several popular books, including Vine Deloria's *Custer Died for Your Sins* in 1969 and Dee Brown's *Bury My Heart at Wounded Knee* in 1970, helped to build awareness of the problems of Native Americans. Empathy was further enhanced when the growing environmental movement and many countercultural movements of the 1960s adopted the Native Americans as symbols, albeit for very different reasons and with very different agendas in mind.

In this more favorable atmosphere, a protest movement commonly referred to as the Red Power movement appeared. Like black power, red power encompassed a coalition of groups and a varied collection of ideas. The two movements also shared a similar stress on self-determination and pride in race and cultural heritage.

One important organization in the movement was the National Indian Youth Council (NIYC), founded in the early 1960s. The NIYC helped to formulate and guide a militant phase of the protest movement that resembled the concurrent black protest movement. Some of the more famous and important protest episodes, which also illustrate the nature of Native American demands, included a "fish-in" in the state of Washington in 1965. The state government had tried to limit the fishing rights of several different tribes, even though fishing was crucial for their subsistence, on the grounds that the supply of fish was diminishing and needed to be protected from "overfishing." The tribes argued that their right to fish the waters in question had been guaranteed by treaties signed in the 1850s and that it was the pollution and commercial fishing of the dominant society that had depleted the supply of fish. In violation of the state's policy, the tribes organized a "fish-in," which was met by a contingent of police officers and other lawmen. Violent confrontations and mass arrests ensued. Three years later, after a lengthy and expensive court battle, the tribes were vindicated and their treaty rights to fish the rivers of Washington State were confirmed by the U.S. Supreme Court (Nabakov, 1991, pp. 362–363).

Another widely publicized episode took place in 1969, when Indians from various tribes occupied Alcatraz Island in San Francisco Bay, the site of a closed federal prison. The protesters were acting on an old law that granted Native Americans the right to reclaim abandoned federal land. The occupation of Alcatraz was organized, in part, by the American Indian Movement (AIM), which had been founded in 1968. More militant and radical than the previously established protest groups, AIM aggressively confronted the BIA, the police, and other forces that were seen as oppressive. With the backing of AIM and other groups, Alcatraz was occupied for nearly 4 years and generated a great deal of publicity for the Red Power movement and the plight of Native Americans.

In 1972 AIM helped to organize a march on Washington, D.C., called the Trail of Broken Treaties. Marchers came from many tribes and represented both urban and reservation Indians. The intent of the marchers was to dramatize the problems of the tribes. The leaders demanded the abolition of the BIA, the return of lands illegally taken, and increased self-governance for the tribes, among other things. When they reached Washington, some of the marchers forcibly occupied the BIA offices. Property was damaged (by which side is disputed) and records and papers were destroyed. The marchers eventually surrendered and none of their demands was met. The following year, AIM occupied the village of Wounded Knee in South Dakota to protest the violation of treaty rights. The occupation lasted more than 2 months and involved several armed confrontations with federal authorities. Again, the protest ended without achieving any of the demands made by the Indian leadership (Olson & Wilson, 1984, pp. 172–175).

Since the early 1970s, the level of protest activity has declined, just as it has for the black protest movement. Lawsuits and court cases have predominated over dramatic, direct confrontations. The Red Power movement enjoyed some successes but fell short of achieving the goals of tribal autonomy, the restoration of tribal lands, and comprehensive development programs for the reservations.

Ironically, the struggle for red power encouraged assimilation along with pluralism. The movement linked members of different tribes and forced people of diverse heritages to find common ground, often in the form of a "generic" American Indian culture. Inevitably, the protests were conducted in English and the grievances were expressed in ways understandable to the larger society, thus increasing the pressure to acculturate even while arguing for the survival of the tribes.

Native Americans in the late 20th century seek to become a part of the larger society on *their* terms. Relatively few members of the group pursue complete pluralism or total separation from the larger society, but the desire for straightforward, unqualified acculturation and integration seems equally weak. On the one hand, the Red Power movement and its protests, manifestos, and conferences are assimilationist. These activities are necessary in order to influence public opinion and to effectively represent the interests of the group to a huge, highly bureaucratized government structure. On the other hand, many Native Americans are committed to the preservation of their traditional cultures and lifestyles, even as their societies continue to change under the pressure of modernization. The search continues for a way for Native Americans to find common ground somewhere between Americanization and pluralism.

Continuing Competition: The Modern Battle for Resources

In spite of their relative poverty and powerlessness, Native Americans are not entirely without assets. The treaties signed in the 19th century sometimes allotted land to the tribes that, ironically, turned out to be rich in resources that became valuable in the 20th century. These resources include 3% of U.S. oil and natural gas reserves, 15% of coal reserves, and 55% of uranium reserves (Amott & Matthaei, 1991, p. 54). In addition, some tribes hold title to water rights, fishing rights, woodlands that could sustain a lumbering industry, and wilderness areas that could be developed for camping, hunting, and other forms of recreation.

The challenge for Native Americans is to retain control of the resources they hold at present and to develop them for the benefit of the tribes. Threats to the remaining tribal lands and other assets are common. Mining and energy companies continue to cast envious eyes on these holdings, while other tribal assets are coveted by real estate developers, fishermen (recreational as well as commercial), backpackers and campers, and cities facing water shortages.

Some tribes have organized to protect their resources and to negotiate more effectively for their use with the larger society. The Council of Energy Resource Tribes (CERT) was founded by 25 tribes in 1975 to coordinate and control the development of the mineral resources on reservation lands. Since its founding, CERT has successfully negotiated a number of agreements with dominant group firms that have increased the flow of income to the tribes and raised the quality of life (Cornell, 1988; Snipp, 1989).

The treaties signed with the federal government in the 19th century offer another potential resource for some tribes. Many treaties were violated by white settlers, the military, state and local governments, or the BIA. One of the challenges for Native Americans is to pursue this trail of broken treaties and secure reasonable compensation for the wrongs of the past. For example, in 1972, the Passamaquoddy and Penobscot tribes filed a lawsuit demanding the return of 12.5 million acres of land—more than half the state of Maine—and $25 billion in damages. The tribes argued that the land had been illegally taken more than 150 years earlier. After 8 years of litigation, the tribes settled for a $25 million trust fund and 300,000 acres of land. Although far less than their original demand, the award gave the tribes control of resources that could be used for economic development, creating jobs, upgrading educational programs, or developing other programs that would enhance human and financial capital (Worsnop, 1992, p. 391).

Virtually every tribe has similar grievances, and if pursued successfully, the long-dead treaty relationship between the Indian nations and the government could be a significant fount of economic and political resources. Of course, lawsuits require considerable (and expensive) legal expertise and years of effort to bring to fruition. There are no guarantees of success, so this avenue has some sharp limitations and risks.

Another potential resource for Native Americans is the gambling industry. Many state and local laws do not apply on reservations, which are at least nominally governed by the tribes. Increasingly, tribes have attempted to take advantage of this opening to build gambling casinos. As many as one half of all tribes currently either have casinos or are contemplating getting involved in the gambling business (Meier, 1994). Some of these enterprises are extremely profitable. One reservation casino in Minnesota reported gross receipts of $500 million in 1993. Profits were shared equally among all 100 tribal members, each of whom received $400,000 ("Looking for a Piece of the Action," 1994, p. 44). There are attempts at both the state and federal levels to limit the spread and profitability of reservation gambling, so this potential resource may also encounter some sharp limitations.

The natural resources, treaty rights, and gambling establishments may provide a basis for development of the reservation and for further improvements in the quality of life. For most tribes, these assets continue to be merely a potential waiting to be actualized. Problems of poverty and powerlessness, prejudice and discrimination continue to limit the lives of the vast majority of the group.

Native American–White Relations
Since the 1960s

This section analyzes the contemporary situation of Native Americans using many of the terms and concepts we have developed in previous chapters.

Prejudice and Discrimination

There are relatively few studies on anti-Indian prejudices in general and it is difficult to characterize changes over the past several decades. We don't know whether there has been a shift to "modern" forms of anti-Indian racism, as there apparently has been for antiblack prejudice, or if the stereotypes of Indians have declined in strength or changed in content.

One of the very few records of national anti-Indian prejudices over time are social distance scale results (see chapter 2). When the scales were first administered in 1926, American Indians were ranked in the middle third of all groups (18th out of 28), at about the same level as Southern and Eastern Europeans and slightly above Mexicans, another colonized group. The ranking of Native Americans remained stable until 1977, when there was a noticeable rise in their position relative to other groups. This change may reflect the greater empathy for the group generated in the 1960s, the shift from overt forms of prejudice to the more subtle modern racism, or both. Remember, however, that the samples for the social distance scale research consisted of college students for the most part and do not necessarily reflect trends in the general population.

A variety of studies have documented continuing stereotyping of Indians in the popular press, textbooks, the media, cartoons, and various other places. Native Americans are often portrayed as stereotypical bucks and squaws, complete with headdresses, bows, teepees, and other such "generic" Indian artifacts. These portrayals obliterate the diversity of Native American culture and lifestyles. Native Americans are often referred to more in the past than in the present, as if their present situation was of no importance or, worse, as if they no longer existed. Many history books continue to begin the study of American history in Europe or with the "discovery" of America, omitting the millennia of civilization prior to the arrival of European explorers and colonizers. Recent portrayals of Native Americans such as the film *Dances With Wolves* (1990) are sympathetic but still treat the tribes as part of a bucolic past forever lost, not as peoples with real problems in the present.

Research is also unclear about the severity or extent of discrimination against Indians. Certainly, Native Americans' opportunities for upward mobility, choice of occupations, and the range of income available are all limited by the group's lower average levels of education. This exclusion is a form of institutional discrimination in the sense that the opportunities to develop human capital are much less available to Native Americans than to much of the rest of the population. In terms of individual discrimination or more overt forms of exclusion, "there is little research showing that American Indians are systematically segregated into lower status, lesser paid occupations" (Snipp, 1992, p. 363). The situation of Native American women is also underresearched, but Snipp reports that, like their counterparts in other minority groups and the dominant group, Indian women "are systematically paid less than their male counterparts in similar circumstances. (Snipp, 1992, p. 363)

Evidence suggests that overt anti-Indian prejudice has declined, perhaps in parallel with antiblack prejudice. Much stereotyping remains though, and demeaning or negative portrayals of Native Americans are common throughout the dominant culture. Institutional discrimination is a major barrier for Native Americans, who have had limited access to opportunities for education and employment.

Acculturation

Many tribes have been able to preserve a large portion of their traditional culture in spite of more than a century of coercive Americanization. For example, many tribal languages continue to be spoken on a daily basis, especially among Native Americans living on reservations in the west (Snipp, 1989, p. 176). The greater the extent to which the traditional languages are spoken, the more likely the traditional culture is to survive.

Traditional culture is retained in other forms besides language. Religions and value systems, political and economic structures, and culinary and recreational patterns have all survived the military conquest and the depredations of reservation life, although each pattern has been altered by contact with the dominant group. The Native American Church (NAC), for instance, combines elements from both cultures. Although the NAC freely uses Christian imagery, the Bible, and Christian artifacts, a major part of its services are devoted to seeking personal visions induced in part by peyote, a hallucinogenic drug. This practice is consistent with the spiritual and religious traditions of many tribes, and the NAC is an important Native American religion with congregations across the nation (Wax, 1971, pp. 141–144).

Native Americans have been considerably more successful than African Americans in preserving their traditional cultures. The reasons for this may lie in the nature of their respective relationship with the dominant group. African Americans were exploited for labor, whereas the competition with Native Americans centered on land. African cultures, on the one hand, could not easily survive because the social structures that transmitted the cultures and gave them meaning were destroyed by slavery and sacrificed to the exigencies of the slave plantation.

Native Americans, on the other hand, confronted the dominant group as tribal units, intact and whole. The tribes maintained integrity throughout the wars and throughout the reservation period. Tribal culture was indeed attacked and denigrated during the reservation era, but the basic social unit that sustained the culture survived, albeit in altered form. The fact that Indians were administered on separate reservations, isolated from one another and the "contaminating" effects of everyday contact with the larger society, also abetted the preservation of traditional language and culture. (See Cornell, 1990.)

Indian culture and identity have been fortified by increasing interest in ethnicity and "roots." Also, over the past few decades, the federal government has moderated its efforts at acculturation (Snipp, 1989, p. 309). In an atmosphere of greater tolerance and support for pluralism, Indian cultures seem more robust than they have been for decades.

Some social forces are working against pluralism and the survival of tribal cultures, however. The Indian protest movement and other joint efforts have brought the tribes together and increased communication across tribal lines. This pan-tribalism may threaten the integrity of individual tribal cultures even as it successfully represents Indian grievances and concerns to the larger society. Opportunities for jobs, education, and higher incomes draw Indians to more developed urban areas and will continue to do so as long as the reservations are underdeveloped. Many aspects of the tribal cultures can be fully expressed and practiced only with other tribal members on the reservations.

Thus, many Native Americans must make a choice between "Indianness" on the reservation and "success" in the city. Native American traditions and heritages are preserved by those who live on or near the reservations and speak their native language. The younger, more educated members of the group will be more likely to confront the choice between reservation and city, and the future vitality of traditional Indian cultures and languages will hinge on which option is chosen.

Secondary Structural Assimilation

This section assesses the degree of integration of Native Americans in the various institutions of public life, following the general outlines established in chapter 5.

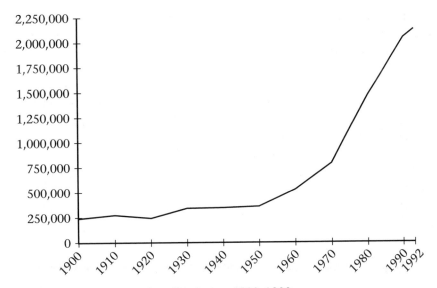

Figure 6.2 Native American Population, 1900–1990
Source: U.S. Bureau of the Census, 1990, 1993, and unpublished data.

Population Size

The changing fortunes of Native Americans are reflected in their population size. In 1492 the group numbered at least a million in what is now the continental United States (Snipp, 1992, p. 354). Losses suffered during the contact period reduced the population to less than 250,000 by 1900. Since that time, population has generally increased, and dramatically so in recent decades. Figure 6.2 charts the changes in Native American population during the 20th century.

The growth of the Native American population reflects their higher fertility rate. It also reflects the changing definitions of race in the larger society. The population figures are based on the official counts taken by the U.S. Bureau of the Census, and the method used to classify people into racial categories has changed over the years. Until 1960, race was determined by applying a standard set of biological definitions to everyone (Simpson & Yinger, 1985, pp. 28–30). After 1960, the census adopted a "self-report" system for determining race. That is, a person's response to the question "What is your race?" was accepted at face value. This looser and more subjective treatment of race is consistent with the social (vs. biological) realities of the concept but makes it difficult to know exactly what the recent population increases mean. Are people now more willing to "admit" Indian ancestry? Are people lying about their racial affiliation? How *should*

"Native American" (or any other so-called race) be defined? These questions raise the possibility that the population increase is as much a social and political phenomenon as it is a biological reality.

Residence

Since the Indian Removal Act of 1830, Native Americans have been concentrated in the western two thirds of the nation, as illustrated in Figure 6.3. A few pockets of population can still be found in the east. The states with the largest concentrations of Native Americans—California, New Mexico, and Arizona—together include about a third of all Native Americans; another 10% live in Oklahoma.

Native Americans belong to hundreds of different tribes. The ten largest are listed in Table 6.1.

Table 6.1 The Ten Largest Tribes

Tribe	Number	Percent of All Native Americans
Cherokee	306,132	16.4
Navajo	219,198	11.7
Chippewa	103,826	5.5
Sioux	103,255	5.5
Choctaw	82,299	4.4
Pueblo	52,839	2.8
Apache	50,051	2.7
Iroquois	49,038	2.6
Lumbee	48,444	2.6
Creek	43,550	2.3

Source: U.S. Bureau of the Census, 1993, p. 48.

Health

Throughout most of this century, the poverty, rural isolation, substandard housing, and lack of health care services on reservations have made Native Americans especially vulnerable to a variety of illnesses and medical problems. Conditions and services have improved considerably in recent years, however, and Native Americans are approaching national norms on a variety of statistics that measure health and well-being (Hodgkinson, Outtz, & Obarakpor, 1990, p. 19). Nonetheless, health remains a major area of concern for this group. On reservations,

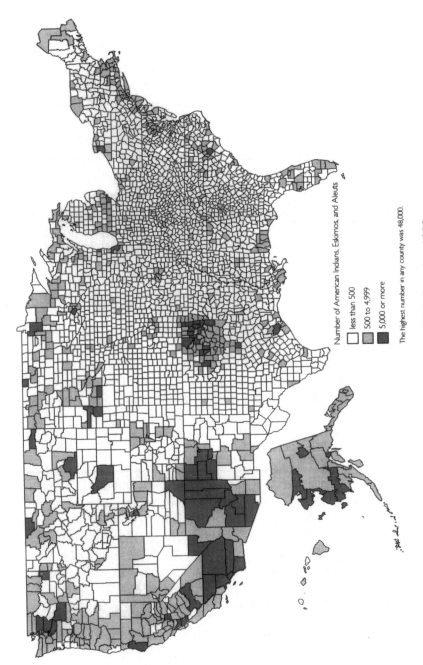

Figure 6.3 American-Indian, Aleut, and Eskimo Population of U.S. Counties, 1990

Note: Excludes Hispanics.

Source: O'Hare, 1992, p. 26

the ratio of doctors and nurses to the population as a whole is less than 40% of the ratio in the larger society. In the judgment of one expert, Indian health care is "abysmal," and alcoholism, deaths from alcohol, and suicide remain particular problems (Worsnop, 1992, p. 400).

Education

Native Americans continue to lag behind national standards in educational levels. Until the last few decades, schools for Native Americans were primarily focused on "civilizing" and Americanizing the children, not on educating them. The percentage of high school graduates has risen (from 22% in 1970 to 56% in 1980, compared to 55% and 69%, respectively, for white adults) and the number of Indians enrolled in college has increased. In 1976 there were about 75,000 Native Americans in college, and in 1988 the number exceeded 90,000 (Hodgkinson et al., 1990, p. 22; Wright & Tierney, 1991, p. 12).

In contrast to this positive sign, school dropout continues to be a major problem (Snipp, 1989, p. 364). The dropout rate in 1988 for Native American children was 35.5% compared to 28.8% for the nation as a whole (Hodgkinson et al., 1990, p. 22). Furthermore, the percentage of Native Americans actually graduating from high school and college is still far below national norms. In 1992 78% of Indians ages 25–44 were high school graduates compared to 91% of non-Hispanic whites in the same age group. The percentage of college graduates was 11% for Indians and 28% for non-Hispanic whites (O'Hare, 1992, p. 29). These differences are especially important because the lower levels of educational attainment limit mobility and job opportunities in the postindustrial job market.

Political Power

The ability of Native Americans to exercise power as a voting bloc or to otherwise directly impact the political structure is limited by group size, for they are a tiny percentage of the electorate. Their political power is further limited by their lower average levels of education, language differences, lack of economic resources, and fractional differences within and between tribes and reservations. The number of Native Americans holding elected office is minuscule: four tenths of 1% in 1987 (O'Hare, 1992, p. 40). In 1992, however, Ben Nighthorse Campbell of Colorado became the first Native American to be elected to the U.S. Senate.

Jobs and Income

Some of the most severe challenges facing Native Americans relate to work and income. The problems are especially evident on the reservations, where jobs are scarce and affluence is rare. In 1989 the BIA con-

Table 6.2 Employment for Indians Living on or Near Reservations

Total able to work[1]	384,686	
Employed	233,476	(61.70% of those able to work)
Earning more than $7,000 per year	152,014	(65.11% of those employed)

1. Total number of people between 16 and 64 years of age who are not in school or otherwise unable to work.

Source: Hodgkinson et al., 1990, p. 25.

ducted a study of the employment of almost 1 million Indians living on or near reservations. Some of the results are displayed in Table 6.2. Nearly 40% of those able to work were unemployed and about one third of those who were employed earned less than $7,000 a year. On some reservations, unemployment rates can reach as high as 80% or 90%. Nationally, Figure 6.4 shows an employment picture with Indians underrepresented in the higher status, more lucrative professions and overrepresented in unskilled labor, agricultural work, and service jobs.

Income data reflect the patterns of unemployment and lower levels of education. In 1979 median household income for Native Americans was $20,500 (68% of median household income for non-Hispanic whites). The figure fell to $20,000 (64% of median household income for non-Hispanic whites) in 1989 (O'Hare, 1992, p. 34). In 1969 about one third of all Indian families had incomes below the federal poverty line, and the percentage was higher on the reservations (Snipp, 1992, pp. 362–363). The percentages remained virtually

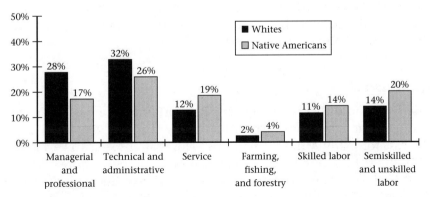

Figure 6.4 Occupational Distribution of Native Americans and Whites, 1990
Source: O'Hare, 1992, p. 33.

the same in 1991, with 32% of Indian families falling below the official poverty income line (O'Hare, 1992, pp. 38).

The interlocking forces of past discrimination, lack of development on the reservation, poor health care, and lower levels of education have severely limited the range of job opportunities and career possibilities for Native Americans. Over the last 20 years, the situation of the group has improved on many indicators and there is some promise for the future (e.g., natural resources, treaty rights, gambling). However, the rural isolation of the reservations and their distance from the centers of growth and development limit these possibilities for improvement and raise the likelihood that the reservations will remain the rural counterpart of the urban ghetto.

Primary Structural Assimilation

Rates of intermarriage for Native Americans are quite high compared to those of other groups. In 1980 only about half of all married Indians were married to other Indians. In contrast, the rate of within-group marriage for whites and blacks was about 99%. Native Americans' higher rate of marriage outside the group is partly the result of the small size of the group. In New England, which has the lowest relative percentage of Indians in any region, less than 10% of Indian marriages are within the group. In the mountain states, which have a greater number of Native Americans who are also highly concentrated on reservations, more than 60% of Indian marriages are within the group (Snipp, 1989, pp. 156–159).

The higher rate of marriage outside the group is also an indication of the extent of acculturation and integration for Native Americans. Marriages with non-Indians are much more common in metropolitan areas, away from the reservations. They are also associated with higher levels of education, greater participation in the labor force, higher income levels, and lower rates of poverty (Snipp, 1989, pp. 160–164). Thus, marriage with non-Indians is more characteristic for Native Americans who have left the reservation to pursue opportunities for education and careers in the cities.

Conclusion

The situation of Native Americans has certainly changed over the course of the 20th century, but is it "better" or just "different," as is the case for many African Americans? The answer seems to be a little of both as the group grows in size and becomes even more diversified. Let's assess the usefulness of some of our theoretical models and concepts.

The linear, simplistic thinking of traditional assimilation theory does not fit the current situation or the past experiences of Native Americans very well. Some Native Americans are intermarrying with whites and integrating into the larger society, while others strive to retain a tribal culture in the midst of an urbanized, industrialized society. Members of the group can be found at every degree of acculturation and integration, and Native Americans seem to be moving toward assimilation in some ways and away from it in others.

From the standpoint of the Noel and Blauner hypotheses, Native Americans have had to struggle from their origins as a conquered and colonized minority group. For most of this century, they have been left to survive as best they could at the margins of the larger society, too powerless to establish meaningful pluralism yet too colonized to pursue equality.

Economic development of the reservations would seem to be the key for the survival of the tribes. Some tribes do have some assets that could fuel development efforts. However, these more fortunate tribes sometimes do not have the expertise or the capital to finance the exploitation of these resources. They must rely, in whole or in part, on non-Indian expertise and white-owned companies and businesses. Thus, non-Indians, rather than the tribes, may be the primary beneficiaries of some forms of development. (This would, of course, be consistent with American history.) For those reservations for which gambling is not an option and for those without natural resources, investment in human capital (education, for example) may offer the most compelling direction for future development.

Urban Indians face the barriers of discrimination and racism that confront other minority groups of color. Members of the group with lower levels of education and job skills face the prospects of becoming a part of a permanent urban underclass. More educated and skilled Native Americans share with black Americans the prospect of a middle-class lifestyle more partial and tenuous than that of comparable segments of the dominant group.

The situation of Native Americans today may be superior to the status of the group at the end of the 19th century. Given the depressed and desperate conditions of the reservations in the 1890s, it wouldn't take much to show an improvement. Native Americans are growing rapidly in number and are increasingly diversified by residence, education, and degree of assimilation. Yet, enormous problems remain both on and off the reservations. The challenge for the future, as it was in the past, will be to find a course between pluralism and assimilation that will balance the issues of quality of life against the importance of retaining a Native American identity.

MAIN POINTS

- At the beginning of the 20th century, Native Americans faced the paternalistic reservation system, poverty, rural isolation, and coercive acculturation. Their situation has been shaped by federal legislation including the Indian Reorganization Act (IRA) of 1934 and the disastrous policy of termination.

- Native Americans began to urbanize rapidly in the 1950s, but they are the least urbanized American minority group.

- The Red Power movement began in the 1960s and sought to redress past grievances, increase awareness of the problems of Native Americans, and address the problems of poverty and powerlessness. Current conflicts between Native Americans and the dominant group center on control of natural resources, preservation of treaty rights, and gambling.

- Native American acculturation is low, and their traditions and heritages show few signs of disappearing. Secondary structural assimilation of Native Americans is also low and, on many measures of quality of life, they are the most impoverished American minority group. Primary structural assimilation is comparatively high, especially in areas were Native Americans make up a small percentage of the population.

FOR FURTHER READING

Brown, Dee. 1970. *Bury My Heart at Wounded Knee* New York: Holt, Rinehart & Winston.

Cornell, Stephen. 1988. *The Return of the Native: American Indian Political Resurgence.* New York: Oxford University Press.

Deloria, Vine. 1969. *Custer Died for Your Sins.* New York: Macmillan Pub. Co.

Nabakov, Peter. 1991. *Native American Testimony.* New York: Penguin Books.

Snipp, C. Matthew. 1989. *American Indians: The First of This Land.* New York: Russell Sage Foundation.

Wax, Murray. 1971. *Indian Americans: Unity and Diversity.* Englewood Cliffs, NJ: Prentice Hall.

CHAPTER 7

Hispanic Americans
Colonization, Immigration, and Ethnic Enclaves

The United States is home to many different Spanish-origin groups. Some of these groups have existed in North America for centuries, whereas others are among the newest immigrants. Hispanic Americans trace their origins to many different places and connect themselves to a diversity of traditions. Though these groups share a language, they have not generally thought of themselves as a single social entity (Portes, 1990, p. 160).

In contrast to the colonized origins of African-American and Native American minority groups, Hispanic-American groups combine elements of immigration with colonization, resulting in a variety of present-day relationships with the larger society. The various Hispanic-American groups are further differentiated by physical (or racial) criteria. Some (like Mexican Americans) combine Spanish and Native American ancestry, whereas others (like Puerto Ricans) are a mixture of European and African racial backgrounds. These physical differences often, but not always, overlap with cultural distinctions (like language or religion) and reinforce the separation of Hispanic Americans from Anglo-American society. Even Hispanic Americans who are completely acculturated may still experience discrimination based on their physical appearance.

In this chapter we focus on the three largest Hispanic groups, concentrating particularly on Mexican Americans and covering Puerto Ricans and Cuban Americans in somewhat less detail. We also look at recent immigration from Latin America and the Caribbean and answer questions similar to those asked about African Americans and Native Americans. How has the situation of Hispanic Americans changed over the course of the 20th century? How does their present status compare to that of other minority groups? How do the various Hispanic groups differ from one another? How have these groups been affected by immigration?

Table 7.1 Size and Recent Growth of the Hispanic-American Population[1]

Group	Population		Percent Increase 1980–1990	Percent of Total Population, 1990
	1980	1990		
Mexican Americans	8,740	13,496	54	5.4
Puerto Ricans[2]	2,014	2,728	35	1.1
Cuban Americans	803	1,044	30	0.4
Other Hispanics[3]	3,051	5,086	67	2.1

1. In thousands.
2. Living on U.S. mainland only.
3. Includes people from the Dominican Republic, Colombia, El Salvador, Nicaragua, and other countries.
Source: U.S. Bureau of the Census, 1993, p. 18.

Table 7.1 shows the relative size of the three largest Hispanic groups and their rates of growth since 1980. Hispanic Americans are currently about 9% of the total population and, considered as a whole, they are the second largest American minority group after African Americans who constitute about 12% of the total population. With present rates of growth, the number of Hispanic Americans is projected to surpass the number of African Americans early in the 21st century (U.S. Bureau of the Census, 1993, p. 19).

A final introductory comment is in order. As is the case with most groups in the United States, labels and group names are important. The term *Hispanic American* is widely used and might seem neutral and inoffensive to non-Hispanics. However, the term can have negative meanings and controversial connotations. This group label is similar to the "American Indian" label in that it is a designation invented and applied by the dominant group. The term reinforces the mistaken perception that all Spanish-speaking peoples are alike and imposes a common identity where none in fact exists. Also, the "Hispanic" label highlights Spanish heritage and language but does not acknowledge the roots of these groups in African and Native American civilizations.

Another commonly used term for this group is *Latino Americans*, which stresses common origins in Latin America and the fact that each culture is a unique blend of diverse traditions (*Latino* is used to refer to the whole group or to males; *Latina* is the female form). In this chapter I use both terms when referring to the category as a whole. In other cases I specify the Spanish-origin group to which I am referring. (See Murguia, 1991, for more on group labels.)

Mexican Americans: Developments During the 20th Century

As discussed in chapter 3, Mexicans in the Southwest were conquered and colonized in the 19th century as the United States expanded from the East. Mexicans became a minority, displaced and exploited in lands that had once been theirs. Following the conquest, the group became a cheap labor force in agriculture, ranching, mining, railroad construction, and other areas of the expanding dominant-group economy.

In some ways the situation of Mexican Americans in 1900 resembled that of Native Americans. Both were small groups, numbering much less than 1% of the total population (Cortes, 1980, p. 702). Both differed from the dominant group in culture and language and both were impoverished, relatively powerless, and isolated in rural areas, distant from the centers of industrialization and modernization.

In other ways, though, the status of Mexican Americans was reminiscent of African Americans in the South. Although they supplied much of the labor power for the regional economy, Mexican Americans were limited to low-paid occupations and a subordinate status in the social structure. Like both Native Americans and African Americans, Mexican Americans lacked the resources to end their exploitation, and their cultural heritage came under continual attack by the dominant society (Mirande, 1985, p. 32). In short, Mexican Americans were a colonized minority group similar to other colonized minority groups of the time period.

There were also, of course, important differences in the experiences of the three groups. Perhaps most crucial was the proximity of the sovereign nation of Mexico. Population movement across the border was constant, and Mexican culture and the Spanish language were continually rejuvenated even as they were disparaged by Anglo-American society.

Cultural Patterns

Mexican-American and Anglo-American cultures differ in a number of ways. While the dominant society is largely Protestant, the overwhelming majority of Mexican Americans are Catholic, and the Church remains one of the most important institutions in any Mexican-American community. Religious practices vary though, and Mexican Americans (especially the men) are relatively inactive in church attendance, preferring to express their spiritual concerns in less routinized ways.

Everyday life in Mexican-American communities has been described in terms of the culture of poverty (see chapter 5). This perspective asserts that Mexican Americans suffer from an unhealthy value system that encourages fatalism and other negative attitudes and re-gards planning for the future as futile (Lewis, 1959, 1965, 1966). Cur-rently, many analysts regard these characterizations as exaggerated and more descriptive of people who are poor and uneducated, not Mexican Americans per se (Moore & Pachon, 1985; Valentine, 1968).

Another area of cultural difference involves <u>**machismo, a value sys-tem that stresses male dominance, honor, virility, and violence.**</u> The stereotypes of the dominant group exaggerate the importance of ma-chismo and often fail to recognize that machismo can be expressed through being a good provider, a respected father, and in other non-destructive ways. In fact, the concern for male dignity is not unique to Hispanics and can be found, in varying strengths and expressions, in many cultures, including Anglo American. Thus, this difference is one of degree rather than kind (Moore & Pachon, 1985).

Compared to Anglo Americans, Mexican Americans tend to place more value on family relations and obligations. Strong family ties can be the basis for support networks and cooperative efforts but can also conflict with the emphasis on individualism and individual success in the dominant culture. For example, familism may inhibit geographi-cal mobility and people's willingness to pursue educational and occu-pational opportunities distant from their home communities (Moore, 1970, p. 127).

These cultural differences have inhibited communication with the dominant group and have served as the basis for excluding Mexican Americans from the larger society. They also have provided a basis for group cohesion and unity that has sustained common action and protest activity.

Immigration

Since 1900, the situation of Mexican Americans has been shaped by immigration, and a large percentage of the group are either immi-grants or the children of immigrants. The number of legal border crossings from Mexico to the United States is shown in Table 7.2. Note how the rate of immigration fluctuates. For the most part, the changing rates reflect the varying demand for labor in the low-pay-ing, unskilled sector of the U.S. labor market. During periods of high demand, such as the 1920s, Mexicans were encouraged to immigrate and were actively recruited by U.S. employers. During hard times, such as the 1930s, demand for labor decreased and the flow of immi-gration slowed, and Mexicans in the United States returned home, sometimes voluntarily, often by force. Thus, for the last century, Mexico has served as a reserve labor pool for the benefit of U.S. busi-nesses, agricultural interests, and other groups.

Table 7.2 Legal Mexican Immigration

Years	Total Number	Mexican Immigrants as a Percent of All Legal Immigrants
1901–1910	46,642	0.6
1911–1920	219,004	3.8
1921–1930	459,287	11.2
1931–1940	22,319	4.2
1941–1950	60,389	5.9
1951–1960	299,811	11.9
1961–1970	453,937	13.7
1971–1980	640,294	14.2
1981–1990	1,655,843	22.6

Source: 1900–1980: Tienda, 1989, p. 115. 1981–1990: U.S. Immigration and Naturalization Service, 1992, p. 30.

Causes of Immigration From Mexico (Push and Pull)

Until the 1920s, movement across the border was informal and largely unregulated (Grebler, Moore, & Guzman, 1970, p. 63). As the economies of the West and Southwest developed, however, efforts to control the border increased even as a number of forces combined to "pull" Mexicans to the United States.

Agriculture in the Southwest began to expand rapidly soon after 1900 and demand for labor in the fields expanded. The volume of immigration from Mexico increased accordingly (Acuna, 1988, pp. 141–143). The importance of Mexican labor for U.S. employers increased again when the combination of World War I and restrictive immigration legislation in the 1920s (see chapter 4) reduced or eliminated the supply of labor from Europe and Asia.

Events in Mexico also affected immigration. The Mexican Revolution began in 1910 and the resulting political turmoil and instability was a significant "push" factor. Mexico also began to industrialize at about the same time and the rural population was displaced by the mechanization of agriculture. These political and economic forces combined to "push" people out of Mexico and toward the United States (Cortes, 1980, p. 702; Moore, 1970, pp. 39–41).

The Influence of Federal Programs and Policies

Government policy on Mexican immigration has changed as often as the demand for cheap labor has fluctuated. It has been shaped by domestic and international politics and by the volume of immigration from other parts of the globe. The flow of people across the border has been alternately encouraged, discouraged, and ignored. Sometimes, more than one policy has been pursued simultaneously.

During the Great Depression, unemployment rates soared and efforts were made to reduce the Mexican-American population. The government instituted a **repatriation** campaign aimed specifically at deporting illegal Mexican immigrants. In many localities repatriation was pursued with great zeal, and many legal immigrants and native-born Mexican Americans were intimidated into moving to Mexico. As one indication of the effectiveness of repatriation, it is estimated that the Mexican-American population of the United States declined by about 40% during the 1930s (Cortes, 1980, p. 711).

When the Depression ended and U.S. society mobilized in the face of World War II, federal policy toward immigrants from Mexico changed once more. Labor shortages began to occur and employers again turned to Mexico for workers. In 1942 a formal program was initiated to bring in contract laborers. Called the **bracero program** (*bracero* means "laborer"), the policy permitted contract laborers to work in the United States for a limited amount of time. These workers generally filled labor shortages in agriculture and other areas requiring unskilled labor. When their contract expired, they were required to return to Mexico.

The bracero program continued for several decades after the end of the war and was a crucial source of labor for the American economy. In 1960 alone, braceros supplied 26% of the nation's seasonal farm labor (Cortes, 1980, p. 703). The program generated millions of dollars of profit for growers and other employers by paying braceros much less than American workers would have received (Amott & Matthaei, 1991, pp. 79–80). While the bracero program permitted immigration from Mexico, other programs and agencies worked to deport undocumented (or illegal) immigrants, large numbers of which entered the country with the braceros. The government effort reached a peak in the early 1950s with **Operation Wetback,** a program under which federal authorities deported some 3.8 million Mexicans (Grebler et al., 1970, p. 521).

In 1965 the quota system established by the National Origins Act of 1924 was finally abolished. A new immigration policy was established that limited each nation to a yearly maximum of 20,000 immigrants, with a worldwide limit of 270,000 per year. The new policy gave a high priority to family and kin, allowing immediate family (parents, spouses, children) of U.S. citizens to enter without numerical restriction. About 80% of the restricted 270,000 immigrant visas were reserved for other close relatives of permanent U.S. residents and citizens. The remaining 20% of the visas went to people who had skills needed in the labor force, including professionals, technical workers, and engineers. Also, people who were classified as political refugees could enter without regard to the numerical limits (Bouvier & Gardener, 1986, pp. 13–15; Rumbaut, 1991, p. 215).

The priority given to families under the new policy reinforced the tendency for immigrants to move along chains of kinship and other social relations. The social networks connecting Latin America with the United States expanded and the rate of immigration for Mexicans and other Hispanics increased after 1965.

Another change in federal immigration policy that has had a notable impact on Mexican Americans was the 1986 Immigration Reform and Control Act (IRCA). Under this act, illegal immigrants who had been in the country continuously since 1982 could legalize their status. Some 3 million people, most of them Mexican, have taken advantage of this provision (U.S. Immigration and Naturalization Service, 1993, p. 17).

Mexican Immigrants Since 1965

Most Mexican immigrants continue to seek work in the low-paying, unskilled sectors of the labor market in the cities and fields of the Southwest. For many, work is seasonal or temporary. When the work ends, they return to Mexico, commuting across the border as has been done for decades.

Contrary to popular perception, Mexican immigrants—the undocumented as well as the legal—are not particularly destitute or impoverished when compared to the Mexican population as a whole. Their rates of literacy and their educational levels tend to be higher than the average for their homeland. Mexican immigrants often come from urban areas and white-collar occupations. This continuing immigration from Mexico, as from much of Latin America, is motivated not by unemployment or rural poverty but by the absence of jobs that pay well, the huge gap in development and affluence with the United States, and the continuing need for cheap labor in the U.S. economy (Portes, 1990, p. 180; Portes & Rumbaut, 1990, p. 11).

Immigration, Colonization, and Intergroup Competition

Three points can be made about the flow of immigration from Mexico over the course of this century. First, Mexican immigration was and is stimulated and sustained by powerful political and economic interests in the United States. Mexican laborers have been actively recruited and elaborate networks of communication and transportation routinize the flow of people and make it a predictable source of labor for the benefit of U.S. agriculture and other employers. The flow of people back and forth across the border was well established long before efforts began to regulate and control that movement. The problem of "illegal" immigration is the result of changing U.S. policy as much as it is the result of people moving from one place to another (Portes, 1990, pp. 160–163).

Second, unlike immigrants from other parts of the globe, Mexican immigrants enter a social system in which the colonized status of their group has already been established. The positions open to Mexican immigrants were determined by the paternalistic traditions and racist systems that began during the original 19th-century conquest. Mexican Americans continued to be treated as a colonized group in spite of the streams of new arrivals, and the history of the group in the 20th century has many parallels with African Americans and Native Americans. Thus, Mexican Americans might be thought of as a colonized minority group that happens to have a large number of immigrants (Alvarez, 1973, pp. 927–928; see Almaguer, 1989, for a different view).

Third, the twisting, often contradictory history of U.S. policy on Mexican immigration should serve as a reminder that levels of prejudice and discrimination increase as competition and the sense of threat between groups increases. The very qualities that make Mexican labor attractive to employers have caused bitter resentment among those segments of the Anglo population who feel that their jobs and financial security are threatened. Often caught in the middle, Mexican Americans have not had the resources to avoid exploitation by employers or rejection and discrimination by others. The ebb and flow of the efforts to stem the tide of immigration can be understood in terms of competition, power, and prejudice.

Developments in the United States

As the flow of immigration from Mexico fluctuated with the need for cheap labor, Mexican Americans struggled to improve their status. Like other colonized minority groups, they faced a system of repression and control in which they were accorded few legal rights and had little political power. Throughout the 20th century, the group was concentrated in the least desirable jobs and received the lowest wages. Split labor markets, in which Mexican Americans are paid less for the same jobs than Anglos are, have been common. The workforce has often been further split by gender, with Mexican-American women assigned to the worst jobs and receiving the lowest wages in both urban and rural areas (Takaki, 1993, pp. 318–319).

Men's jobs often took them away from their families to work in the mines and fields. In 1930, 45% of Mexican-American men worked in agriculture, with another 28% in unskilled nonagricultural jobs. The women were often forced by economic necessity to enter the job market, and in 1930 they were concentrated in farm work (21%), unskilled manufacturing jobs (25%), and domestic and other service work (37%) (Amott & Matthaei, 1991, pp. 76–77). They were typically paid less than both Mexican-American men and Anglo women. In addition to their job responsibilities, Mexican-American women had to maintain their own households and raise their own children, often facing these tasks with an absent spouse (Zinn & Eitzen, 1990, p. 84).

As the United States continued to industrialize and urbanize during the century, employment patterns became more diversified. Mexican Americans found work in manufacturing, construction, transportation, and other sectors of the economy. Some Mexican Americans, especially those whose families had been in this country for three or more generations, moved into middle- and upper-level occupations, and some began to move out of the Southwest. Still, Mexican Americans in all regions (especially recent immigrants) remain concentrated at the bottom of the occupational ladder (Amott & Matthaei, 1991, pp. 76–79; Cortes, 1980, p. 708).

Like African Americans in the segregated South, Mexican Americans were excluded from the institutions of the larger society by law and by custom for much of this century. There were separate (and unequal) school systems for Mexican-American children and, in many communities, Mexican Americans were disenfranchised. Residential segregation has been widespread, and discrimination in the criminal justice system and civil rights violations have been common grievances of Mexican Americans.

Protest and Resistance

Like all minority groups, Mexican Americans have attempted to improve their collective position when possible. The beginnings of organized resistance and protest reach back to the original contact period in the 19th century, when protest was usually organized on a local level. Regional and national organizations made their appearance in the 20th century (Cortes, 1980, p. 709). As was the case with African Americans and Native Americans, the early protest organizations were integrationist and reflected the assimilationist values of the larger society.

As the century progressed, the number and variety of groups pursuing the Mexican-American cause have increased. During World War II, Mexican Americans served in the armed forces and, as was the case with other minority groups, this experience increased their impatience with the constraints placed on their freedoms and opportunities. After the war ended, a number of new Mexican-American organizations were founded, including the Community Service Organization in Los Angeles and the American GI Forum in Texas. Compared with older organizations, the new groups were less concerned with assimilation per se, addressed a broad range of community problems, and attempted to increase Mexican-American political power (Grebler et al., 1970, pp. 543–545).

The Chicano Movement

The 1960s were a time of intense activism and militancy for Mexican Americans. A protest movement guided by an ideology called **Chicanismo** began at about the same time as the Black Power and Red Power movements. Chicanismo encompassed a variety of organizations and ideas, united by a heightened militancy and impatience with the racism of the larger society and by strongly stated demands for justice, fairness, and equal rights. The movement questioned the value of assimilation, sought to increase awareness of the continuing exploitation of Mexican Americans, and adapted many of the tactics and strategies (marches, rallies, voter registration drives, etc.) of the civil rights movement of the 1960s.

Chicanismo is similar in some ways to the black power ideology (see chapter 5). It is in part a reaction to the failure of U.S. society to implement the promises of integration and equality. It rejected traditional stereotypes of Mexican Americans, proclaimed a powerful and positive group image and heritage, and analyzed the group's situation in American society in terms of victimization and institutional discrimination. The inequalities that separated Mexican Americans from the larger society were seen as the result of deep-rooted, continuing racism and the cumulative effects of decades of exclusion. According to Chicanismo, the solutions to these problems lay in group empowerment, increased militancy, and group pride, not in assimilation to a culture that had continuously exploited Mexican Americans (Acuna, 1988, pp. 307–358; Moore, 1970, pp. 149–154).

Some of the central thrusts of the 1960s protest movement are captured in the widespread adoption of **Chicano** as the group name for Mexican Americans. Other minority groups underwent similar name changes at about the same time. For example, African Americans shifted from "Negro" to "black" as a group designation. These name changes are not merely cosmetic; they mark fundamental shifts in group goals and desired relationships with the larger society. The new names come from the minority groups themselves, not from the dominant group, and they express the pluralistic themes of group pride, self-determination, militancy, and increased resistance to exploitation and discrimination.

Organizations and Leaders

The Chicano movement saw the rise of many new groups and leaders. One of the most important leaders was Reies Lopez Tijerina, who in 1963 formed the Alianza de Mercedes. The goal of this group was to correct what Tijerina saw as the unjust and illegal seizure of land from Mexicans in the 19th century. The Alianza was militant and confrontational and members of the group seized and occupied federal lands. Tijerina spent several years in jail as a result of his protest activities, and the movement faded from view in the 1970s.

Another key figure was Jose Angel Gutierrez, organizer of the La Raza Unida (People United) party. La Raza Unida offered alternative candidates and ideas to Democrats and Republicans. Its most notable success was in Crystal City, Texas, where in 1973 it succeeded in electing its entire slate of candidates to local office (Acuna, 1988, pp. 332–451).

Without a doubt, the best known Chicano leader of the 1960s and 1970s was the late Cesar Chávez, who organized the United Farm Workers (UFW), the first union to successfully represent migrant workers. Chávez was as much a labor leader as he was a leader of the Mexican-American community, and he also organized African Americans, Filipinos, and others. Migrant farm workers have few economic or political resources, and the migratory nature of their work isolates them in rural areas and makes them difficult to contact. In the 1960s (and still today) many were undocumented immigrants. As a group, farm workers were nearly invisible in the social landscape of the United States in the 1960s. Organizing this group was a demanding task, and Chávez's success is one of the more remarkable studies in group protest.

Like Dr. Martin Luther King, Chávez advocated nonviolent direct protest. His best-known tactic was the organization of a grape pickers' strike and a national grape boycott that began in 1965. The boycott lasted 5 years and ended when the growers recognized the UFW as the legitimate representative for farm workers. The agreement was a major victory and resulted in significant improvements in the situation of the workers.

Gender and the Chicano Protest Movement

Mexican-American women have been heavily involved in the Chicano protest movement. Jessie Lopez and Dolores Huerta were central figures in the movement to organize farm workers and worked closely with Cesar Chávez. However, as was the case for African-American women, Chicano women encountered sexism and gender discrimination within the movement even as they worked for the benefit of the group as a whole. Nevertheless, they have contributed to the movement in a variety of areas. Chicana women helped to organize poor communities and have worked for welfare reform. Continuing issues include domestic violence, child care, the criminal victimization of women, and the racial and gender oppression that limits all women of all minority groups (Amott & Matthaei, 1991, pp. 82–86).

Mexican Americans and Other Minority Groups

Like the Black Power and Red Power movements, Chicanismo began to fade from public view in the 1970s and 1980s. The movement could claim some successes, but perhaps the clearest victory was in raising awareness in the larger society about the grievances of and problems encountered by Mexican Americans. Today, Chicanos still face poverty and powerlessness and continue to be exploited as a cheap agricultural labor force. The urban poor of the group share with other minority groups of color the prospect of becoming a permanent underclass. We address this later in the chapter.

The history and present situation of Chicanos have strong parallels with both African Americans and Native Americans. All three groups became minorities as the result of conquest in the past and remain largely colonized minority groups today. But the groups also vary in that they have different histories, face different issues, and have different agendas for the future. For example, bilingual education and immigration policy are prominent issues for Chicanos but not for the other groups.

Regardless of the differences, it is clear that the experiences of Mexican Americans are poorly described by the traditional model of assimilation. Mexican Americans as a group experienced less social mobility over the century than European immigrant groups and have maintained their traditional culture and languages. A large segment of the group has spent most of this century in roughly the same social and economic position: as an unskilled labor force for the development of the Southwest, augmented with "immigrants" from Mexico at the convenience of U.S. employers. Today, almost a third of employed Mexican Americans, double the national percentage, remain in the "unskilled labor" and "farm" sectors of the labor force (Garcia, 1993; U.S. Bureau of the Census, 1993). The cultural and linguistic differences of Mexican Americans combine with racial differences to increase social visibility and are used to rationalize the continuing patterns of discrimination and exclusion.

Puerto Ricans

Puerto Ricans began their contact period in the context of war and conquest during the Spanish-American War of 1898. A former Spanish colony, Puerto Rico became a territory of the United States after the defeat of Spain. The island was small and impoverished and it was difficult for its inhabitants to avoid domination by the United States. By the time Puerto Ricans began to migrate to the mainland in large numbers, their relationship to U.S. society was largely that of a colonized minority group. They generally retained that status on the mainland.

Migration (Push and Pull)

At the time of initial contact, the population of Puerto Rico was overwhelmingly rural and supported itself by subsistence farming and by exporting coffee and sugar. As the century wore on, U.S. firms began to invest in and develop the island economy, and their agricultural endeavors took more and more of the land. Opportunities for economic survival in the rural areas declined and many peasants were forced to move into cities (Portes, 1990, p. 163).

Movement to the mainland began gradually and increased slowly until the 1940s. During that decade, the number of Puerto Ricans on the mainland increased more than fourfold to 300,000. In the 1950s, the group continued to grow and nearly tripled in size (U.S. Commission on Civil Rights, 1976, p. 19). This movement was the result of a combination of circumstances. First, Puerto Ricans became U.S. citizens in 1917, so their movements were not impeded by international boundaries or other restrictions. Second, unemployment continued to be a major problem on the island and the population continued to grow. By the 1940s, a considerable number of Puerto Ricans were available to seek work off the island and, like Chicanos, could serve as a cheap labor supply for U.S. employers.

Third, Puerto Ricans were "pulled" to the mainland by the same workforce shortages that attracted Mexican immigrants during and after World War II. While the latter stream responded to job opportunities in the West and Southwest, Puerto Ricans moved to the Northeast. The job profiles of these two groups were similar and both were concentrated in the low-wage, unskilled sector of the job market. However, Puerto Rican migration began many decades after the Mexican migration, at a time when the United States was much more industrialized and urbanized. As a result, Puerto Ricans have been more concentrated in urban labor markets than Mexican immigrants have been (Portes, 1990, p. 164).

Most Puerto Ricans enter the mainland through New York City. A small Puerto Rican community had existed in that city since the turn of the century, and when migration began to increase in the 1940s, organizations and networks were established to help newcomers with housing, jobs, and other issues. Although they eventually dispersed to other regions and cities, the Puerto Rican population on the mainland remains centered on New York City, and more than two thirds currently reside in the urban Northeast (U.S. Bureau of the Census, 1993, p. 32).

Economics and jobs were at the heart of the move to the mainland. The rate of Puerto Rican migration followed the cycle of boom and bust, just as it has for Mexican immigrants. The 1950s, the peak decade for Puerto Rican migration, was a period of rapid U.S. economic growth. Migration was encouraged and job recruiters traveled to the island to attract even more workers. By the 1960s, however, the supply of jobs on the island had expanded appreciably and the average number of migrants declined from the peak of 41,000 per year in the 1950s to about 20,000 per year. In the 1970s, the U.S. economy faltered, unemployment grew, and the flow of Puerto Rican migration actually reversed itself, with the number of returnees exceeding the number of migrants in several different years (U.S. Commission on Civil Rights, 1976, p. 25). Still, the migration continued and by the early 1990s, more than 2.7 million Puerto Ricans, about half of all Puerto Ricans, were living on the mainland.

Cultural Transitions

Although Puerto Ricans are not "immigrants," the move to the mainland does involve a change in culture and language (Fitzpatrick, 1980, p. 858). In spite of nearly a century of political affiliation, Puerto Rican and Anglo cultures differ along many dimensions. Puerto Ricans are overwhelmingly Catholic, but the religious practices and rituals on the mainland are quite different from those on the island. Religious observances on the mainland are more restrained and organized, whereas those on the island are more spontaneous and expressive (Fitzpatrick, 1980, p. 865). Also, there are relatively few Puerto Rican priests on the mainland, and members of the group often feel estranged from and poorly served by the Church (Fitzpatrick, 1987, pp. 117–138).

Another cultural difference between the island and the mainland involves skin color and perceptions of race. Puerto Rico has a long history of intermarriage between racial groups. On the island, race is perceived as a continuum, not as a simple dichotomous split between white and black. Furthermore, in Puerto Rico factors such as social class are considered to be more important than race as criteria for judging and classifying others. In fact, social class can affect perceptions of skin color, and people of higher status might be seen as "whiter" than those of lower status, regardless of their actual skin color. The primacy of race in U.S. culture and the simplistic and rigid racial thinking of much of the mainland population are disconcerting and even threatening to many Puerto Ricans.

The confusion and discomfort that can result are illustrated by a study of Puerto Rican college students in New York. Dramatic differences were found between the personal racial identification of the students and their perceptions of how Anglos saw them. When asked for their racial identification, most of the students classified themselves as "tan," with a third labeling themselves "white," and only 7% as "black." When asked how they thought they were racially classified by Anglos, however, none of the students used the "tan" classification: 58% felt that they were seen as white, and 41% felt that they were seen as black (Rodriquez, 1989, pp. 60–61; see also Rodriquez & Cordero-Guzman, 1992).

In the racially dichotomized U.S. culture, many Puerto Ricans feel that they have no clear place. The racial perceptions of the dominant culture can be threatening to Puerto Ricans to the extent that they are victimized by the same webs of discrimination and disadvantage that affect African Americans. There are still clear disadvantages to being classified as "black" in U.S. society. Institutionalized racial barriers can be extremely formidable and may combine with cultural and linguistic differences to sharply limit opportunities and mobility for Puerto Ricans.

Puerto Ricans and Other Minority Groups

Puerto Ricans arrived in the cities of the Northeast long after European immigrants and several decades after African Americans began migrating from the South. Since they are more recent arrivals, they have not been subjected to the more repressive paternalistic or rigid competitive systems of race relations like slavery or Jim Crow. Instead, the subordinate status of the group is manifested in their occupational, residential, and educational profiles and by the institutionalized barriers to upward mobility that they face.

Like Mexican Americans, Puerto Ricans on the mainland combine elements of both an immigrant and a colonized minority experience. Since there is considerable movement back and forth between the island and the mainland, Puerto Rican culture retains a strong vitality. Puerto Ricans have much in common with other urban minority groups of color: high rates of urban poverty, failing educational systems, crime, and social disorganization. Like African Americans, their fate is dependent on the future of the American city, and a large segment of the group is in danger of becoming part of a permanent urban underclass.

Cuban Americans

The contact period for Cuban Americans also dates back to the Spanish-American War, when Cuba, along with Puerto Rico, was a Spanish colony. At the end of the war, Cuba became, nominally, an independent nation. The United States remained heavily involved in Cuban politics and economics for decades and U.S. troops actually occupied the island on two different occasions.

The development of a Cuban-American minority group bears little resemblance to the experiences of either Chicanos or Puerto Ricans. As recently as the 1950s, there had been little immigration from Cuba to the United States, even during labor shortages, and Cuban Americans were a very small group (Perez, 1980, p. 256).

Immigration (Push and Pull)

The conditions for a mass immigration were created in the late 1950s when a successful revolution in Cuba resulted in the rise to power of a Marxist government led by Fidel Castro. The new government began to restructure Cuban society along socialist lines. Members of the middle and upper classes lost political and economic power and the changes created by the revolution made it difficult, even impossible, for them to continue business as usual. Cuban immigration came from the more elite classes and included people who had been affluent and powerful and who still controlled many resources.

Prior social, cultural, and business ties helped to pull these immigrants in the direction of the United States. U.S. companies had helped to develop the Cuban economy and, at the time of the revolution, Cuban political and economic elites were profoundly Americanized in their attitudes and lifestyles (Portes, 1990, p. 165). Furthermore, many Cubans viewed south Florida as an ideal spot from which to launch a counterrevolution to oust Castro.

Immigration was considerable for several years. By 1962 more than 215,000 Cubans had arrived. Then, an escalation of hostile relations resulted in the cutoff of all direct contact between Cuba and the United States. In 1965 an air link was reestablished and an additional 340,000 Cubans made the journey. When the air connection was terminated in 1973, immigration slowed to a trickle once more. In 1980, however, another period of open immigration was permitted by the

Cuban government. Using boats of every shape, size, and degree of seaworthiness, some 124,000 Cubans crossed to Florida. These immigrants are often referred to as the **Marielitos,** after the port of Mariel from which many of them debarked. This wave of immigrants generated a great deal of controversy in the United States because the Cuban government used the opportunity to rid itself of a number of convicted criminals and outcasts. The Marielitos included people from every segment of Cuban society, but there was so much concern about the "undesirables" that people lost sight of this fact (Portes & Manning, 1986, p. 58).

Regional Concentrations

The huge majority of Cuban immigrants settled in southern Florida, especially in Miami and surrounding Dade County. Today, Cubans remain one of the most spatially concentrated minority groups in the United States, with more than two thirds of all Cuban Americans residing in Florida. Forty-nine percent of the population of Miami and surrounding Dade County is Hispanic, most of them Cuban (Winsberg, 1994, p. 4).

Socioeconomic Characteristics

Compared to other immigrants from Latin America, Cubans are, on the average, unusually affluent and well educated. Among the immigrants in the early 1960s were large numbers of professionals, landowners, and businesspeople. In later years, as Cuban society was transformed by the Castro regime, the immigrant stream included fewer elites—largely because there were fewer left in Cuba—and more political dissidents and working-class people.

Today, Cuban Americans rank higher than other Latino groups on many measures of affluence. The higher status reflects the higher levels of educational and economic resources they brought with them from Cuba and the favorable and supportive reception they enjoyed from the federal government and the public at large (Portes, 1990, p. 169).

These assets gave Cubans an advantage over Chicanos and Puerto Ricans, but the differences among the three Latino groups run deeper and are more complex than a simple accounting of initial resources would suggest. Cubans adapted to U.S. society in a way that is fundamentally different from the other two Latino groups.

The Ethnic Enclave

The minority groups we have discussed to this point have been concentrated in the unskilled, low-wage segments of the economy where jobs are insecure and not linked to opportunities for upward mobility.

Many Cuban Americans have bypassed this sector of the economy and much of the discrimination and limitations associated with it. Like several other groups, Cuban Americans are an enclave minority (see chapter 1). An ethnic enclave is a social, economic, and cultural subsociety controlled by the group itself. Located in a specific geographical area or neighborhood inhabited solely or largely by members of the group, the enclave encompasses sufficient economic enterprises and social institutions to permit the group to function as a self-contained entity largely independent of the surrounding community.

The first wave of Cuban immigrants brought with them considerable resources and business expertise. Although much of their energy was focused on ousting Castro and returning to Cuba, they generated enough economic activity to sustain restaurants, shops, and other small businesses that catered to the exile community.

As the years passed and the hope of a return to Cuba dimmed, the enclave economy grew. Between 1967 and 1976, the number of Cuban-owned firms in Dade County increased ninefold, from 919 to about 8,000. Six years later, the number had reached 12,000. Most of these enterprises are small but there are some factories that employ hundreds of workers. In addition to businesses serving their own community, Cuban-owned firms are involved in construction, manufacturing, finance, insurance, real estate, and an array of other activities. Over the decades, Cuban-owned firms have become increasingly integrated into the local economy and increasingly competitive with nonethnic firms. The growth of economic enterprises has been paralleled by a growth in the number of other types of groups and organizations and in the number and quality of services available (schools, law firms, medical care, funeral parlors, etc.). The enclave has become a largely autonomous community capable of providing for its members from cradle to grave (Portes & Bach, 1985; Portes & Manning, 1986, p. 59; Wilson & Portes, 1980).

The fact that the enclave economy is controlled by the group itself is crucial; it separates the ethnic enclave from "the ghetto," or neighborhoods that are impoverished and segregated. In ghettos, economic enterprises are typically controlled by members of other groups and the profits, rents, and other resources flow *out* of the neighborhood. In the enclave, profits are reinvested and kept *in* the neighborhood. Group members can avoid the discrimination and limitations imposed by the larger society and can apply their skills and talents in an atmosphere free from language barriers and prejudice. Those who might wish to venture into business for themselves can utilize the networks of mutual aid for advice, credit, and other forms of assistance. Thus, the ethnic enclave provides a platform from which Cuban Americans can pursue economic success independent of their degree of acculturation or English-language ability.

The effectiveness of the ethnic enclave as a pathway for adaptation is illustrated by a study of a group of Cuban and Mexican immigrants, all of whom entered the United States in 1973. At the time of entry, the groups were comparable in levels of skills, education, and English-language ability. Over time, the groups remained comparable on many variables, but some dramatic differences, which reflected their positions in the labor market, began to appear. Most of the Mexican immigrants were employed in the low-wage job sector. Most of the Cuban immigrants, however, were self-employed or employed by another Cuban (i.e., they were involved in the enclave economy). The highest monthly incomes were reported by self-employed Cubans ($1,495) and the second highest incomes were earned by Cubans otherwise employed in the enclave ($1,111). The lowest incomes ($880) were earned by Mexican immigrants employed in small nonenclave firms; many of these people worked as unskilled laborers in seasonal, or temporary, jobs (Portes, 1990, p. 173).

The ability of the Mexican immigrants to rise in the class system was constrained by discrimination and by their lack of economic and political power. Cuban immigrants who found jobs in the enclave did not expose themselves to American prejudices or rely on the job market of the larger society. They entered an ethnic community that featured networks of mutual assistance and support and that linked them to opportunities more consistent with their ambition and their qualifications.

From the viewpoint of many theories and much of the common wisdom about assimilation, the fact that success and prosperity came faster to the group that was *less* integrated and acculturated is an irony that, by this point in the text, need hardly be stressed. These lessons have not been lost on others and many of the themes of Black Power, Red Power, and Chicanismo emphasize self-help, self-determination, nationalism, and separation.

Ethnic enclaves cannot be a panacea for all groups, however. They develop only under certain limited conditions; namely, when business and financial expertise and reliable sources of capital are combined with a labor force willing to work for low wages in exchange for on-the-job training, future assistance and loans, or other delayed benefits. Enclave enterprises usually start on a small scale and cater only to other ethnics. The early economic returns are small and prosperity follows only after years of hard work, if at all. Most important, eventual success and expansion beyond the boundaries of the enclave depend on the persistence of strong ties of kinship and solidarity. These networks and the strength of group cohesion might well be weakened or destroyed by the pressure to assimilate (Portes & Manning, 1986, pp. 61–66).

A final qualification on the Cuban "success story" is necessary. Success has been selective and inequality, poverty, and unemployment continue to be problems. For example, median family income for Cuban Americans in 1991, while higher than that of Mexican Americans and Puerto Ricans, was still only 77% of non-Hispanic whites.

Cuban Americans and Other Minority Groups

The adaptation of Cuban Americans contrasts sharply with the experiences of colonized minority groups and with the common understanding of how immigrant groups are "supposed" to acculturate and behave. Cuban Americans are neither the first nor the only group to develop an ethnic enclave, and their success has generated prejudice and resentment from other groups. Whereas Puerto Ricans and Chicanos have been the victims of stereotypes labeling them "inferior," higher status Cuban Americans have been stereotyped as *too* successful, *too* clannish, and *too* ambitious. The former stereotype commonly emerges to rationalize exploitative relationships; the latter expresses disparagement and rejection of groups that are more successful in the struggle to acquire resources. Nonetheless, the Cuban-American stereotype is an exaggeration and misperception obscuring the fact that poverty and unemployment are major problems for many members of the group.

Recent Immigration From Latin America and the Caribbean

Immigration from Latin America and the Caribbean to the United States has been considerable since the 1960s (Figure 7.1). This immigrant stream is diverse as well as large, with French and British traditions represented as well as Spanish. The immigrants come from a score of nations and reflect the cultural and racial diversity of their homelands. Some are highly educated professionals, and others are farmhands, skilled technicians, or the kinfolk of U.S. citizens. Mexico alone accounts for about half of the people who have legally immigrated from Latin America and the Caribbean since the 1960s. Other large contingents come from Cuba (more than 600,000), the Dominican Republic (about 575,000), Jamaica (about 461,000), Haiti (about 370,000), and Colombia (about 300,000) (U.S. Immigration and Naturalization Service, 1992, pp. 27–28). In this section we examine the characteristics of these immigrants and their impacts on U.S. society.

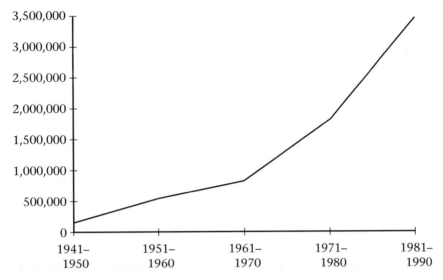

Figure 7.1 Recent Legal Immigration From Latin America and the Caribbean
Source: U.S. Immigration and Naturalization Service, 1992, pp. 27–29.

Socioeconomic Characteristics

Most recent immigrants from the Western Hemisphere come from the less developed nations in the immediate vicinity of the United States, most of which have long-standing relations with this country. We have already discussed the role Mexico and Puerto Rico have played as sources of cheap labor and the ties that led Cubans to immigrate. Each of the sending nations has been similarly linked to the United States, the dominant economic and political power in the region (Portes, 1990, p. 162).

Although the majority of these immigrants bring educational and occupational qualifications that are modest by U.S. standards, they are more educated, more urbanized, and more skilled than the average citizens of the nations from which they come. Contrary to widely held beliefs, these immigrants do not represent the poorest of the poor, the "wretched refuse" of their homelands. They tend to be rather ambitious and most are not so much fleeing poverty as they are attempting to pursue their ambitions and seek opportunities for advancement that are simply not available in their country of origin (Rumbaut, 1991, p. 229). This characterization applies to legal and unauthorized immigrants alike. In fact, the latter may illustrate the point more dramatically since the cost of illegally entering the United States can be considerable.

Location and Impacts

Latino immigrants tend to follow the well-worn paths and networks of previous generations. New York City and Los Angeles remain major points of entry, and Houston and Miami also receive large numbers of Latino immigrants. The impact of these newcomers on local communities is significant and immigration has generated considerable controversy in recent years.

Some of the common and most vociferous concerns of the public are that immigrants take jobs away from U.S. citizens and that they slow economic growth and reduce economic vitality. Research conducted in a variety of places and over time suggests that these fears are exaggerated and that, overall, the economic impact of immigration has been positive. Latino immigrants tend to take low-wage jobs abandoned by native-born workers, or they work in the enclave economies of their own group, taking jobs that would not have existed without the economic activity of their fellow ethnics (Bouvier & Gardner, 1986, pp. 28–30; Muller & Espenshade, 1985; Portes & Rumbaut, 1990, pp. 235–239).

Another concern is the strain immigrants place on taxes and services such as schools and welfare programs. Again research suggests that immigrants often cost less than they contribute. Taxes are automatically deducted from paychecks, and use of such services as unemployment compensation, Medicare, food stamps, Aid to Families with Dependent Children, and Social Security is actually lower than immigrants' proportional contributions. This is also true for undocumented immigrants whose use of services is sharply limited by their vulnerable legal status (Bouvier & Gardner, 1986, p. 31; Simon, 1989).

These findings are not conclusive and it is possible, as some have suggested, that immigration in very recent years has been so great that previous studies are no longer valid. Nonetheless, to give some perspective to these concerns, we should remember that the percentage of the U.S. population that is foreign born is lower today than it was at the turn of the century. In 1920, toward the end of the last great wave of immigration, 13.2% of the population was foreign born. In 1990 the comparable figure was 7.9% (U.S. Bureau of the Census, 1993, p. 50). The current opposition to immigration may be a reaction to *who* as much as to *how many*.

We have been through these debates before. Proposals to reduce (or even reverse) the flow of immigration become prominent when the U.S. public is concerned or anxious about the impact of immigration. Contemporary proposals to curb immigration include Proposition 187 in California—which denies educational, health, and other services to anyone who cannot prove legal residency—as well as a variety of anti-immigrant programs at the federal level. Some of these proposals are reminiscent of the Chinese Exclusion Act of the 1880s and the National Origins Act of the 1920s. The arguments, both for and against immigration, and the proposed remedies and policy changes have a familiar, even nostalgic flair. The idea that prejudice and discrimination are related to the degree of competition for scarce resources seems relevant as an analytical perspective on these debates.

As the debate rages, immigrants—legal and illegal alike—continue to find work in American society. The networks that have delivered cheap immigrant labor for the low-wage sector of the economy continue to operate as they have for more than a century. The primary beneficiaries of this long-established system are not the immigrants.

Recent Immigration in Historical Context

The current wave of immigration to the United States is only one aspect of a centuries-old process that spans the globe. Underlying this population movement is the powerful force of the continuing industrial revolution. We have already discussed 19th-century immigration in the context of industrialization (see chapter 4), and the population movements since the 1960s continue many of the features of the old pattern. The United States and other industrialized nations continue to be centers of growth in the global economy, and immigrants, as always, continue to flow to areas of greater opportunity. During the 19th century, the population movement was largely from Europe to the Western Hemisphere. In the 20th century, the movement has been from south to north. This pattern reflects the simple geography of industrialization and opportunity; the more developed nations are in the Northern Hemisphere.

The United States has been the world's dominant economic, political, and cultural power for much of the century and, consistent with its prominence, has been the preferred destination of most immigrants. By 1960 the United States had received half of all legal immigrants in the world; by the 1980s the percentage had risen to two thirds (Rumbaut, 1991, p. 210). This massive population movement is the result of the combined decisions of millions of individuals, families, and groups. The immigrants forged and then followed networks of social relations linking workers with opportunity. The movements are coordinated and directed by webs of communication and transportation and by chains of people and social relationships stretching across national boundaries and through time and space (Yans-McLaughlin, 1990, p. 6).

Immigrants from Latin America and the Caribbean continue the collective, social nature of past population movements. The direction of their travels reflects contemporary global inequalities between nations and regions: labor continues to flow from the less developed nations to the more developed nations of the world. The direction of this flow is not accidental or coincidental; it is determined by the differential rates of industrialization and modernization across the globe. Its existence contributes to the wealth and affluence of the more developed societies and, especially, to the dominant groups and elite classes of those societies.

Contemporary Hispanic American–Dominant Group Relations

In this section we review the current situation of Hispanic Americans using the concepts developed in previous chapters.

Prejudice and Discrimination

The American tradition of prejudice against Latinos was born in the 19th-century conflicts that created minority group status for Mexican Americans. The themes of the original anti-Mexican stereotype were consistent with the nature of the contact situation: As Mexicans were conquered and subordinated, they were characterized as inferior, lazy, irresponsible, low in intelligence, and dangerously criminal (McWilliams, 1961, pp. 212–214). Prejudice and racism, supplemented with racist ideas and beliefs brought to the Southwest by many Anglos, helped to justify and rationalize the colonized, exploited status of the Chicanos.

These prejudices were incorporated into the dominant culture and were transferred to Puerto Ricans when they began to arrive on the mainland. This stereotype of inferiority didn't quite fit Cuban Americans. Instead, the affluence and prosperity of this group are exaggerated and Cuban success was perceived to be undeserved or achieved by unfair or "un-American" means, a characterization just as stereotypical as that which alleges Latino inferiority.

On the one hand, there is some evidence that the level of Latino prejudice has been affected by the decline of overt American racism. The social distance scale results reported in chapter 2 show a decrease in the scores of Mexican Americans and an increase in rank position. On the other hand, overall levels of prejudice and racism against Latinos seem to have increased recently in reaction to the high rate of immigration.

Although discrimination of all kinds, institutional as well as individual, has been common against Latino groups, it has not been as rigid as the systems that controlled black labor under slavery and segregation. However, discrimination has not decreased as it has against European immigrant groups and their descendants (see chapter 9). Because of their longer tenure in the United States and their original status as a rural labor force, Mexican Americans have probably been more victimized by the institutionalized forms of discrimination than other Latino groups.

Acculturation

Latino groups are highly variable in their extent of acculturation but are often seen as "slow" to learn English and adapt Anglo customs. This perception results in part from comparing Hispanic groups to what many understand to have been the experiences of pre–World War I immigrants from Europe. In American popular thought, as well as in some traditional sociological theories, assimilation is "supposed" to occur by generation and be completed by the third generation. In contrast, Latino groups have been part of American society for decades and the language and cultural differences remain prominent.

On closer examination, research shows that the rate of acculturation does increase with length of residence and is highest for the native born (de la Garza, DeSipio, Garcia, Garcia, & Falcon, 1992; Strategy Research Corporation, 1991). On the specific acculturation issue of language, for example, Latinos are aware that assimilation in the United States has historically followed the Anglo-conformity model and that English is a virtual precondition for many opportunities in the larger society. English-language fluency does increase as the generations pass, and most Americans of Hispanic descent speak English or a combination of English and Spanish. Even those who speak Spanish at home report that they also speak English well or very well (Martin & Midgley, 1994, pp. 37–39; Portes & Schauffler, 1994).

While many are concerned about preserving the English language, others focus on the issue of literacy. In 1986, the year in which California voters made English the official state language, 40,000 immigrant adults were turned away from English classes in Los Angeles alone. The services provided by the state could not keep up with the demand (Rumbaut, 1991, p. 243).

To some extent, the perception of slower acculturation is accurate. Colonized groups such as Chicanos and Puerto Ricans were not encouraged (and often not permitted) to assimilate. Valued only for the cheap labor they supplied, they were seen as otherwise inferior or undesirable, unfit for integration (Zinn & Eitzen, 1990, p. 73). For much of this century, Jim Crow–type laws and other devices were used to exclude Latinos from the experiences (e.g., school) that could have led to greater equality and higher rates of acculturation. Prejudice, racism, and discrimination combined to keep most Latino groups away from the centers of modernization and change and away from opportunities to improve their situation.

In addition, the continuing flow of immigrants, the proximity of the homelands, and pride in Latino heritage helped to sustain separate Hispanic communities in the United States. Modern forms of communication have also helped to sustain language and keep people connected to the "old country" in ways that were not possible in earlier times. Telephones, television, and the speed of modern travel have helped immigrants maintain contact with their home cultures. A study of Mexican women working in the crabbing industry in eastern Virginia found that the women stayed abreast of developments back home and even watched their favorite Mexican soap operas every day via satellite TV (Pellett, 1990).

Racial factors have complicated and slowed the process of acculturation for many Latinos. Latinos who are less "Anglo" in appearance may retain or even emphasize their Spanish heritage to avoid being classified as African or Native American with all the difficulties associated with American racism. Thus, the weight of our racist past and present may put some Latinos in a position where they increase the salience of their ethnic identity, and thus slow the process of Anglo conformity, as a way of avoiding the disadvantages associated with their racial identity.

Finally, for Cuban Americans and other groups, cultural differences reflect the recency of immigration. The first generations are alive and well and, as is typical for immigrant groups, they retain their language and traditions. For example, Cuban Americans have been a sizable group in the United States for only about 35 years, barely enough time for a third generation to develop.

Secondary Structural Assimilation

In this section we survey the situation of Latinos in the public areas and institutions of American society, beginning with where people live.

Residence

Figure 7.2 shows the regional concentrations of Latinos in 1990. The legacies of their varied patterns of entry and settlement are evident. The higher concentrations in the Southwest reflect the presence of Mexican Americans, those in Florida are the results of the Cuban immigration, and those in the Northeast display the settlement patterns of Puerto Ricans. Within these regions, Latino groups are highly urbanized. Cubans are the most urbanized (96%), followed by Puerto Ricans (94%) and Mexican Americans (90%) (Garcia, 1993, p. 12).

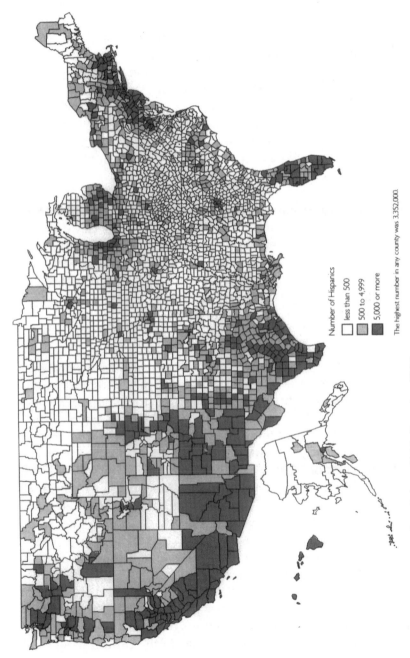

Figure 7.2 Hispanic Population of U.S. Counties, 1990

Note: Hispanics may be of any race.
Source: O'Hare, 1992, p. 22.

Education

Levels of education among all three groups have risen in recent years but still lag behind national standards. While 83% of all non-Hispanic whites over age 25 had completed high school in 1992, the comparable figures were 62% for Cubans, 61% for Puerto Ricans, and 45% for Mexican Americans (Garcia, 1993, pp. 12–13).

About 23% of the non-Hispanic white population was college educated in 1992, compared to 18% of Cuban Americans, 8% of Puerto Ricans, and 6% of Mexican Americans (Garcia, 1993, pp. 12–13). Note that these comparisons rank the three groups in an order consistent with Blauner's idea that colonized minority groups (Mexican Americans and Puerto Ricans) would experience greater inequality than minority groups created by immigration (Cuban Americans).

The lower levels of education are the cumulative results of decades of systematic discrimination and exclusion and are further reduced by the high percentage of recent immigrants who bring modest educational backgrounds. Given the role that educational credentials have come to play in the job market, these figures suggest that, without substantial change in the accessibility of schooling, opportunities for upward mobility for many Latinos, and especially for Mexican Americans and Puerto Ricans, will continue to be limited.

Political Power

The political resources available to Hispanic Americans have increased in recent years, but the group is still proportionally underrepresented. The number of Hispanics in the U.S. House of Representatives has increased from 6 in 1981 to a total of 17 in 1993 (U.S. Bureau of the Census, 1993, p. 277). Although this is nearly a threefold increase, Hispanics still hold only 4% of the total House seats despite the fact that they make up more than 9% of the population.

In similar fashion, the number of Hispanic Americans of voting age doubled between 1978 and 1992, and Hispanics were nearly 8% of the voting age population in 1992. Yet because registration rates and actual turnout have been low, the Hispanic vote remains mostly a potential power resource. For example, in the past four presidential elections, around 30% of eligible Latinos voted, about half of the comparable rate for non-Hispanic whites (U.S. Bureau of the Census, 1993, p. 283). These lower participation rates are due to many factors, including the illegal and/or marginal status of many Latinos and the "English only" nature of the political process in the United States.

Jobs and Income

Unemployment and poverty continue to be major issues. The socioeconomic profiles of Mexican Americans and Puerto Ricans reflect

Table 7.3 Economic Characteristics of Three Hispanic Groups

	Mexican Americans	Puerto Ricans	Cubans	Non-Hispanic Whites
Percent Unemployed, 1992				
Males	12	14	9	8
Females	11	10	10	5
Occupational Distribution, 1992				
Managerial and professional	11	18	25	27
Technical, sales, and admininstration	23	32	33	31
Service	19	20	12	14
Skilled labor	14	11	13	11
Unskilled labor	24	18	15	14
Farm	8	1	2	3
Median Family Income, 1991	23,018	20,654	30,095	39,239
Percent Earning More than $50,000				
Males	3	5	12	15
Females	1	2	3	3
Percent Living in Poverty	30	39	18	9

Source: Garcia, 1993; U.S. Bureau of the Census, 1993.

their historic concentration in the low-wage sector of the economy, the long tradition of discrimination and exclusion, recent immigration, and the lower amounts of human capital (education, job training) controlled by these groups. Cuban Americans, buoyed by a more privileged social class background and their enclave economy, rank higher on virtually all measures of wealth and prosperity. Table 7.3 displays unemployment, occupational, income, and poverty data for these groups.

The high rates of unemployment reflect not only discrimination but also the insecurity and seasonal nature of many of the jobs held by

Latinos. Occupationally, the Cuban-American profile is most similar to that of non-Hispanic whites, and both Mexican Americans and Puerto Ricans are underrepresented in the higher occupational categories and overrepresented in the lower. The income figures are consistent with the relative degree of colonization for the three groups. Note that the median income for Cuban Americans is still almost $10,000 less than that for non-Hispanic whites, a gap that illustrates the exaggeration and misperception in the stereotypes of Cuban affluence.

It is not surprising to find high levels of poverty among Hispanic Americans. The percentage of Mexican Americans living in poverty is comparable to that of African Americans, and the poverty rate for Puerto Ricans is even higher. The poverty rate is lowest for Cubans but is still twice that of non-Hispanic whites.

Status and opportunity also vary by gender. Latina women participate in the labor force at lower rates than both Latino males and women in general. The rate of participation is about 45% for Puerto Rican women and 52% for Cuban- and Mexican-American women versus 58% for non-Hispanic white women (Garcia, 1993, pp. 14–15). In addition to the greater family responsibilities fulfilled by women, these lower rates may reflect the traditional Latino ideas concerning "proper" gender roles (Valdivieso & Davis, 1988, p. 178).

Also, income varies by gender within each Latino group. Hispanic men in general earn about 60% of what non-Hispanic white men earn, and the income gap is even larger for Hispanic women. Table 7.4 shows that Mexican-American women are at the greatest disadvantage, both with respect to Mexican-American males and to non-Hispanic white males. These figures point to a split labor market differentiated by gender within the dual market differentiated by race and ethnicity.

The impacts of poverty are especially severe for Latina women, who often find themselves with the responsibility of caring for their chil-

Table 7.4 Median Earnings of Latina Women

	Mexican Americans	Puerto Ricans	Cubans
Median earnings, 1991	12,959	18,256	17,638
As a percentage of the median earnings for men of the same group	72	79	74
As a percentage of median earnings for non-Hispanic white men	38	66	54

Source: Garcia, 1993, pp. 14–15.

dren alone. The percentage of female-headed households ranges from a high of 40% for Puerto Rican families to about 20% for Mexican-American and Cuban-American families. The rate for non-Hispanic whites is 13% (Garcia, 1993, pp. 20–21). This pattern is the result of many factors, but none is more important than the status of Latino men in the labor force. As we have seen, the jobs available to Latino men often do not pay enough to support a family and many jobs are seasonal, or otherwise insecure.

Female-headed Latino families are affected by a triple economic handicap: they have only one wage earner whose potential income is limited by discrimination against both women and Latinos. The result of these multiple disadvantages is an especially high rate of poverty. Whereas about 25% of non-Hispanic white female-headed households fall below the poverty line, the percentage for Mexican female-headed households is 48% and for Puerto Rican female-headed households, 66% (Garcia, 1993, pp. 20–21).

The socioeconomic situation of Latinos is complex and diversified. Although members of all groups have successfully entered the mainstream economy, poverty and exclusion continue to be major issues. Segments of these groups are highly concentrated in deteriorated urban areas and, like other minority groups of color, they face the possibility of permanent poverty and economic marginality.

Primary Structural Assimilation

Overall, the extent of intimate contact between Hispanic Americans and the dominant group is probably higher than for either African Americans or Native Americans. This pattern may reflect the fact that Latinos are partly ethnic minority groups and partly racial minority groups. Some studies report that contact is greater for the more affluent social classes, in the cities, and for the younger generations (who are presumably more Americanized) (Fitzpatrick, 1976; Grebler et al., 1970, p. 397; Rodriquez, 1989, pp. 70–72).

Rates of intermarriage are higher for Latinos than for African Americans but neither constitutes a high percentage of all marriages. Black-white interracial couples are less than one half of 1% of all marriages and the comparable figure for Latinos is about 2% of all marriages. Intermarriage for Latinos has increased since 1970 when the rate was close to 1% of all marriages (U.S. Bureau of the Census, 1993, p. 44).

Conclusion

As test cases for what we have called the traditional view of American assimilation, Latinos fare poorly. Mexican Americans and Puerto Ricans continue to be overrepresented in the low-wage sector of the labor market. Both have struggled to rise from their colonized past and some members have succeeded in doing so. Yet both groups continue to share many problems with other colonized minority groups of color.

The traditional views of assimilation likewise fail to describe the experiences of Cuban Americans, who violate some of the most basic assumptions of the assimilationist model. On the average they are more prosperous than either Mexican Americans or Puerto Ricans, but they integrated economically before acculturating and became successful by remaining separate.

Clearly, there is no single Hispanic-American experience or pattern of adjustment to the larger society. The diversity of the experiences of the many Hispanic groups in U.S. society suggests the variety and complexity of what it means to be a minority group. These groups also illustrate some of the fundamental forces that shape minority experience: the split labor market and the U.S. appetite for cheap labor, the impact of industrialization, the dangers of a permanent urban underclass, the relationships between competition and prejudice, and the persistence of race as a primary dividing line between people and groups.

MAIN POINTS

- Hispanic-American groups have some characteristics of colonized groups and some of immigrant groups. Also, these groups are racial minorities in some ways and ethnic minorities in others.

- Since the turn of the century, Mexico has served as a reserve labor force for the development of the U.S. economy. For much of the century, however, Mexican Americans were a colonized group in spite of the large number of immigrants.

- Puerto Ricans began to move to the mainland in large numbers in the 1940s. The group is concentrated in the urban Northeast and in the low-wage sector of the job market.

- Cubans began immigrating in the late 1950s. They settled primarily in south Florida, where they created an ethnic enclave.

- Immigration from Latin America and the Caribbean, and especially Mexico, has increased greatly since 1965 and has generated considerable controversy in the larger society.

- Anti-Hispanic prejudice and discrimination seem to have declined in the long term but may have increased because of recent immigration. Levels of acculturation are highly variable, as are levels of secondary structural assimilation. Primary structural assimilation with the dominant group is greater than for African Americans and Native Americans.

FOR FURTHER READING

Acuna, Rodolfo. 1988. *Occupied America* (3rd ed.). New York: Harper & Row.

Boswell, Thomas D., & Curtis, James R. 1984. *The Cuban American Experience*. Totowa, NJ: Rowman and Allanheld.

Fitzpatrick, Joseph P. 1987. *Puerto Rican Americans: The Meaning of Migration to the Mainland* (2nd ed.). Englewood Cliffs, NJ: Prentice Hall.

Mirande, Alfredo, & Enriquez, Evangelica. 1979. *La Chicana: The Mexican-American Woman*. Chicago: University of Chicago Press.

Moore, Joan W., & Pachon, Harry. 1985. *Hispanics in the United States*. Englewood Cliffs, NJ: Prentice Hall.

Portes, Alejandro, & Bach, Robert L. 1985. *Latin Journey: Cuban and Mexican Immigrants in the United States*. Berkeley: University of California Press.

CHAPTER 8

Asian Americans
Modes of Incorporation

As was the case with Hispanic Americans, there are many different Asian-origin groups in the United States. Asian Americans come from a variety of cultures, as distinct from one another as they are from Anglo-American culture, and combine elements of both immigration and colonization in their relationships with the dominant society. Table 8.1 lists most Asian-origin groups.

Several features of the table are worth noting. First, as is common in U.S. government reports on Asian Americans, Pacific Islanders (e.g., Samoans) are included along with groups whose origins are in Asia (e.g., Chinese and Japanese Americans). Although this is a common combination, it is arbitrary and based on a coincidence of geography and some superficial racial similarities. Second, note that all of these groups are tiny fractions of the total population. Even when aggregated into a single unit, Asian Americans and Pacific Islanders were not quite 3% of the total population in 1990. In contrast, African Americans are 12% of the total population, Latinos, almost 10%.

Third, most Asian-American and Pacific Islander groups have grown dramatically in recent years, largely as a result of high rates of immigration since the 1965 changes in immigration policy. During the 1980s, nearly three quarters of the growth for Asian Americans came from immigration (O'Hare, 1992, p. 13). Fourth, the Asian-American groups for which we have data are highly concentrated on the West Coast. West Coast cities have been the most common ports of entry for Asian groups since this population movement began about 150 years ago.

This chapter focuses on the experiences of Chinese and Japanese Americans, the Asian groups with the longest histories in the United States. Other Asian groups and recent immigrants are then examined more briefly, and the chapter ends with an assessment of the present

Table 8.1 Major Asian and Pacific Islander Groups

Group	Numbers 1980[1]	Numbers 1990[1]	Percent of Total Population, 1990	Percent Change, 1980–1990	Percent Living on West Coast
Chinese	806	1,645	0.7	104	52
Filipino	775	1,407	0.6	82	71
Japanese	701	848	0.3	21	76
Asian Indian	362	815	0.2	126	23
Korean	355	799	0.2	125	44
Vietnamese	262	615	0.2	135	54
Hawaiian	167	211	0.1	27	90
Cambodian[2]	16	147	*	819	**
Laotian[2]	48	149	*	210	**
Thai[2]	45	91	*	102	**
Hmong[2]	5	90	*	1,700	**
Pakistani[2]	16	81	*	406	**
Samoan	42	63	*	50	88
Guamanian	32	49	*	53	70
Indonesian[2]	10	29	*	190	**
Others	86	233	*	171	**
Totals	3,500	7,274	2.9	108	56

1. In thousands.
2. 1980 figures for these groups are estimates based on random samples. All other figures are exact tabulations.
* Less than one tenth of 1%.
** Data not available.
Source: U.S. Bureau of the Census, 1993, pp. 18, 32.

status of Asian Americans. We ask questions comparable to those asked in previous case studies: How has the situation of Asian Americans changed during the 20th century? How have they been colonized and excluded? How have they been affected by recent immigration?

As in previous chapters, we compare the situation of Asian Americans with that of other minority groups. However, these comparisons take on a new dimension in this chapter because Asian Americans are commonly regarded as "model minorities": successful, highly educated people with few of the problems often associated with minority groups. It is true that on many indicators of success, some Asian-American groups have attained equality, on the average, with the dominant group. Throughout this chapter we explore the true extent of Asian-American success: How widespread is it? How can we explain the apparent success of some groups? Have Asian Americans forged a pathway to upward mobility that could be followed by other groups? Does the success of Asian Americans mean that the United States is truly a fair and just society?

Before we can sort out these issues, we need to examine some of the general cultural traits that have shaped the Asian-American experience. An appreciation of their cultural backgrounds will enhance understanding of Asian Americans' experiences in U.S. society.

Cultural Patterns

Asian Americans speak many different languages and practice religions as diverse as Buddhism, Confucianism, Islam, Hinduism, and Christianity. While no two Asian cultures are the same, some general similarities can be identified. These cultural traits have shaped the behavior of Asian Americans as well as the perceptions of members of the dominant group.

Asian cultures tend to stress group membership over individual interest. For example, Confucianism, the dominant ethical and moral system in traditional China, counsels people to see themselves as elements in larger social systems and status hierarchies. Confucianism emphasizes group loyalty, conformity, and respect for superiors. In traditional China, as in other Asian societies, everyday life was organized around kinship relations, and most interpersonal relations were with family members and other relatives (Lyman, 1974, p. 9). The family or the clan often owned the land on which all depended for survival and determined inheritance patterns, arranged marriages, settled disputes, and performed a number of crucial social functions.

Asian cultures stress sensitivity to the opinions and judgments of others and to the importance of avoiding public embarrassment and not giving offense. Especially in regard to Japanese culture, these tendencies are often contrasted with Western practices in terms of guilt versus shame (Benedict, 1946). In Western cultures, each individual is encouraged to develop and abide by a conscience, or an inner moral voice, and behavior is guided by a person's sense of guilt. In contrast, Asian cultures stress the importance of maintaining the respect and good opinion of others, conforming to convention, and avoiding shame and public humiliation ("saving face").

Traditional Asian cultures were male dominated, and women were consigned to subordinate roles. A Chinese woman, for example, was expected to serve first her father, then her husband, and, if widowed, her eldest son (Amott & Matthaei, 1991, p. 200). In traditional China, women of high status symbolized their subordination by binding their feet. This crippling practice began early in life and required women to wrap their feet tightly in order to keep them artificially small. The bones in the arch of the foot were intentionally broken so that the toes could be bent back under the foot, further decreasing the size of the foot. Bound feet were considered beautiful, but they also immobilized women and were intended to prevent them from wandering away from their domestic and household duties (Takaki, 1993, pp. 209–210).

These cultural traits were modified by the experiences of these groups in America. For the Asian groups with the longest histories in U.S. society, the effects of these values on individual personality is slight; for more newly arrived groups, the effects are more powerful.

Chinese Americans

The Chinese were the first Asian group to immigrate to the United States in substantial numbers. The early history of the group is replete with discrimination, subordination, and exclusion and gives few hints that Chinese Americans would become a "model minority."

Population Trends

As discussed in chapter 4, Chinese immigration was curtailed by the Chinese Exclusion Act of 1882. After the 1890s, the number of Chinese in the United States actually declined and did not start to grow again until the 1930s and 1940s (see Figure 8.1). Large-scale immigration resumed after federal policy was revised in 1965.

Most 19th-century Chinese immigrants to North America were young adult male sojourners who intended to return to China. Immigration was curtailed before women could arrive in substantial numbers. At the turn of the century, Chinese males outnumbered Chinese females by more than 250 to 1. The sex ratio did not approach parity until recent decades (Lai, 1980, p. 223).

The scarcity of women delayed the appearance of a second generation (the first born in the United States) until the 1920s and 1930s (Lai, 1980, p. 223). This is important because the children of immigrants are usually much more acculturated than their parents and can serve a number of important functions for the group as a whole. Their language facility and greater familiarity with the larger society often permit the second generation to represent the group more effectively.

In the case of Chinese Americans (and other Asian groups), members of the second generation were citizens of the United States by birth, a status from which the immigrants were barred, and they had legal and political rights not available to their parents. The decades-

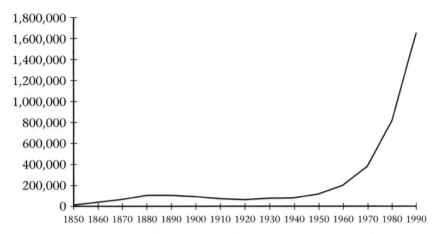

Figure 8.1 Chinese-American Population Growth in the United States
Sources: Lai, 1980, p. 223; O'Hare, 1992, p. 12.

long absence of a generation of more Americanized, English-speaking children may have reinforced the exclusion and isolation of the Chinese-American community that resulted from the overt discrimination of the dominant group.

The Ethnic Enclave

In response to the 19th-century anti-Chinese campaign, the Chinese became increasingly urbanized. Forced out of many towns and smaller cities, they settled in larger cities such as San Francisco, which offered the safety of urban anonymity and ethnic neighborhoods where the old ways could be practiced and contact with the hostile larger society minimized. Chinatowns had existed since the start of the immigration and took on added significance as a shield from the storm of anti-Chinese venom. The Chinese withdrew to the relative safety of these neighborhoods where, in the words of one scholar, they became an "invisible minority" (Tsai, 1986, p. 67).

Like the more recently founded Cuban community in Miami, these early Chinatowns were ethnic enclaves and were formed by a similar process. The earliest urban Chinese were merchants and skilled artisans experienced in commerce (Chan, 1990, p. 44). They established businesses and retail stores typically small in scope and modest in profits. As the number of urban Chinese increased, the market for these enterprises became larger and more spatially concentrated. New services were required and the size of the cheap labor pool available to Chinese merchants and entrepreneurs increased. Thus, the Chinatowns became the economic, cultural, and social centers of the Chinese-American community.

Within the Chinatowns, an elaborate social structure developed that mirrored traditional China in many ways. The enforced segregation of the Chinese in America helped preserve much of the traditional culture of their homeland against the pressures of Americanization. The social structure was built around several traditional forms, some based on family and clan membership and others based on the region or district in China from which the immigrant had come. The most prominent of the regional associations were the **huiguan**, which were generally controlled by merchants. The huiguan performed various social and welfare services, including aiding new arrivals and facilitating the development of mutual aid networks (Lai, 1980, p. 221; Lyman, 1974, pp. 32–37, 116–118).

The functions of the family and clan groups overlapped with and supplemented the huiguan. The organizational life of the community was further enriched by a variety of other religious, social, and recreational groups. The growth of these associations and the process of community development weren't always smooth, and there was conflict, some of it violent, over control of resources and the organizational infrastructure of the Chinatowns. In particular, secret societies called **tongs** contested the leadership of the merchant-led huiguan and the clan associations. The conflicts were sometimes bloody and were sensationalized in the American press, where they reinforced the popular stereotypes of exotic Orientals, mysterious and dangerous (Lyman, 1974, pp. 37–50).

In spite of internal dissension and conflict, the associational life of the American Chinatowns evolved into highly organized, largely self-contained communities complete with their own leadership and decision-making structure. The internal "city government" of each Chinatown was the Chinese Consolidated Benevolent Association (CCBA). Dominated by the larger huiguan and clans and the merchants, the CCBA coordinated and supplemented the activities of the various organizations and represented the interests of community to the larger society.

The CCBAs, as well as other Chinese-American organizations, attempted to combat anti-Chinese discrimination and racism. The effectiveness of these protest efforts was handicapped by the relative lack of resources in the Chinese community and by the fact that Chinese immigrants could not become citizens.

Survival and Development

The Chinese-American community survived in spite of widespread poverty and discrimination. The enclave economy provided at least a bare subsistence for the community, and members of the group began to seek opportunity in other regions of the United States. The percentage of Chinese living on the West Coast decreased from 97% in 1880 to 73% in 1910 and 60% in 1940 (Lai, 1980, p. 223). Chinatowns appeared and grew in New York, Boston, Chicago, Philadelphia, and many other cities.

The patterns of exclusion and discrimination that began on the West Coast were common throughout the nation and continued for much of this century. Chinese Americans responded by finding economic opportunity in areas where dominant group competition for jobs was weak, continuing their tendency to be an "invisible" minority group. Very often, they started small businesses that served either other members of their own group (e.g., restaurants) or that relied on the patronage of the general public (like laundries).

The jobs provided by these small businesses were the economic lifeblood of the community but were limited in the amount of income and wealth they could generate. Until relatively recent decades, for instance, the restaurants served primarily other Chinese. Since their main clientele was poor, the profit potential of these businesses was sharply limited. Laundries served the more affluent dominant group but the returns from this enterprise declined as washers and dryers became increasingly widespread in homes throughout the nation. The population of Chinatown was generally too small to sustain more than these two primary commercial enterprises (Zhou, 1992, pp. 92–94).

As the decades passed, the enclave economy and the complex subsociety of Chinatown evolved. However, the barriers of discrimination, combined with defensive self-segregation, ensured the continuation of poverty, limited job opportunities, and substandard housing for Chinese Americans. Relatively hidden from the view of the dominant group, the Chinatowns became the world in which the second generation grew to adulthood.

The Second Generation

Compared with the immigrant generation, the second generation was much more influenced by the larger culture. The institutional and organizational structures of Chinatown had been created to serve the older generation, and younger Chinese Americans tended to look beyond the enclave to fill their needs. They came in contact with the larger society through schools, churches, and other organizations. They abandoned many traditional customs and were less loyal to the associations constructed by the immigrant generation. They founded organizations of their own that were more compatible with their Americanized lifestyles (Lai, 1980, p. 225).

As was the case for other minority groups, World War II became an important watershed for Chinese Americans. During the war, job opportunities outside the enclave increased and, after the war, many of the 8,000 Chinese Americans who served in the armed forces were able to take advantage of the GI Bill to further their education (Lai, 1980, p. 226). In the 1940s and 1950s, many second-generation Chinese Americans moved out of the enclave and pursued careers in the larger society. This group was mobile and Americanized and, with educational credentials comparable to those of the general population, was prepared to seek success outside Chinatown.

In another departure from tradition, the women of this generation also pursued education and, by 1960, median years of schooling for Chinese-American women was slightly higher than for Chinese-American men (Kitano & Daniels, 1988, p. 45). Chinese-American women also became more diverse in occupational profile as the century progressed. In 1900 three quarters of all employed Chinese-American women worked in manufacturing (usually in garment industry sweatshops or in canning factories) or in domestic work. By 1960 less than 2% were in domestic work, 33% were in clerical occupations, and 18% held professional jobs, often as teachers (Amott & Matthaei, 1991, pp. 209–211).

The second generation, men and women alike, achieved considerable educational and occupational success and helped to lay the groundwork for the idea that Chinese Americans are a model minority. A closer examination reveals, however, that the old traditions of anti-Chinese discrimination and prejudice continued to limit the life chances of even the best educated members of this generation. Second-generation Chinese Americans earned less on the average and had less favorable occupational profiles than comparably educated white Americans. The gap between qualifications and rewards is usually attributed to discrimination. Kitano and Daniels conclude, for example, that although well-educated Chinese Americans could find good jobs in the mainstream economy, the highest, most lucrative positions—and those requiring direct supervision of whites—were still closed (Kitano & Daniels, 1988, pp. 45–47; see also Hirschman & Wong, 1984).

Not all members of the second generation enjoyed educational or economic success, and poverty and unemployment continued to be major problems in the Chinese-American community. Some of the less fortunate included those who stayed in the Chinatowns to operate the enclave economy. Others are among the recent immigrants who began arriving after 1965, many of whom have very modest educational and occupational credentials. In a 1980 study, recent (1975–1980) Chinese immigrants were found to have only about half the income of native-born Chinese Americans (Barringer, Takeuchi, & Xenos, 1990, p. 34).

The success of Chinese Americans has not been unqualified or universal. The upwardly mobile second generation and their children are concentrated in occupations toward the top of the job structure. Other members of the group are concentrated in less affluent positions in the garment industry, the service sector, and the small businesses of the enclave. This concentration at the top and the bottom of the occupational structure has been described as bipolar and the situation of those at the lower end is quite consistent with a history of colonization, exploitation, and exclusion. (See Barringer et al., 1990; Duleep, 1988; Ko & Clogg, 1989; Takaki, 1993, pp. 415–416; Zhou & Logan, 1989.)

Japanese Americans

Immigration from Japan began to increase shortly after the 1882 Chinese Exclusion Act took effect, in part to fill the gap in the labor supply created by the restrictive legislation (Kitano, 1980). The 1880 census counted only a few hundred Japanese in the United States, but the group increased rapidly in the next few decades (see Figure 8.2). Most Japanese immigrants, like the Chinese and many other groups, were young male laborers (Duleep, 1988, p. 24).

The Anti-Japanese Campaign

The Japanese immigrated to the same West Coast regions of the United States as the Chinese and entered the labor force in a similar position. Predictably, the feelings and emotions generated by the anti-Chinese campaign were transferred to the Japanese. By the early

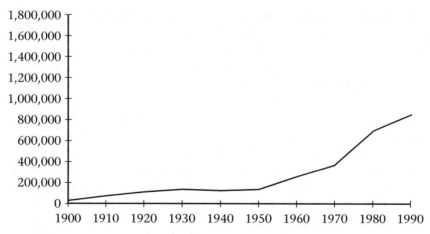

Figure 8.2 Japanese-American Population Growth in the United States

Sources: Kitano, 1980, pp. 562, 564; O'Hare, 1992, p. 12.

1900s, an anti-Japanese campaign was in full swing and demands were being made to exclude Japanese immigrants in the same way the Chinese had been barred (Kitano, 1980, p. 563; Kitano & Daniels, 1988, pp. 55–56; Petersen, 1971, pp. 30–55).

Japanese immigration was partly curtailed in 1907 when a "Gentlemen's Agreement" was signed between Japan and the United States. The events leading up to this agreement began in San Francisco in 1905 when an attempt was made to segregate Japanese children in school. Japan reacted strongly to this discrimination and exerted considerable pressure on the U.S. government for fair treatment of Japanese nationals (Chan, 1990, p. 62). The dispute was resolved in the 1907 agreement, in which Japan consented to limit the number of "laborers" it would allow to immigrate to the United States (Kitano, 1980, p. 563; Kitano & Daniels, 1988, pp. 55–56; Petersen, 1971, pp. 42–44).

The language used in the agreement is important because it was interpreted to apply only to males. Females were not considered to be "laborers" and they continued to immigrate for almost two decades until the National Origins Act of 1924 went into effect and barred virtually all immigration from Japan. The Gentlemen's Agreement left the door partially open and permitted the Japanese, unlike the Chinese, to maintain a relatively balanced sex ratio, marry, and begin families. Thus, a second generation of Japanese Americans began to appear without much delay. U.S.-born Japanese numbered about half of the group by 1930 and made up a majority of 63% on the eve of World War II (Kitano & Daniels, 1988, p. 55).

Many immigrants from Japan entered the rural economy. Their farms tended to be small but successful, and part of the anti-Japanese movement attempted to dislodge the group from agriculture. In 1913 California passed the **Alien Land Act,** which declared aliens who were ineligible for citizenship (effectively meaning only immigrants from Asia) to be also ineligible to become landowners (Kitano, 1980, p. 563). The Japanese were able to dodge the discriminatory intent of the law by putting the title of the land in the names of their American-born children, who were citizens by birth, and farming remained a crucial part of the Japanese-American subeconomy (Jibou, 1988, p. 359).

Although the Alien Land Act failed, the campaign against the Japanese continued. In the early decades of this century, the Japanese were politically disenfranchised and segregated from dominant group institutions in schools and residential areas. The group was excluded from the mainstream economy and confined to a limited range of poorly paid occupations. Japanese Americans were discriminated against in movie houses, swimming pools, and other public facilities (Kitano & Daniels, 1988, p. 56). Thus, there were strong elements of systematic discrimination and colonization in their overall relationship with the larger society.

The Ethnic Enclave

Like the Chinese, the Japanese constructed a separate subsociety. The immigrant generation, called the **Issei**, established an economic enclave in agriculture and related enterprises, a rural enclave in contrast to the urban versions constructed by other groups we have examined. As late as 1940, more than 40% of the Japanese-American population was involved directly in farming and many more were dependent on the economic activity stimulated by agriculture, such as transportation and marketing (Jibou, 1988, p. 360).

Other Issei lived in urban areas, where they were concentrated in a narrow range of businesses and services. In addition to serving their own group, the Issei catered to the dominant group in such enterprises as domestic service and contract gardening (Jibou, 1988, p. 362). The group maximized its economic clout by doing business as much as possible with firms owned by other Japanese Americans. The networks they created helped the enclave economy to grow and also permitted Japanese Americans to avoid the hostility of the larger society. These very same patterns, though, helped sustain the stereotypes that depicted the Japanese as clannish and unassimilable. In the years before World War II, the Japanese-American community was largely dependent for survival on networks of cooperation based on mutual ethnicity, not on Americanization and integration.

The Second Generation (Nisei)

In the 1920s and 1930s, anti-Asian feelings continued to run high, and Japanese Americans continued to experience exclusion and discrimination in spite of (or, perhaps, because of) their relative success. Unable to find acceptance in Anglo society, the second generation, called the **Nisei**, established their own social and recreational organizations (Kitano & Daniels, 1988, pp. 59–60).

Although the Nisei were generally successful in school, the intense discrimination and racism of the 1930s prevented them from translating their educational achievements into better jobs and higher salaries. Many Nisei were forced to remain within the enclave and, in many cases, jobs in the produce stands and retail shops of their parents were all they could find. Their demoralization and anger over their exclusion were eventually overshadowed by the larger events of World War II.

The Internment Camps

On December 7, 1941, Japan attacked the U.S. naval base at Pearl Harbor. The next day, President Franklin D. Roosevelt asked Congress for a declaration of war. The ensuing mobilization stirred up a wide range of fears and anxieties in the American public, including concerns about the loyalty of Japanese Americans. Decades of exclusion and anti-Japanese prejudice had conditioned the dominant society to see Japanese Americans as clannish, foreign, and racially inferior. Enhanced by the ferocity of war itself and fears about a Japanese invasion, the tradition of anti-Japanese racism laid the groundwork for a violation of civil rights unparalleled in 20th-century America.

Two months after the attack on Pearl Harbor, President Roosevelt signed Executive Order 9066, which led to the relocation of all people of Japanese ancestry living on the West Coast. By the late summer of 1941, more than 110,000 Japanese Americans—virtually the entire West Coast population—had been transported to internment camps, where they were imprisoned behind barbed-wire fences patrolled by armed guards.

The government gave families little time to prepare for evacuation and safeguard their homes, businesses, and belongings. They were allowed to bring only what they could carry, and many possessions simply had to be abandoned. Businessowners sold their establishments and farmers their land at "panic sale" prices or locked up their stores and houses and walked away, hoping the evacuation would be short-lived and their possessions undisturbed.

The internment lasted for nearly the entire war. Some Japanese Americans were able to escape the camps by agreeing to move to areas distant from the West Coast and about 25,000 volunteered for military service, nearly all of them serving in segregated units (Kitano, 1980, p. 567). Still, when the camps closed at the end of the war, about half of the original internees remained (Kitano & Daniels, 1988, p. 64).

The strain of living in the camps affected Japanese Americans in a variety of ways. Lack of activities and privacy, overcrowding, and boredom were all common complaints. The camps disrupted the traditional forms of family life as people had to adapt to barracks living and mess hall dining. Conflicts flared between those who counseled caution and temperate reaction to the incarceration and those who wanted to protest in more vigorous terms.

Some Japanese Americans protested the incarceration from the start and brought lawsuits to end the relocation program. These efforts failed at first, but in 1944 the U.S. Supreme Court did rule that detention was in fact unconstitutional. After the camps closed, Japanese Americans began to seek compensation for the economic losses the group had suffered. By the late 1940s, some 26,500 people had filed claims for damages against the federal government. These claims were eventually settled for about $38 million, less than one tenth of the actual economic losses suffered. The demand for meaningful compensation pressed on, and in 1988 Congress passed a bill granting reparations of about $20,000 in cash to the 60,000 remaining survivors of the camps. The law also acknowledged that the relocation program had been a grave injustice to Japanese Americans (Biskupic, 1989, p. 2879).

Japanese Americans After World War II

The wartime evacuation devastated the Japanese-American community and left it with few material resources. The emotional and psychological damage inflicted by the relocation is incalculable. Today, only five decades later, the fact that Japanese Americans are equal or superior to national averages on measures of educational achievement, occupational prestige, and income is one of the more dramatic transformations in minority group history.

For virtually every American minority group, World War II brought new experiences and a broader sense of themselves, the nation, and the world. A similar transformation occurred for the Nisei, who had used their greater facility in English to take leadership of the group in the camps. When the war ended, the Nisei were unwilling to rebuild the Japanese community as it had been before.

Like second-generation Chinese Americans, the Nisei had a strong record of success in school, and they also took advantage of the GI Bill to further their education. The job market eventually began to open to the Nisei as strong anti-Asian discrimination declined in the 1950s, and the Nisei were educationally prepared to take advantage of these employment opportunities (Kitano, 1980, p. 567).

The Issei-dominated enclave economy did not reappear after the war. By 1960 Japanese Americans had an occupational profile very similar to that of whites, with the exception that they had an above average proportion of professionals. Many were employed in the primary economy, not in the ethnic enclave, but there was a tendency to choose "safe" careers (e.g., in engineering, optometry, pharmacy, accounting) that did not require extensive contact with the public or supervision of whites (Kitano & Daniels, 1988, p. 70).

Within these limitations, the Nisei, their children (Sansei), and grandchildren (Yonsei) have enjoyed relatively high status and upward mobility. Also, immigration from Japan in recent years has been relatively low and the immigrants who have come are generally highly educated professional and business people. The combined prosperity of Americans of Japanese descent and recent immigrants from Japan has contributed greatly to the perception that Asian Americans are a model minority, successful and affluent.

The Sansei and Yonsei are highly integrated in the occupational structure of the larger society. Their connections with their ethnic past are more tenuous than for the Nisei, and their values, beliefs, and personal goals are more similar to those of dominant group members of similar age and social class than to the Nisei and Issei. Many report that they have never been the victims of discrimination or racism (Kitano & Daniels, 1988, p. 71).

Other Asian Groups

In this section we briefly examine some of the larger Asian-American groups and thereby outline some of the diversity within the group.

Filipino Americans

Today, Filipinos are the second largest Asian-American group (see Table 8.1), but their numbers became sizable only in the last few decades. There were fewer than 1,000 Filipinos in the United States in 1910, and by 1960 the group still numbered less than 200,000. Since 1970 the group has almost tripled in size, with most of the growth coming from increased immigration.

Many of the earliest immigrants were agricultural workers recruited for the sugar plantations of Hawaii and the fields of the West Coast. The more recent wave of immigrants is diversified and, like Chinese Americans, Filipino Americans are bipolar in their educational and occupational profiles. Many recent immigrants have entered the United States under the family preference provisions and, by and large, these immigrants compete for jobs in the low-wage secondary labor market.

More than half of all Filipino immigrants since 1965, however, have been professionals entering this country with skills that are in short supply. These immigrants are especially concentrated in the fields of health and medicine. Many female immigrants from the Philippines are nurses actively recruited by U.S. hospitals to fill gaps in the labor force (Amott & Matthaei, 1991, p. 245). Thus, the Filipino-American community is diverse, with some members—in many cases, recent immigrants—in the higher wage primary labor market and others competing for work with members of the colonized minority groups.

Korean Americans

Immigration from Korea to the United States began at the turn of the century, but this group was small until very recent decades. In the 1950s, following the Korean War, the rate of immigration rose because of refugees and war brides. Immigration did not become substantial, however, until the new immigration policy of 1965 went into effect. The size of the group increased fivefold in the 1970s and by 125% in the 1980s (see Table 8.1).

Immigrants from Korea since 1965 consist mostly of families and include many highly educated people. Like Cubans, Chinese, Japanese, and other groups, Korean Americans have formed an ethnic enclave, and the group is heavily involved in small businesses and retail stores, particularly fruit and vegetable retail stores or green groceries.

By many measures, Koreans have been successful in building their businesses and securing at least minimal economic returns. A 1987 study compared 15 minority groups and found that Koreans had the highest rate of business ownership, followed by Asian Indians, Japanese Americans, and Cuban Americans. At the bottom of the rankings were racial minority groups with strong histories of colonization and exclusion: Mexican Americans, African Americans, and Native Americans (O'Hare, 1992, p. 37).

The enclave has its limits, though. Success depends heavily on mutual assistance and financial support of other Koreans, resources that are constantly threatened by acculturation and integration. Furthermore, the economic niches in which "mom-and-pop" green groceries and other small businesses can survive are often in deteriorated neighborhoods populated largely by other minority groups. There has been a good deal of hostility and resentment expressed against Korean shop owners by African Americans, Puerto Ricans, and other urbanized minority groups. For example, anti-Korean sentiments were widely expressed in the 1992 Los Angeles riots following the acquittal of the police officers charged in the beating of motorist Rodney King. Korean-owned businesses were among the first to be looted and burned. Thus, part of the price of survival for many Korean merchants is to place themselves in positions in which antagonism and conflict with other minority groups are common (Kitano & Daniels, 1988, pp. 105–120; Light & Bonacich, 1988).

Vietnamese Americans

A flow of refugees from Southeast Asia and particularly from Vietnam began in the 1960s as a result of the involvement of the United States in the region. The war in Vietnam eventually enveloped Cambodia and Laos and disrupted social life throughout Southeast Asia. In 1975, when the U.S. military withdrew, many Southeast Asians who had collaborated with the United States and its allies fled in fear for their lives. This group included high-ranking officials and members of the region's educational and occupational elites. Later groups of refugees tended to be less well educated and more impoverished. Many Vietnamese, Cambodians, and Laotians waited in refugee camps for months or years before being admitted to the United States. They often arrived with few resources and no social networks to ease their transition to the new society (Kitano & Daniels, 1988, pp. 135–158).

The Vietnamese are the largest of the Asian refugee groups and, contrary to Asian-American success stories and notions of model minorities, they have incomes and educational levels comparable to colonized minority groups (see tables 8.3, 8.4, and 8.5 later in this chapter). One study has found that the Vietnamese are the "most segregated group in the society" (Massey & Denton, 1992, p. 170).

Asian Indians

Immigration from India was low until the mid-1960s. Today, Indians are the fourth largest Asian group and the size of the group more than doubled in the 1980s. Unlike many other immigrant groups, Indian immigrants tend to be highly educated and skilled. For instance, in 1980, 11% of male Asian Indians in the United States were physicians, as were 8% of the females (Kamen, 1992, p. A1). In comparison, physicians are less than 1% of the total population of the United States (U.S Bureau of the Census, 1993, p. 118).

These skilled immigrants from India are part of a worldwide movement of educated peoples from less developed countries to more developed countries. One need not ponder the differences in career opportunities, technology, and compensation for very long to get some insight into the reasons for this movement. Other immigrants from India are more oriented to commerce and small business, and there is a sizable Indian ethnic enclave in many cities (Kitano & Daniels, 1988, pp. 89–104).

Recent Immigration From Asia

About half of all recent immigrants to the United States have come from Latin America and the Caribbean. Much of the other half has come from Asia and the Pacific Islands. Furthermore, the proportion of all immigrants who come from Asia has increased from a mere 6% in the 1950s, when quotas were still in effect, to roughly one third in recent times. This growth pattern suggests that Asian-American groups will become a more visible element in the ethnic, racial, and cultural mix of the United States in the years to come.

The major countries of origin for Asian immigrants have shifted somewhat, but China and the Philippines have remained major contributors since 1965. Since the 1970s, Korea and India have become major sources of immigrants, and Vietnam and Pakistan have also been important sending nations. The proportional share of immigrants from Japan has declined since the 1950s and constitutes only about 3% of the total Asian immigration.

Old Ports of Entry and New Groups

Asian immigrants share many ports of entry with Latin American immigrants. Los Angeles tends to be the most common destination along with New York City and San Francisco (U.S. Immigration and Naturalization Service, 1992, p. 63).

Most recent Asian immigrants are genuine newcomers to the United States. Only the Chinese and Japanese had large communities in the mainland United States prior to the 1960s. Table 8.2 shows the percentage of various Asian-American groups that are foreign born (i.e., first generation).

Less than a majority of Japanese Americans are foreign born, while about 70% of Koreans and almost 90% of Vietnamese are foreign born. Thus, most Asian immigrant groups are still in their first generations and it will be years before the second and third generations grow to adulthood.

Table 8.2 Percent Foreign Born of Selected Asian-American Groups

Group	Percent Foreign Born	
	1980	1990
Chinese[1]	55	56
Asian Indian	57	55
Japanese	32	34
Korean	82	71
Filipino	65	65
Vietnamese	88	88

1. Includes Hong Kong and Taiwan.
Source: U.S. Bureau of the Census, 1993, p. 50.

Modes of Incorporation Into U.S. Society

Although their U.S. destinations are similar, recent immigrants from Asia and Latin America bring with them very different occupational and educational backgrounds. On average, Asian immigrants are more educated and proportionally fewer compete for jobs in the low-paid secondary sector of the economy. Some analysts have argued that there is a two-tier system of immigration today: Latino immigrants compete with colonized minority groups for lower-level jobs, while Asian immigrants enter the society at the middle- and upper-class levels and compete for jobs in the primary sector of the economy (Bouvier & Gardner, 1986, p. 26).

These differences in socioeconomic characteristics are so sharp that they can draw attention away from the diversity within each stream. Rather than constituting a single tier, Asian immigrants enter U.S. society in three general ways: (1) through the primary labor market, (2) through the secondary labor market, and (3) through ethnic enclaves. Each of these modes of incorporation represents a different contact situation and has different implications for upward mobility, conflict, prejudice, and acculturation. Although some of these contact situations reinforce the idea that Asian Americans are a model minority, others raise the same questions and concerns as those generated by the recent wave of unskilled laborers immigrating from Latin America.

Immigrants and the Primary Labor Market

Asian immigrants entering the primary labor market are educated, skilled professionals and businesspeople who are highly integrated into the global urban-industrial economy. In many cases, they are employees of multinational corporations who are transferred to this nation by their companies. They are dramatically different from most of the immigrants we have considered to this point in the text. However, these professional-level immigrants do share one characteristic with many other immigrants, regardless of country of origin or occupational background: Many of them—just like braceros and other laborers—are seeking job opportunities and career experiences that are simply not available in their less developed homelands.

The Asian groups with the highest percentages of educated and skilled immigrants include the Japanese, the Filipinos, and the Chinese. In 1992, for example, between 20% and 30% of immigrants from Japan, the Philippines, China, and India were in the two highest occupational categories: professionals (such as medical doctors and college professors) and administrators or managers. In contrast, only about 1% of immigrants from Mexico in that same year were in these occupational categories (U.S. Immigration and Naturalization Service, 1992, pp. 68–69).

The relative socioeconomic standing—and the image of "success"— of some Asian-American groups is inflated by these immigrants. In 1980 native-born Japanese Americans had a mean income of $15,656, whereas Japanese immigrants who had arrived within the preceding 5-year period reported an average income of $19,236 (Barringer et al., 1990, p. 34).

Using Blauner's distinction between colonized and immigrant minority groups (see chapter 3), these affluent Asian immigrants with professional backgrounds probably come closer to the pure immigrant group than most other minority groups we have considered. Still, their assimilation is complicated by their racial background and the discrimination it provokes. Anecdotal evidence of racial discrimination for these immigrants is common. In a *New York Times* article on anti-Asian prejudice, Tun-Hsu McCoy, who immigrated almost 30 years ago and holds a Ph.D. in physics, is quoted as saying: "Every Asian can tell you that we have all encountered subconscious discrimination. People don't equate an Asian face with being an American" (Polner, 1993, p. 1).

Immigrants and the Secondary Labor Market

A second mode of incorporation more closely follows the Latino immigration experience. Frequently ignored in the glitter of Asian success stories are large groups of uneducated and unskilled laborers. This group includes undocumented aliens, the less skilled and less educated kinfolk of the higher status immigrants, and a high percentage of the refugee groups from Vietnam and other Southeast Asian nations.

The refugees are, of course, involuntary immigrants, motivated by the misery of war or persecution and not by a decision to seek their fortune in the capitalist West. They are very recent arrivals with few networks to connect them to the job market. They bring lower levels of educational achievement and skills with them, which is a reflection of the lower level of development of their home societies and the difficulties of pursuing an education in the midst of war.

The experiences of these less skilled immigrants are strongly affected by gender, with female immigrants often more vulnerable and more exploited. For example, immigrant Chinese women in New York City are heavily concentrated in the garment industry, where the nature of their work allows them to balance the conflicts inherent in their multiple roles. The industry pays by the piece, not by the hour, and the women can work at a pace that allows them to subordinate work to their other roles. This pattern is consistent with traditional

Chinese male supremacy but it also reflects a family-oriented strategy for survival and mobility in the United States. The women generate income not for themselves but for the benefit of the family as a whole and especially for the younger family members (Zhou & Logan, 1989, p. 818).

Immigrants and Ethnic Enclaves

Some Asian immigrants have been able to establish ethnic enclaves. Like Cuban immigrants in the 1960s and 1970s and Chinese and Japanese immigrants at the turn of the century, these groups enter U.S. society as entrepreneurs, that is, owners of small retail shops and other businesses. The enclave provides contacts, financial and other services, and social support for the new immigrants. As we saw above, Koreans and Asian Indians have been particularly likely to follow this path.

Contemporary Asian American–Dominant Group Relations

The diversity of Asian Americans makes it difficult to characterize the group as a whole. Nonetheless, we again use our guiding concepts to see what conclusions we can reach about these groups and about the larger society.

Prejudice and Discrimination

American prejudice against Asians first became prominent during the 19th century anti-Chinese movement. The Chinese were castigated as racially inferior, cruel, crafty, and threatening (Lai, 1980, p. 220; Lyman, 1974, pp. 55–58). Many of these stereotypes and fears were transferred to the Japanese later in the 19th century and then to other groups as they, in turn, arrived in the United States.

The social distance scales presented in chapter 2 provide the only long-term record of anti-Asian prejudice in the society as a whole. In 1926 Asian groups were clustered in the bottom third of the scale, along with other racial and/or colonized minority groups. Since that time, the position of the groups reflects shifting patterns of warfare and alliance. By 1977 the Asian groups were still clustered in the bottom third of the scale, but their scores were lower. The falling scores probably reflect the societywide increase in tolerance and/or the shift to modern racism. The relative position of Asians in the American hierarchy of group preferences has remained remarkably consistent and this stability may reflect the cultural or traditional nature of anti-Asian prejudice in the United States.

Although prejudice against Asian groups may have weakened over-all, there is considerable evidence that it remains a potent force in American life and, in fact, that it has been exacerbated by recent economic and political rivalries with Asian nations, most noticeably Japan. Domestically, hate crimes against Asian Americans seem to increase during hard economic times. Asian Americans have been attacked, beaten, and even murdered in recent years (U.S. Commission on Civil Rights, 1992).

Acculturation

The extent of Asian-American acculturation is highly variable from group to group. On the one hand, the Chinese and Japanese have been part of U.S. society for more than a century, and their third and fourth generations are highly Americanized (Kitano & Daniels, 1988, pp. 72–75). On the other hand, recent Asian immigrants are still in the first generation and many have scarcely had time to learn the American culture and the English language.

The Chinese in particular present a mixed picture: one segment of the group has American roots going back about 150 years, whereas another sizable segment consists of very new Americans. The Japanese-American minority group is almost as old as the Chinese-American group but immigration from Japan has been low. Thus, Japanese Americans have not received as strong an infusion of traditional culture or language and are, as a group, more acculturated than Chinese Americans (Kitano & Daniels, 1988, p. 73).

Secondary Structural Assimilation

We cover this complex area in roughly the order followed in previous chapters.

Residence

Figure 8.3 shows the regional concentrations of Asians and Pacific Islanders. The tendency to reside on either coast and around Los Angeles, San Francisco, and New York stand out clearly. Asian Americans are highly urbanized, a reflection of the entry conditions of recent immigrants as well as the appeal of urban ethnic neighborhoods like Chinatown.

Education

Unlike other U.S. racial minority groups, Asian Americans compare favorably with societal standards of educational achievement, and on many measures they are above those standards. Table 8.3 displays information regarding high school and college graduation rates for

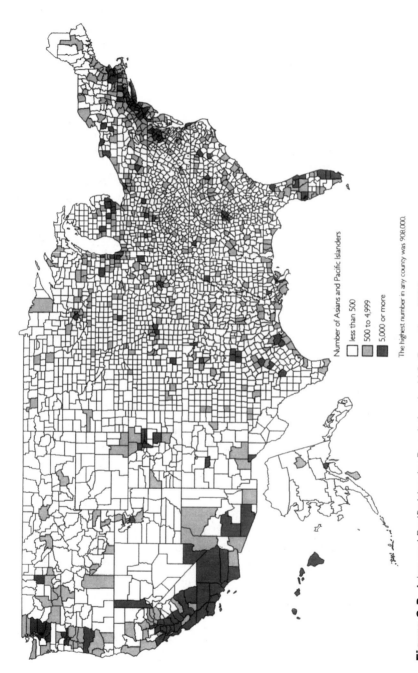

Figure 8.3 Asian and Pacific Islander Population by U.S. Counties, 1990

Source: O'Hare, 1992, p. 24.

Table 8.3 Educational Attainment of Asian Americans, 1990

	Percent High School Graduates		Percent College Graduates	
	Male	Female	Male	Female
Whites	79	79	25	19
African Americans	66	67	12	11
Japanese	90	86	43	28
Asian Indian	89	79	66	49
Korean	89	74	47	26
Filipino	84	81	36	42
Chinese	77	70	47	35
Vietnamese	69	53	22	12

Sources: Paisano, 1993, p. 4; U.S. Bureau of the Census, 1993, p. 153.

several Asian-American groups compared with whites and African Americans. For males, almost all of the Asian groups have higher rates of high school and college graduation than do whites. The Vietnamese males are the only Asian-American group to resemble black Americans more than white Americans. The picture for females is more varied but, in general, we again find a pattern of equal or higher achievement by the Asian groups.

These statistics are consistent with the stereotype of Asian Americans as a model minority. However, this image should be balanced by the recognition that there is a full range of success and failure among Asian Americans and by the fact that average levels of achievement are inflated for some groups by recent immigrants who are highly educated, skilled professionals. Also, there is considerable variety in Asian educational performance by gender and group. With the sole exception of college-educated Filipinos, women fare less well than men and the pattern of high accomplishment and success does not apply to the Vietnamese.

Jobs and Income

If we look at all Asian Americans as a single category, the picture of success and equality is again sustained. One report shows that Asian Americans and Pacific Islanders have median household incomes about $5,000 per year higher than those for non-Hispanic whites and more than 75% greater than those for African Americans and Native Americans (O'Hare, 1992, p. 33–34).

Table 8.4 Income and Poverty Data for Selected Groups, 1989

	Median Family Income	Percent of U.S. Median Income	Percent in Poverty
United States[1]	35,225	—	10
Asian Americans			
Chinese	41,316	117	11
Japanese	51,550	146	3
Koreans	33,909	96	15
Cambodians	18,126	52	42
Vietnamese	30,550	87	24

1. Data are for the entire U.S. population, including Asian Americans.
Source: Paisano, 1993, p. 9.

These overall comparisons may not be very meaningful, however, given the great diversity among the Asian-American groups that we have observed. As tables 8.4 and 8.5 illustrate, while some groups (Chinese and Japanese Americans) do indeed seem prosperous and successful, others (Vietnamese and Cambodians) more closely resemble colonized, impoverished, racial minority groups.

Also, Asian Americans generally reside in areas with higher than average costs of living (e.g., Los Angeles, New York) and their higher incomes have relatively less purchasing power. Furthermore, they are more likely than the general population to have multiple wage earners in each household (Takaki, 1993, pp. 414–417).

Evidence of Anti-Asian Discrimination

Asian Americans are generally "overeducated" for their occupational positions and earn less than comparably educated whites. To illustrate, one 1990 study found that, for employed individuals ages 25 to 64, the average yearly earnings of Asian Americans increased by $2,300 for each additional year of schooling, whereas earnings for non-Hispanic whites increased by $3,000. This gap is assumed to be the result of anti-Asian discrimination (O'Hare & Felt, 1991, p. 8).

The relative prosperity of some Asian groups needs to be seen in the context of the various caveats we have established throughout the chapter. Asian-American groups vary considerably in the extent of their "success" in the United States, with Filipinos and Vietnamese, for example, generally at a greater disadvantage than native-born third- and fourth-generation Chinese and Japanese Americans. There

Table 8.5 Comparative Occupational Profiles of Whites, Asian Americans, and African Americans

| Occupational Category | Whites | Asian Americans | | | | | African Americans |
		Chinese	Japanese	Koreans	Cambodians	Vietnamese	
Professional, technical, sales, and administration	58	67	71	63	33	47	32
Skilled labor	11	6	8	9	17	16	16
Unskilled labor and service	28	27	18	28	48	36	48
Farm	3	< 1	3	< 1	2	1	4
	100	100	100	100	100	100	100

Note: For the sake of clarity, this table collapses occupational categories and presents information for only five Asian groups. More detailed information is available in Paisano, 1993.
Source: Paisano, 1993, p. 9; U.S. Bureau of the Census, 1993, p. 409.

is evidence of continuing anti-Asian discrimination even for the best educated groups, and poverty and economic marginality continue to be the lot of the less well educated.

Primary Structural Assimilation

Asian-American groups have experienced considerable assimilation in the areas of primary relations, friendship choices, and marriage. Using 1980 census data, Lee and Yamanaka (1990) report higher rates of intermarriage for Asian Americans than for other minority groups. They report out-marriage rates at 2% for black Americans, 13% for Hispanic Americans, and from 15% (for Chinese and Indians) to 34% (for Japanese) for Asian Americans. They also found that native-born Asian Americans were much more likely to marry outside their group than the foreign born. (See also Kitano & Daniels, 1988; Sung, 1990.)

Comparing Minority Groups

To conclude this chapter, let's return to one of the questions raised in the opening pages: how can we explain the apparent success of some Asian-American groups? We have seen that the label of "model minority" is simplistic and that the high levels of occupational prestige and economic affluence for some Asian-origin groups are inflated by professional, high-status immigrants moving into the primary economic sector. Still, other racial minority groups are rarely perceived as successful and, at least at first glance, there would seem to be little in our theories and concepts to help us understand the situation of Asian Americans.

Let's see what we can learn by comparing Asian-American experiences to those of other minority groups. What are the important differences among Asian-American groups, European immigrant groups, and the racial and colonized minority groups? Although we won't resolve the issue in its entirety, we can still identify some of the factors that account for the relatively high status of Asian Americans.

The debate over the causes of Asian-American success often breaks down into two opposing viewpoints. One view accepts Asian-American success at face value and attributes their present status to the "good values" they inherit from traditional Asian cultures. These values, all highly compatible with U.S. middle-class Protestant heritage, include discipline, thriftiness, conformity, deference, and politeness. This line of argument is consistent with traditional assimilation theory and human capital theory and can be called a *cultural* explanation of the Asian-American experience, since it argues that Asian Americans gained acceptance and opportunities because of their values.

In opposition to cultural explanations are a variety of views that, first of all, question the notion that Asian Americans are particularly successful. These views stress the facts of Asian-American poverty and the continuing barriers of racism and exclusion. To the extent that some Asian-American groups have achieved some measure of affluence, explanations are posed in *structural* terms related to the original contact situations and the modes of incorporation followed by Asian-American groups, rather than to their values and norms. The focus of this approach is on such structures as enclave economies, networks of mutual assistance, group cohesion, position in the labor market, and the extent of institutionalized discrimination aimed at the group. This second approach is more compatible with the theories and concepts we have used throughout the text and identifies several of the important pieces needed to solve the puzzle of Asian "success" and put it in perspective. This is not to suggest that the cultural approach is wrong or irrelevant; the issues we raise are complex and will probably require many approaches and perspectives before they are fully resolved.

Asian and European Immigrants

Chinese and Japanese immigrants arrived in America at about the same time as immigrants from Southern and Eastern Europe. Both Asian and European groups consisted mainly of sojourning young men who were largely unskilled, from rural backgrounds, and not highly educated. European immigrants, like Asian immigrants, encountered massive discrimination and rejection and were also the victims of restrictive legislation (e.g., the National Origins Act of 1924). Yet the barriers to upward mobility for European immigrants (or at least for their descendants) fell away more rapidly than the barriers for immigrants from Asia.

The reasons for the different rates of mobility are only now being fully explored (see Chan, 1990). Some important differences between the two immigrant experiences are, however, quite clear. For one thing, the Southern and Eastern European immigrants who arrived before the 1920s entered the industrializing East Coast economy, where they took industrial and manufacturing jobs. Even though these first jobs were poorly paid and insecure, this position in the labor force gave Eastern European immigrants and their descendants a potential for upward mobility into skilled, well-paid, unionized jobs and even managerial and professional careers.

In contrast, Chinese and Japanese immigrants on the West Coast (like Mexican Americans) relied at first on the unskilled, often seasonal work available in the mines and rural areas. Later, they were forced into ethnic enclaves and came to rely on jobs in the small business and service sector and, in the case of the Japanese, in the rural economy. By their nature, these jobs did not link Chinese and Japanese immigrants or their descendants to the industrial sector or to better paid, more secure, unionized jobs. Furthermore, their exclusion from the mainstream economy was reinforced by overt discrimination from both employers and labor unions (see Fong & Markham, 1991).

Also, the fact that Asian Americans are racial (as opposed to ethnic) minority groups is significant. As the cultural markers that identified European ethnic groups faded with each passing generation, the more visible physical characteristics of the Asian immigrant groups continued to separate them from the larger society and bar them from the pathways followed by European-origin groups. Thus, Asian Americans cannot be considered purely "immigrant" groups (Blauner, 1972, p. 55). For most of this century, Chinese and Japanese Americans were in a less favorable position than European immigrants and their descendants and were excluded from the mainstream economy until the decades following World War II.

Asian Americans and Colonized Minority Groups

Comparisons between Asian Americans and African, Native, and Hispanic Americans have generated a level of controversy and passion that may be surprising at first. When the issues and their implications are examined, however, it is clear that the debate involves hidden political and moral agendas and evokes clashing views on the nature of U.S. society. What might appear on the surface to be merely an academic comparison of different minority groups turns out to be an argument about the quality of American justice and fairness, the very essence of the value system of U.S. society.

What is not in dispute in this debate is that some Asian groups (e.g., Chinese Americans and Japanese Americans) rank far above other racial minority groups on all of the commonly used measures of secondary structural integration and equality. Based on national trends for males from 1960 to 1976, for example, Hirschman and Wong conclude that there were "two worlds of ethnic inequality," one for Asian Americans, which is marked by upward mobility and achievement, and one for colonized minority groups, which is "bleak and unpromising" (1984, p. 595). More recent studies find similar patterns (Barringer et al., 1990).

What is disputed is how to interpret these comparisons and assess their meanings. First of all, we need to be aware that gross statistical comparisons between entire groups can be misleading. The extent of Asian-American "success" is exaggerated and needs to be seen in a proper context.

Even when these qualifications are acknowledged, though, discussion often slides onto more ideological ground. Asian-American success is often taken as proof that American society is essentially fair and open, truly the land of opportunity. The upward mobility of Japanese and Chinese Americans is cited as evidence for the belief that, in the United States, individuals and groups who work hard and obey the rules will get ahead, and that people can be anything they want to be as long as they work hard enough.

In our discussion of modern racism, we saw that the belief in U.S. openness and fairness can be a way of blaming the victim and putting the responsibility for change on the minority groups rather than on the structure of society. Asian success has become "proof" of the validity of this ideology. The none-too-subtle implication is that other groups (blacks, Hispanics, Native Americans) can achieve the same success but choose not to. Thus, the relative success of Chinese and Japanese Americans has become a device for scolding other minority groups.

A more structural approach to investigating Asian success begins with an examination of the respective economic positions of the various racial minority groups. When Chinese and Japanese Americans were building their enclave economies in the early part of this century, African Americans and Mexican Americans were primarily concentrated in the unskilled agricultural occupations of the mainstream economy; Native Americans were isolated from the larger society on their reservations; and Puerto Ricans had not yet begun to immigrate to the mainland. The social class differences among these groups today is intimately linked to their respective situations in the past.

For Chinese and Japanese Americans, much of their success is due to the high levels of education achieved by the second generation. While education is traditionally valued in Asian cultures, the decision to invest in schooling is also quite consistent with the economic niche occupied by these immigrant groups. Education is a relatively low-cost strategy to upgrade the productivity and profit of a small business economy and improve the status of the group as a whole. An educated, English-speaking second generation could bring expertise and business acumen to the family enterprises and lead them to higher levels of performance. Education might also be the means by which the second generation could enter professional careers. This strategy may have been especially attractive to a generation that was itself relatively uneducated and barred from citizenship (Hirschman & Wong, 1986, p. 23; see also Bonacich & Modell, 1980, p. 152).

The efforts to educate the next generation were largely successful. Chinese and Japanese Americans achieved educational parity with the larger society as early as the 1920s (Hirschman & Wong, 1986, p. 11). For many decades afterward, though, both Asian groups continued to be barred from the mainstream economy. But once anti-Asian prejudice and discrimination declined after World War II, the Chinese- and Japanese-American second generations had the educational backgrounds necessary to take advantage of the increased opportunities.

Thus, Chinese and Japanese Americans and the colonized minority groups developed differently and the difference was crucial. When native-born Chinese and Japanese Americans reached educational parity with white Americans in the 1920s, African Americans, Native Americans, and Mexican Americans were still victimized by Jim Crow laws and legalized segregation and excluded from opportunities for anything but the most rudimentary education. The Supreme Court decision in *Brown v. Board of Education of Topeka* was decades in the future, and Native American schoolchildren were still being subjected to intense Americanization in the guise of a curriculum. Even by the 1990s, the colonized minority groups have not escaped from the disadvantages imposed by centuries of institutionalized discrimination. African Americans have approached educational parity with white Americans only in recent years, and the status of Native and Mexican Americans is still below national averages.

Conclusion

Asian Americans are a diverse group having a variety of experiences with the dominant society. Chinese and Japanese Americans, the groups with the longest histories in the United States, once more expose the limitations of traditional views of the assimilation process. The immigrant generation of these groups responded to the massive discrimination they faced by withdrawing, developing ethnic enclaves, and becoming "invisible" to the larger society. They used their traditional culture and patterns of social life to build their own subcommunities from which they launched the next generation. Contrary to traditional ideas about how assimilation is "supposed" to happen, we see again that integration can precede acculturation and that the smoothest route to integration and equality may be the creation of a separate subsociety independent of the surrounding community.

MAIN POINTS

- Both Chinese and Japanese immigrants were the victims of a massive campaign of discrimination. Both groups established ethnic enclaves and faced many barriers to employment in the dominant society until opportunities began to increase after World War II.

- Other Asian-origin groups come from the Philippines, Korea, Vietnam, India, and a host of other places. These groups are diverse in occupation, education, and degree of acculturation. Asian immigrants have entered the U.S. society through the primary labor market, the secondary labor market, and the enclave economies.

- There are suggestions that the overall levels of anti-Asian prejudice and discrimination have declined in recent years. Still, hate crimes, racism, and discrimination against Asians are widespread. Levels of acculturation and secondary structural assimilation are highly variable.

- The notion that Asian Americans are a model minority is exaggerated. The relative affluence and success of many Asian-origin groups is distorted by recent immigrants with high-status occupations. Comparisons with European immigrants and colonized minority groups suggest some of the important reasons for the relative success of some Asian-American groups.

FOR FURTHER READING

Kitano, Harry H. L. 1969. *Japanese Americans.* Englewood Cliffs, NJ: Prentice Hall.

Kitano, Harry H. L., & Daniels, Roger. 1988. *Asian Americans: Emerging Minorities.* Englewood Cliffs, NJ: Prentice Hall.

Kwong, Peter. 1987. *The New Chinatown.* New York: Hill and Wang.

Lyman, Stanford. 1974. *Chinese Americans.* New York: Random House.

Zhou, Min. 1992. *Chinatown.* Philadelphia: Temple University Press.

CHAPTER 9

European Immigrants
Assimilation and the Persistence of Ethnicity

Between the 1820s and the 1920s, almost 40 million people immigrated from Europe to the United States. At the beginning of this population movement, the United States was an agrarian nation clustered along the East Coast. When the mass immigration from Europe ended, America had industrialized, become a world power, and stretched from coast to coast with colonies in the Pacific and the Caribbean.

It was no coincidence that European immigration, American industrialization, and the rise to global prominence occurred simultaneously. These processes were interlinked, and they were the mutual causes and effects of one another. Industrialization fueled the growth of U.S. military and political power and the industrial machinery of the nation depended heavily on cheap labor from Europe.

As the nation industrialized and modernized during the 20th century, the immigrants from Europe overcame the barriers of discrimination and rejection and gradually carved out a place for themselves and for their children and grandchildren. As the generations passed, Americanization and access to the institutions of the larger society increased. Today, the descendants of the European immigrants are no longer the victims of widespread discrimination and might no longer fit the definition of a minority group.

However, there are a number of reasons for including these groups in this series of case studies. These ethnic groups have not entirely disappeared, and their political, religious, and even their gastronomical traditions continue to manifest themselves, especially in the industrial cities of the Northeast and the Midwest. Also, many descendants of the European immigrants continue to think of themselves in ethnic terms and identify with the countries from which their immigrant ancestors came. The prejudices against these groups also persist, albeit in weakened form. Stereotypes (e.g., Jews as shrewd money handlers, Italians as quick-tempered and emotional, Irish as argumentative drunks, Poles as not very bright) and insulting names (wop, mick, hunky, kike, kraut, frog, limey, polack, and scores of others) remain a part of U.S. culture and national memory.

Finally, we can use the experience of the immigrants from Europe to further test the theories and concepts we have developed in previous chapters. We began this series of case studies by considering what Blauner called colonized minority groups; we then moved to "mixed types," or groups affected by both colonization and immigration. European immigrants most closely approximate "purely" immigrant groups, the end point of Blauner's typology. In this chapter we test Blauner's idea that immigrant groups acculturate and integrate more rapidly than colonized groups.

We begin this final case study by examining the history of the white ethnic groups over the last century or so. What modes of incorporation into U.S. society did these groups follow? How did they acculturate and integrate into the larger society? How did their experiences compare with those of other minority groups? Because these groups are now so assimilated, we do not examine contemporary patterns of prejudice, discrimination, and inequality in a separate section. Instead, these concepts are discussed in the context of the experiences of these groups in the United States. Finally, we consider why, in spite of massive assimilation, a sense of ethnicity persists among European Americans.

European Origins

The immigration from Europe included scores of different nationalities, cultures, and religious faiths. The immigrants differed from one another on every conceivable dimension: social class, education, the timing of their arrival, and their motives for immigrating. These diverse characteristics profoundly shaped their experiences in the United States as well as the reactions of the dominant group.

Immigrants from Europe are usually separated into two groups: the old, who came earlier in the 19th century, and the new, who arrived between the 1880s and the 1920s. These two waves differ in the regions from which they came and in a number of other ways. The old immigrants were from Northern and Western Europe and included Germans, Irish, Scots, Welsh, French, Danes, Norwegians, Swedes, and Finns. With the exception of the Irish, these groups were mostly Protestant, a religious affiliation they shared with the dominant group in the United States. Many of the Northern and Western European sending nations were as developed and industrialized as the United States and, again with the exception of the Irish, the immigrants from these nations shared many values (e.g., the Protestant ethic—which stressed hard work, success, and individualism—and support for the principles of democratic government) with the dominant culture. Further, many immigrants from these more developed regions brought high levels of educational credentials and occupational skills, which they were able to apply in the industrializing United States.

In contrast, the new immigrants came from Southern and Eastern Europe. This wave included Italians, Poles, Russians, Hungarians, Serbs, Ukrainians, Croats, Greeks, and Bulgarians. These immigrants were mainly Catholic or Jewish and these religious differences were the focus of severe prejudice, discrimination, and violent attacks in the United States. The rejection and persecution of the new immigrants (and the Irish) were often expressed in religious as well as ethnic terms.

Although many Protestant old immigrants were educated and experienced urbanites, the huge majority of the Irish and the new immigrants were peasants who came from agrarian, village-oriented cultures in which family and kin took precedence over individual needs or desires, not unlike the Asian cultures we discussed in chapter 8. Family life tended to be autocratic and male dominated, and children were expected to subordinate their personal desires and work for the good of the family as a whole. Arranged marriages were common in many of these cultures. Thus, this stream of immigrants had cultural backgrounds less consistent with the industrializing, capitalistic, individualistic Anglo-American culture and they faced more barriers and greater rejection than the Protestant immigrants from Northern and Western Europe.

For both new and old immigrants, religion had a major impact on the experiences of the groups in the United States. Protestant immigrants had an advantage in pursuing integration and opportunity, in part because they shared a faith with the dominant group and in part because they tended to come from more developed and modern countries. Catholic and Jewish immigrants experienced much greater levels of rejection, in part because of their religions and in part because they tended to come from less developed nations and were therefore less educated and skilled than the Protestant immigrants.

Although Catholic and Jewish immigrants were often stereotyped as single groups, they also varied along a number of dimensions. For example, the Catholic faith as practiced in Ireland was significantly different from that practiced in Italy, Poland, and other countries. Catholic immigrant groups often established their own parishes with

priests who could speak the old language. Cultural and national differences often separated Catholic groups in spite of the common faith
(Herberg, 1960).

Jewish immigrants also separated themselves by national origins.
Jewish immigrants from Germany arrived with other Germans before
the Civil War and established themselves as a prosperous, albeit small,
group of merchants. In the 1880s a much larger stream of Jewish immigration began from Eastern Europe. These later immigrants were
mostly Russian or Polish, generally less educated and much poorer
than the Jews from Germany, and much more conservative and strict
in their religious practices. At first, the German Jews felt threatened by
this massive wave of immigrants, fearing that they would stimulate attacks on all Jews. Eventually, however, the more affluent and Americanized Jews took responsibility for their co-religionists and, by the
early 1900s, the German Jewish community was funding numerous
welfare and self-help programs for Eastern European Jews (Herberg,
1960; Howe, 1976; Sklare, 1971).

In these brief pages, we can only suggest the diversity of European
immigrant groups and the multiplicity of their experiences. Still,
these dimensions—national, cultural, and religious—differentiated
these groups from one another as well as from the dominant group
and helped to define and shape their experiences and those of their
children and grandchildren. Other factors were consequential as well,
as we shall see in the next section.

Initial Conditions of Entry

European immigrants followed a variety of pathways into the United
States depending on their cultural and class characteristics, their
country of origin, and the timing of their arrival. Some groups encountered much more resistance than others, and different groups
played different roles in the industrialization and urbanization of
America. To discuss these diverse patterns systematically, the immigrants can be divided into three subgroups: Protestants from Northern and Western Europe, the largely Catholic immigrant laborers
from Ireland and from Southern and Eastern Europe, and Jewish immigrants from Eastern Europe. We look at these subgroups in roughly
the order of their arrival.

Northern and Western Europeans

Because of their physical and cultural characteristics, immigrants
from Northern and Western Europe were more readily accepted into
American society, which until well into the 20th century was highly
intolerant of religious and racial differences. These immigrants gener-

ally experienced a lower degree of ethnocentric rejection and racist disparagement than did the Irish and immigrants from Southern and Eastern Europe.

On the average, Northern and Western European immigrants tended to be more skilled and educated than other groups, and they often brought money and other resources with which to secure a place for themselves in their new society. Many settled in the sparsely populated Midwest and in other frontier areas, where they farmed the fertile land that became available after the conquest and removal of Native Americans and Mexican Americans. By dispersing throughout the midsection of the country, they lowered their visibility and their degree of competition with dominant group members.

By and large, the experiences of these immigrants are consistent with the traditional views of assimilation. Even though they experienced rejection and prejudice, assimilation was relatively smooth, especially when compared to the experiences of racial minority groups who were created by conquest and colonization. Two brief case studies below outline the experiences of these groups.

Immigrants From Norway

Norway had a small population base, and immigration from this Scandinavian nation was never sizable in absolute numbers. However, "America fever" struck here as it did elsewhere in Europe and, on a per capita basis, Norway sent more immigrants to the United States before 1890 than any European nation except Ireland (Chan, 1990, p. 41).

The first Norwegian immigrants were moderately prosperous farmers searching for cheap land. They found abundant acreage in upper Midwestern states such as Minnesota and Wisconsin but then discovered that the local labor supply was too small for their needs. Many used their relatives and friends in the old country to recruit a labor force. Chains of communication and migration linking Norway to the Northern plains were established and supplied immigrants to these areas for decades (Chan, 1990, p. 41). Today, a strong Scandinavian heritage is still evident in the farms, towns, and cities of the upper Midwest.

Immigrants From Germany

Germans were one of the largest groups to immigrate to the United States, and they have left their mark in economics, politics, and culture. In the latter half of the 19th century, at least 25% of the immigrants each year were German (Conzen, 1980, p. 406) and, in a 1994 poll, more white Americans (about 24%) traced their ancestry to Germany than to any other country (National Opinion Research Council, 1994).

The earlier German immigrants moved into the newly opened farmland and the rapidly growing cities of the Midwest, as did many Scandinavians. By 1850 large German communities could be found in Milwaukee, St. Louis, and other Midwestern cities (Conzen, 1980, p. 413). The German immigrants who arrived later in the 19th century found that good land was less available, and they were more likely to settle in urban areas. Many of the city-bound German immigrants were skilled workers and artisans. Others found work as laborers in the rapidly expanding industrial sector. The twin penetrations of German immigrants into the rural economy and the higher sectors of the urban economy is reflected by the fact that by 1870 most employed German Americans were in skilled labor (37%) or farming (25%) (Conzen, 1980, p. 413).

German immigrants took relatively high occupational positions in the U.S. labor force, and their sons and daughters were able to translate that relative affluence into economic mobility. By the turn of the century, large numbers of second-generation German Americans were finding their way into white-collar and professional careers. Within a few generations, German Americans had achieved parity with national norms in education, income, and occupational prestige.

Irish and Southern and Eastern Europeans: Immigrant Laborers

The relative ease of assimilation for Northern and Western Europeans contrasts sharply with the history of the Irish and the Southern and Eastern Europeans, most of whom immigrated as peasants and unskilled laborers with few resources other than their willingness to work. These groups included many sojourners, mostly males, whose personal goals were focused on the old country and an eventual triumphant return to their villages of origin.

By the time most of these new immigrants began to arrive, the better frontier land had already been claimed, so they were much more likely to settle in urban areas than the old immigrants were. Also, a large number of the peasant immigrants had been permanently soured on farming by the oppressive and exploitative agrarian economies from which they were trying to escape. At any rate, those who were interested in agriculture generally lacked the means to purchase even the cheapest of land.

These immigrant groups settled in the cities and towns of the industrializing Northeast and found work in plants, mills, mines, and factories. They supplied the armies of laborers needed to power the industrial revolution, although their view of this process was generally from the bottom looking up. They arrived during the decades in which the industrial and urban infrastructure of the United States was being constructed. They built roads, canals, and railroads, as well as the factories, plants, and mills that housed the machinery of industrialization. The first tunnels of the New York City subway system were dug, largely by hand, by laborers from Italy. Other immigrants found work in the coal fields of Pennsylvania and West Virginia and the steel mills of Pittsburgh, and they flocked by the millions to the factories of the Northeast.

Jobs: Gender and Employment

The Irish and the new immigrants took jobs in which strength and stamina were more important than literacy or skilled craftsmanship. In fact, the minimum level of skills required for employment actually declined as industrialization proceeded through its early phases. In order to keep wages low and take advantage of what seemed like an inexhaustible supply of cheap labor, industrialists and factory owners developed technologies and machines that required few skills and little knowledge of English to operate. As mechanization proceeded, unskilled workers replaced skilled workers in the workforce. Not infrequently, women and children replaced men because they could be hired for lower wages (Steinberg, 1981, p. 35).

The gender of the immigrants shaped their experiences in countless ways. When immigrant women entered the workforce, they generally found jobs in domestic service or in factories where they were assigned to the most menial, lowest paid tasks. Immigrant women were often sent to work by their families at young ages, as were many U.S.–born women of the working class. Women of these groups were expected to work until they married, at which time it was expected that they and their future children would be supported by their husbands. In many cases, however, immigrant men could not earn enough to support their families, and their wives and children were required to contribute to the family budget.

Immigrant wives sometimes continued to work outside the home. Those who did not still found ways to make money. They took in boarders, did laundry or sewing, tended gardens, and were involved in myriad other activities that permitted them to contribute to the family budget while staying home and attending to family and child-rearing responsibilities. A 1911 report on Southern and Eastern European households found that about half kept lodgers and that the income from this activity amounted to about 25% of the husband's wages. Children also contributed to the family income with after-school and summertime jobs (Morawska, 1990, pp. 211–212).

For European immigrant males, entry-level, unskilled jobs in the industrial sector were plentiful but offered little possibility of upward mobility and were insecure and often unsafe. Salary raises were rare, as there was a continuing supply of immigrants just "off the boat" and willing to work for less. Male immigrant laborers usually spent their entire working lives in jobs at the bottom of the occupational structure. The better paid, more secure, and skilled or supervisory positions were reserved for U.S.–born Anglo Americans or for the descendants of Northern and Western European immigrants. The Irish and the Southern and Eastern European immigrants, and most of their descendants, remained a blue-collar, unskilled working class until well into the 20th century (Bodnar, 1985; Morawska, 1990).

In American folklore and in some theories of assimilation, it is common to think of these immigrant laborers as "huddled masses"— helpless, uprooted victims responding to economic and social changes beyond their control. In fact, the new immigrants (like the old and like contemporary immigrants) organized networks of social and kinship relations to ease their movement between the two continents. Before leaving their homeland, the immigrants who moved along these networks knew where they were going, who would meet them, and what their jobs and wages would be when they arrived at their destinations. They were typically on the job, earning money, within days of their arrival (Morawska, 1990, p. 204).

Eventually, the barriers to upward mobility for these groups weakened and the descendants of the immigrant laborers began to rise out of the working class. Today, members of these groups have, on the average, achieved parity with national norms in education, income, and occupational prestige (Alba, 1985, pp. 117–129). However, upward mobility and middle-class prosperity were not universal for the descendants of the immigrant laborers. Today, members of some of these groups remain in the urban, blue-collar workforce throughout the industrial Northeast and Midwest and in the ethnic neighborhoods created by earlier generations. We address these working-class, urban, white European ethnic groups when we discuss the resurgence of ethnicity later in this chapter.

Ethnic and Religious Prejudice

Today it may be hard to conceive the bitterness and intensity of the prejudice that greeted the Irish, Italians, Poles, and other new immigrant groups. Even as they were becoming an indispensable segment of the American workforce, they were castigated, ridiculed, and attacked. The Irish, the first immigrant laborers to arrive, were the first to feel the bitter prejudice and intense discrimination. Anti-Irish campaigns were waged, Irish neighborhoods were attacked by mobs, and Roman Catholic churches and convents were burned. Some employers blatantly refused to hire the Irish, often advertising their ethnic preferences with signs saying No Irish Need Apply. Until they were displaced by later arriving groups, the Irish were mired at the bottom of the job market. Indeed, at one time they were called the "niggers of Boston" (Blessing, 1980; Potter, 1973; Shannon, 1964).

Other groups also felt the sting of discrimination and violence. Italian immigrants were particularly likely to be the victims of violent attacks, one of the most vicious of which took place in New Orleans in 1891. The city's police chief had been assassinated and rumors of Italian involvement in the murder were rampant. Hundreds of Italians were arrested but only nine were brought to trial. All were acquitted. Anti-Italian feeling was running so high, however, that a mob lynched 11 Italians while police and city officials did nothing (Higham, 1963).

Much of the prejudice against the Irish and the new immigrants was expressed as anti-Catholicism. Prior to the mid-19th century, Anglo-American society had been almost exclusively Protestant. Catholicism, with its celibate clergy, Latin masses, and cloistered nuns, seemed alien, exotic, and threatening. The growth of Catholicism, especially since it was associated with non-Anglo immigrants, raised fears that the Protestant religions would lose status. There were even rumors that the pope was planning to move the Vatican to North America and organize a takeover of the U.S. government.

The strength of these fears and rejectionist sentiments waxed and waned throughout the period of mass immigration. As we saw in chapter 4, the anti-Catholic, anti-Semitic, and anti-immigration forces ultimately triumphed with the passage of the National Origins Act of 1924.

Jewish Immigrants

A third pathway into U.S. society was followed by Jewish immigrants from Russia and other parts of Eastern Europe. These immigrants were fleeing religious persecution and most arrived as family units intending to settle permanently and become citizens. Like other European immigrant groups, Eastern European Jews settled in the urban areas of the Northeast and Midwest. New York City was the most common destination and the Lower East Side became the most famous Jewish-American neighborhood. By 1920 almost half of all Jewish Americans lived in New York City alone, and a total of about 60% lived in the urban areas between Boston and Philadelphia (including New York City). Another 30% lived in the urban areas of the Midwest and in Chicago in particular (Goren, 1980, p. 581).

Jobs: Gender and Employment

In Russia and other parts of Eastern Europe, Jews were barred from agrarian occupations and had come to rely on the urban economy for their livelihood. When they immigrated, they brought urban skills and job experiences with them. For example, almost two thirds of the immigrant Jewish men had been skilled laborers (e.g., tailors) in Eastern Europe (Goren, 1980, p. 581). In the rapidly industrializing, early 20th-century economy of the United States, they were able to use these skills to find employment.

Other Jewish immigrants joined the urban working class and took unskilled, manual labor jobs in the industrial sector (Morawska, 1990, p. 202). The garment industry in particular became the lifeblood of the Jewish community and, by itself, provided jobs to about a third of all Eastern European Jews residing in the major cities (Goren, 1980, p. 582). Women as well as men were involved in the garment industry, and Jewish women, like other immigrant women, found ways to combine their jobs and their domestic responsibilities. As young girls, they worked in factories and sweatshops and, after marriage, they did the same work—sewing precut garments together or doing other piecework such as wrapping cigars or making artificial flowers—at home, often assisted by their children (Amott & Matthaei, 1991, p. 115).

Unlike other new immigrant groups, Jewish Americans also became heavily involved in commerce. Drawing on their urban and mercantile experience in the old country, many started businesses and small independent enterprises. The Jewish neighborhoods were densely populated and provided a ready market for services of all kinds. Some Jewish immigrants became street peddlers or opened bakeries, butcher and candy shops, or any number of other retail enterprises. In a process that mirrored the activities of the Chinese and the Japanese on the West Coast at the same time, Eastern European Jews constructed an enclave economy on the East Coast.

The Ethnic Enclave and Upward Mobility

Capitalizing on their residential concentration and close proximity, Jewish immigrants created dense networks of commercial, financial, and social cooperation. Like the other ethnic enclaves we have examined in previous chapters, the Jewish-American ethnic enclave survived because of the cohesiveness of the group, the willingness of wives and children to work for no monetary compensation, and the commercial savvy of the early immigrants. Also, a large pool of cheap labor and sources of credit and other financial services were available within the community. The Jewish-American enclave grew and provided a livelihood for many of the children and grandchildren of the immigrants (Portes & Manning, 1986, pp. 51–52). As was also the case with other enclave groups, economic advancement preceded extensive acculturation, and Jewish Americans made significant strides toward economic equality before they became fluent in English or were otherwise Americanized.

As we discussed in chapter 8, an obvious way in which an enclave immigrant group can improve its position is to develop an educated and acculturated second generation. The Americanized, English-speaking children of the immigrants could use their greater familiarity with the dominant society and their language facility to help preserve and expand the family enterprises. Thus, the same logic that led Chinese and Japanese Americans to invest in education for the next generation also applied to the situation of Jewish immigrants. Further, as the second generation appeared, the public school system was expanding and, in New York City and other cities, education through the college level was free or very cheap (Steinberg, 1981, pp. 136–138).

There was also a strong push for the second and third generations to enter the professions, and as Jewish Americans excelled in school, resistance to and discrimination against them increased. By the 1920s many elite colleges and universities, such as Dartmouth, had established quotas that limited the number of Jewish students they would admit (Dinnerstein, 1977, p. 228). These quotas were not abolished until after World War II.

The enclave economy and the Jewish neighborhoods established by the immigrants proved to be an effective base from which to integrate into American society. The descendants of the immigrants moved out of the traditional ethnic neighborhoods years ago, and their positions in the economy—their pushcarts and stores and their jobs in the garment industry—have been taken over by more recent immigrants. When they left the enclave economy, many second- and third-generation Eastern European Jews did not enter the mainstream occupational structure at the bottom, as the immigrant laborer groups tended to do. They used the resources generated by the entrepreneurship of the early generations to gain access to prestigious and advantaged social class positions (Portes & Manning, 1986, p. 53). Studies show that as a group, Jewish Americans today surpass national averages in income, levels of education, and occupational prestige (Sklare, 1971, pp. 60–69; see also Cohen, 1985; Masserik & Chenkin, 1973).

Anti-Semitism

One barrier Jewish Americans were forced to overcome was prejudice and racism (or **anti-Semitism**). Biased sentiments and negative stereotypes of Jews have been a part of Western tradition for centuries and actually have been stronger and more vicious in Europe than in the United States. For nearly two millennia, European Jews have been chastised and persecuted as the killers of Christ and stereotyped as materialistic moneylenders and crafty businesspeople. The stereotype that links Jews with moneylending has its origins in the fact that, in premodern Europe, Catholics were forbidden by the Church to engage in usury (charging interest for loans). Jews were under no such restriction and thus filled the gap created in the economy.

The ultimate episode in the long history of European anti-Semitism was, of course, the Nazi Holocaust, in which some 6 million Jews died. However, European anti-Semitism did not end with the demise of the Nazi empire; today it remains a prominent concern in Russia, Germany, and other nations.

Before the mass immigration of the late 19th century, anti-Semitism in the United States was relatively mild, perhaps because the group was so small. As the immigration continued, anti-Jewish prejudice increased in intensity and viciousness. In the late 19th century, Jews began to be banned from social clubs and the boardrooms of businesses and other organizations. Summer resorts began posting notices that "we prefer not to entertain Hebrews" (Goren, 1980, p. 585).

By the 1920s and 1930s, anti-Semitism had become quite prominent and was being preached by the Ku Klux Klan and other extremist groups. In recent decades, overall levels of anti-Semitism seem to have tapered off (Morin, 1994). For example, Table 2.2 shows that social distance scores have declined between 1926 and 1977. Note, however, that this table also indicates that anti-Semitism has not disappeared. In 1977 Jews ranked at about the same relative level as they had in 1926. The persistence of anti-Semitism may be due to the cultural nature of prejudice; that is, the tendency of stereotypes and prejudicial sentiments to become embedded in the culture and be passed on from generation to generation through socialization.

Anti-Semitism can also be found in the ideologies of a variety of extremist groups, including skinheads, various contemporary incarnations of the Ku Klux Klan, and others. Some of this targeting of Jews seems to increase during economic recession and may be a type of scapegoating related to the stereotypical view of Jewish Americans as extremely prosperous and materialistic.

Developments Since 1900: Mobility and Integration

Apart from their initial mode of incorporation, the acculturation and integration of white ethnics were affected by these factors:

1. The degree of dissimilarity between the immigrant group and the dominant group,

2. The processes of ethnic succession and secondary structural assimilation, and

3. The broad structural changes in the American economy caused by industrialization.

Degree of Dissimilarity

When the European immigration began, the dominant group consisted largely of Protestants with ethnic origins in Northern and Western Europe, especially England. The degree of resistance encountered by the different European immigrant groups varied in part by the degree to which they differed from these dominant group characteristics. The most significant differences related to religion, language, cultural values, and, for some groups, physical characteristics. Thus, Protestant immigrants from Northern and Western Europe experienced less resistance than the English-speaking but Catholic Irish, who in turn were accepted more readily than the new immigrants, who were both non-English-speaking and overwhelmingly non-Protestant.

These ethnocentric preferences of the dominant group correspond roughly to the arrival times of the immigrants. The more preferred groups immigrated earliest and the least preferred groups tended to be the last to arrive. Because of this coincidence, resistance to any one group of immigrants tended to fade as new groups arrived. For example, anti-German prejudice never became particularly vicious or widespread because the Irish began arriving in large numbers at about the same time. Concerns about the Protestant immigrants were overshadowed by the fear that the Catholic Irish could never be assimilated. Then, as the 19th century drew to a close, immigrants from Southern and Eastern Europe—still more different from the dominant group—began to arrive and made concern about the Irish seem trivial.

In addition, the New Immigration was far more voluminous than the Old Immigration. Southern and Eastern Europeans arrived in record numbers in the early years of this century, and the sheer volume of the immigration raised fears that American cities and institutions would be swamped by hordes of racially inferior, unassimilable immigrants (a fear that has echoes in the present).

Thus, a preference hierarchy was formed among the European-American ethnic groups by religion and region of origin. The hierarchy is illustrated by the social distance scale results presented in Table 2.2. These rankings reflect more than the degree of dominant group ethnocentrism; they also reflect the ease with which the group has been integrated. The sequence of mobility is captured by the concept of ethnic succession, the topic of the next section.

Ethnic Succession and Secondary Structural Assimilation

The process of **ethnic succession** refers to the myriad ways in which European ethnic groups unintentionally affected one another's position in the social class structure of the larger society. The overall pattern was that each European immigrant group tended to be pushed to higher social class levels and more favorable economic situations by the groups that arrived after them.

As more experienced groups became upwardly mobile and began to move out of the neighborhoods that served as their "ports of entry," they were often replaced by a new group of immigrants who would begin the process of assimilation all over again. Some neighborhoods in the cities of the Northeast served as *the* ethnic neighborhood—the first safe haven in the new society—for a variety of different groups in succession. Some of these same neighborhoods continue to fill this role today.

We look to the Irish, the first immigrant laborers to arrive in large numbers, as a case study to trace ethnic succession and integration. The patterns they followed apply generally to all of the immigrant laborer groups.

In many urban areas of the Northeast, the Irish moved into the neighborhoods and jobs left behind by German laborers. After a period of adjustment, the Irish began to create their own connections with the mainstream society, improve their position economically and socially, and be replaced in their neighborhoods and at the bottom of the occupational structure by Italians, Poles, or other immigrant laborers arriving after them.

Local Politics

As the years passed and the Irish gained more experience, they began to forge links to the larger society through several institutions, particularly politics. The Irish allied themselves with the Democratic party and helped to construct the political machines that came to dominate many city governments in the 19th and early 20th centuries.

Machine politicians were often corrupt and even criminal, regularly subverting the election process, bribing city and state officials, using the city budget to line their own pockets, and passing out public jobs as payoffs for favors and faithful service. While not exactly models of good government, the political machines performed a number of valuable social services for their constituents and loyal followers. Machine politicians, such as Boss Tweed of Tammany Hall in New York City, could find jobs, provide food and clothing for the destitute, aid victims of fires and other calamities, or intervene in the criminal and civil courts.

Much of the power of the urban political machines was derived from their control of the city payroll. The leaders of the machines used municipal jobs and the city budget as part of a "spoils" system (as in "to the winner go the spoils") and as a means of rewarding their supporters and allies. The faithful Irish party worker might be rewarded for service to the machine with a job in the police department (thus, the stereotype of the Irish cop) or some other agency. Private businessowners might be rewarded with lucrative contracts to supply services or perform other city business.

The political machine served as an engine of economic opportunity. In addition, the machines, and the city governments they controlled, linked Irish Americans to a central and important institution of the dominant society. Using the resources controlled by local government as a power base, the Irish began to integrate themselves into the larger society and carve out a place in the mainstream structures. The pathways thus created were followed by many of the later-arriving European immigrant groups.

Labor Unions

A second link among the Irish, other European immigrant groups, and the larger society was provided by the labor movement. Although virtually all of the white ethnic groups contributed to the success of this movement, many of the founders and early leaders were Irish. In the early years of this century, the Irish comprised about a third of the union leadership, and more than 50 national unions had Irish presidents (Brody, 1980, p. 615).

As the labor movement grew in strength and gradually acquired legitimacy in the 20th century, the leaders of the movement also gained status, power, and other resources while the rank-and-file membership gained job security, increased wages, and better fringe benefits. The labor movement provided another channel through which resources, power, status, and jobs flowed to the white ethnic groups.

Because of the way in which jobs were organized in industrializing America, union work typically required communication and cooperation across ethnic lines. The American workforce at the turn of the century was multiethnic and multilingual, and in order to enhance efficiency, workers were often organized along ethnic lines and worked together in crews of coethnics. Since the workforce was often ethnically segregated, union leaders not only had to represent the interest of the workers as a social class, but they also had to coordinate and mobilize the efforts of many different language and culture groups. Thus, labor union leaders became important intermediaries between the larger society and European immigrant groups.

Women were also heavily involved in the labor movement. Immigrant women, who were among the most exploited segments of the labor force, were at the core of the unionization effort. They filled leadership roles and served as presidents and in other offices, although usually in female-dominated unions. Some of the most significant events in American labor history involved European immigrant

women laborers. One of the first victories of the union movement occurred in New York City in 1909. The "Uprising of the 20,000" was a
massive, 4-month-long strike of mostly Jewish and Italian women
(many in their teens) against the garment industry (Goren, 1980,
p. 584).

One of the great tragedies in the history of labor relations in the
United States also involved European immigrant women. In 1911 a
fire swept through the Triangle Shirtwaist Factory, a garment industry
shop located on the 10th floor of a building in New York City. About
140 young immigrant girls died, many of them choosing to leap to
their deaths rather than be consumed by the flames. The disaster outraged the general public, and the funerals of the victims were attended by more than a quarter of a million people. The intense reaction fueled a drive for reform and improvement of work conditions
and safety regulations (Amott & Matthaei, 1991, pp. 114–116).

Women workers faced opposition from men as well as from employers. The major unions of the day were not only racially discriminatory
but also often hostile to women. For instance, women laundry workers
in San Francisco at the turn of the century were required to live in dor-
mitories and work from 6 A.M. until midnight. When they applied to
the international laundry workers union for a charter, they were
blocked by the male members. They eventually went on strike and
won an 8-hour workday in 1912 (Amott & Matthaei, 1991, p. 117).

The Catholic Church

A third avenue of mobility for the Irish and other white ethnic
groups was provided by the religious institution. The Irish were the
first large group of Catholic immigrants to enter the United States
and eventually came to dominate the Church administrative structure. The Catholic priesthood became largely Irish, and as they were
promoted through the hierarchy, these Irish priests became bishops
and cardinals.

As other Catholic immigrant groups began to arrive, conflict
within the Irish-dominated Church increased. Both Italian and Polish
Catholic immigrants demanded their own parishes, where they could
speak their own language and celebrate their own customs and festivals. Dissatisfaction was so intense that some Polish Catholics broke
with Rome and formed a separate Polish National Catholic Church
(Lopata, 1976, p. 49).

The other Catholic immigrant groups eventually began to supply
priests and to occupy leadership positions within the Church. Although the Church continued to be disproportionately influenced by

the Irish, other white ethnic groups also used the Catholic Church as part of their power base for gaining acceptance and integration in the larger society.

Other Pathways of Mobility

European immigrant groups also forged some not-so-legitimate pathways of upward mobility. One alternative to legitimate success was offered by crime, a pathway that has attracted every ethnic group to some extent. Crime became particularly lucrative and attractive when Prohibition, the attempt to eliminate all alcohol use in the United States, went into effect in the 1920s. The criminalization of liquor failed to lower the demand for it, and Prohibition created a golden economic opportunity for those willing to take the risks involved in manufacturing and supplying alcohol to the American public.

Many of the criminal organizations that took advantage of Prohibition were headed by Italian Americans, especially those from Sicily, a region with a long history of secret, antiestablishment societies (the ancestors of the Mafia) (Alba, 1985, pp. 62–64). Although the connection between organized crime, Prohibition, and Italian Americans is well known, it is not so widely recognized that ethnic succession operated in organized crime as it did in the legitimate opportunity structures. The Irish and Germans had been involved in organized crime for decades before the 1920s, and the Italians competed with these established gangsters and with Jewish crime syndicates for control of bootlegging and other criminal enterprises. The pattern of ethnic succession continued after the repeal of Prohibition, and the Italian-dominated criminal "families" have recently been challenged by members of groups still newer to urban areas, including African Americans, Hispanic Americans, and Caribbean immigrant groups (Eitzen & Timmer, 1985, pp. 241–247).

Ethnic succession can also be observed in the institution of sports. Since the turn of the century, sports have offered a pathway to success and affluence that has attracted millions of young men. Success in sports does not require formal credentials, education, or English fluency, and sports have been particularly appealing to the young men in those minority groups that have few resources or opportunities.

For example, at the turn of the century, the Irish began to dominate the sport of boxing. They were eventually replaced by boxers from the Italian-American community and other new immigrant groups, with each successive wave of boxers reflecting the concentration of a particular ethnic group at the bottom of the class structure. In more recent decades, the succession of minority groups continues, and boxing has been dominated by African-American and Latino fighters (Rader, 1983, pp. 87–106).

A similar progression or "layering" of ethnic and racial groups can be observed in other sports and in the entertainment industry. The institutions of American society, legitimate and illegal alike, reflect the relative position of minority groups at a particular moment in time. Just a few generations ago, European immigrant groups dominated both crime and sports because they were blocked from legitimate opportunities. Now, the racial minority groups that are still excluded from the mainstream job market and mired in the urban underclass are supplying disproportionate numbers of young people to these alternative opportunity structures.

Continuing Industrialization and Structural Mobility

The social class position and speed of integration of the European immigrants and their descendants were also affected by changes in the American economy and occupational structure. Industrialization is a continuous process, and as it has proceeded, the nature of work in America has evolved and changed. These developments in turn shaped the lives of European immigrant groups and created opportunities for upward mobility. One important process that benefited the European ethnic groups and improved their class positions is called **structural mobility,** or upward mobility that results from changes in the structure of the job market rather than any individual's desire to "get ahead."

Structural mobility was caused in part by the continuing mechanization and automation of the workplace. As the 20th century progressed, machines continued to replace people in virtually all areas of the economy. This process reduced the supply of the manual, blue-collar jobs that had provided employment for so many European immigrant laborers and their sons and grandsons.

As manual labor jobs declined, the supply of other types of jobs increased. We saw in chapter 4 that the relative number of jobs in the extractive or primary sector (e.g., farming and mining) and the secondary sector (manufacturing and industrial jobs) of the American economy has declined since the 1930s. Following World War II, job growth has been in the tertiary or service sector and in white-collar jobs.

Many of the newer jobs in the service sector are minimum wage, part-time, seasonal, or otherwise insecure. Access to the better jobs in the service sector and in the white-collar area is often determined by educational credentials. As the economy shifted away from an emphasis on manual labor, education became more accessible to European ethnic groups. A high school education became much more available in the 1930s. College and university programs, spurred in part by the educational benefits made available by the GI Bill, began to expand rapidly after World War II. Each generation of white ethnics, especially those born after 1925, were significantly more educated than their parents and were able to translate that increased human capital into upward mobility in the mainstream job market (Morawska, 1990, pp. 212–213).

Thus, European-American ethnic groups were able to advance in the occupational structure relative to their parents and grandparents. As the economy shifted from manufacturing to services, information, and high-tech areas, midlevel service and white-collar jobs have grown. Much of the upward mobility of the American population over the past several decades has been the result of the changing location of jobs in the labor market.

The pace and timing of this upward movement was, however, highly variable from group to group and place to place. Ethnic succession continued to operate and the most recent European immigrants tended to be the last to benefit from the general upgrading in education and the job market. The racial minority groups, with the notable exceptions of the enclave-structured Chinese and Japanese Americans, were generally excluded from the dominant group's educational system and from the opportunity to compete for better jobs.

Comparing European Immigrants and Colonized Minority Groups

Could the pathways to integration and mobility forged by European immigrants and their descendants be followed by other groups? How relevant are these experiences for today's racial minorities and for America's newest immigrant groups? Let's address these questions by comparing the relative positions of the European immigrants and the racial minority groups at the turn of the century.

At the beginning of this century, when European immigrants were forging their links to the larger society, most African Americans still resided in the South, where Jim Crow segregation excluded them from education, industrial jobs, and political and legal power. Mexican Americans were also victimized by systematic segregation and exclusion, and Native Americans were dealing with military defeat, attacks on their culture, and the isolation and enforced dependency of the reservation. Chinese and Japanese immigrants had been the victims of concerted campaigns of rejection and discrimination and had responded by withdrawing to ethnic enclaves.

Immigrant groups from Europe were generally in a better position to pursue integration and equality than any of the racial and/or colonized minority groups. Their relative advantage was the result of many factors, not the least of which was the fact that they entered the United States through the industrializing, urbanizing sectors of the economy, whereas the colonized minority groups remained largely isolated in rural areas.

Their status as (relatively) free immigrants gave the European groups more control of their fate. At a time when the racial minority groups faced nearly complete exclusion and massive discrimination, the European immigrants, or their children and their grandchildren, were finding pathways into the dominant society.

Why didn't the racial minority groups follow the same pathways? While the European immigrant groups were "pushing" one another up in the mainstream economy during the first half of this century, the racial and colonized minority groups, particularly African Americans from the rural South, began to move to the cities and seek places in the industrial workforce. Often, African-American migrants moved into the very neighborhoods abandoned by the upwardly mobile European-American ethnic groups and began to compete with them and with elements of the dominant group for jobs and other resources.

In their efforts to penetrate the urban-industrial labor market, members of racial minority groups would often find themselves caught between the labor unions and the factory owners and employers. After European immigration was curtailed in the 1920s, the industrialists used African Americans and other racial minorities as strikebreakers (or scabs) and as a source of cheap, easily exploited labor. Labor unions tried to eliminate this threat by barring African Americans from membership and trying to exclude them from the job market. As the labor movement gradually gained power, more and more workplaces became "closed shops," in which all workers were required to join the union. Minority groups of color were barred from better-paying, more secure union jobs and, in nonunion jobs, were frequently the victims of discrimination by employers. In combination, these forces made it extremely difficult for the racial minority groups to emulate white ethnics and penetrate the mainstream occupational structure (Geschwender, 1978, p. 184). As the white ethnic groups rose in the social class structure, they tended to close the doors behind them.

The job prospects of the colonized minority groups were further limited by the continuing mechanization of the economy, the same process that tended to benefit European immigrant groups and their descendants. By the time the nonwhite groups arrived in the manufacturing and industrial sectors of the economy, the unskilled, manual labor jobs that had sustained generations of white ethnic groups were already disappearing. The industrial escalator to comfortable middle-class prosperity ceased to function just as minority groups of color began arriving in the urban areas. The process of ethnic succession—one group pushing earlier arrivals up—came to a halt as the urban working class became non-Caucasian.

Thus, instead of following the white ethnic groups out of the ghettos and slums, many members of the racial minority groups have been trapped in an impoverished, powerless urban underclass. The job structure of the larger society has split into primary and secondary sectors, with the latter consisting disproportionately of minority groups of color. Blocked from the legitimate opportunity structure, the racial minority groups have penetrated other institutions (e.g., crime and sports).

Assimilation and the Persistence of Ethnicity

By the 1950s and 1960s, the great majority of the descendants of the original immigrants from Europe had left the old ethnic neighborhoods for better housing more in keeping with their relative prosperity. Many of these grandchildren and great-grandchildren of immigrants came to live in a nonethnic world, almost indistinguishable in their values, voting patterns, and personal lives from others of their social class and educational background. They did not organize their lives around their ethnicity or satisfy their needs in the context of the ethnic communities. They were less aware of their ethnic identity and more likely to think of themselves as "just American" (Lieberson & Walters, 1988). Especially for those who achieved suburban, middle-class status, ethnicity has become "merely" expressive, a symbol of one's origins and a way of expressing ties with kinfolk and others of similar ethnicity (Gans, 1979).

Whereas earlier generations had been trapped by their group membership, ethnicity for the descendants of the European immigrants has become voluntary and variable. They can stress their ethnicity, completely ignore it, or maintain any degree of ethnic identity. Many people have ancestors in more than one ethnic group and may change their sense of affiliation periodically (Waters, 1990). This progressive weakening in the strength and meaning of ethnic heritage and identity is consistent with the predictions of the traditional views of assimilation: As groups become more integrated into the institutions of the larger society, their separate, "hyphenated" identities fade and can be expected to eventually disappear altogether.

Yet surprisingly, European-American ethnicity has not disappeared. In the 1960s it actually increased in strength, a phenomenon often referred to as the **ethnic revival**. The revival took a variety of forms.

For some the phenomenon was primarily genealogical, as they expressed a greater interest in their ethnic heritage and their family's roots. Others increased their participation in ethnic traditions and organizations. Candidates for political office courted the "white ethnic vote" and made well-publicized visits to the churches, meeting halls, and neighborhoods of these groups. Demonstrations and festivals celebrating white ethnic heritages were organized, and buttons and bumper stickers proclaiming the ancestry of everyone from the Irish to the Italians were widely displayed.

The causes, extent, and meaning of this renewed interest in ethnicity remain somewhat controversial, but some conclusions are possible. Three factors in particular seem to account for much of the revival: (1) the advanced status of assimilation for these groups; (2) the increasing cultural pluralism of other minority groups in the 1960s; and (3) increased intergroup competition.

Ethnic Identity and Increased Assimilation

Some of the energy behind the rising interest in heritage derives from the dynamics of personal identity and self-image. By the 1960s prejudice and discrimination against most European-American ethnic groups had fallen to negligible levels, and ethnicity was no longer considered to be shameful or socially unacceptable. Proclaiming an ethnic identity and resurrecting and examining one's heritage carried little risk of negative reaction from others. As assimilation progressed, there was no longer much reason to hide one's ethnic ancestry or immigrant origins, and the resurgence of ethnic identity was partly the result of the fact that ethnicity was declining in importance (Alba, 1985, p. 171).

The dynamics of this part of the ethnic revival are captured by Marcus Hansen's **principle of third-generation interest:** What the second generation tries to forget, the third generation tries to remember (Hansen, 1952, pp. 493–500). Although this generalization does not literally apply to the 1960s (by then, most European immigrant groups had produced a fourth or even a fifth generation), Hansen points to some social psychological forces that may be relevant to understanding the persistence of white ethnicity.

Hansen's principle is based on his observation that the second generation tended to de-emphasize ("forget") its ethnicity in order to avoid the prejudice and intolerance of the larger society and compete on more favorable terms for jobs and other opportunities. As they became adults and started families of their own, the children of the immigrants tended to raise the third generation in nonethnic settings with English as their first and only language.

By the time the third generation of European-American ethnic groups reached adulthood, the larger society had become much more tolerant of ethnicity and diversity. Having little to risk, the third generation tried to reconnect with their grandparents and their roots. The third generation wished to remember their ethnic heritage and understand it as part of their personal identity, their sense of who they were and where they belonged in the larger society.

Contrary to some views of assimilation, Hansen argues that ethnic identity and the ethnic groups themselves do not fade and disappear in a linear or simple way. Ethnicity may be a more persistent part of the self, a more valued aspect of identity than anticipated by many theorists and observers. Ironically, the revival of ethnicity may have been possible precisely *because* European-American ethnics had been largely assimilated.

Ethnic Identity and Cultural Pluralism

The renewal of white ethnicity was also stimulated by the activities of other minority groups. The 1960s were a decade of increasing pluralism, even separatism, in group relations. Virtually every minority group generated a protest movement (Black Power, Red Power, Chicanismo, etc.) and proclaimed a commitment to its own heritage and to the authenticity of its own culture and experience. Furthermore, these pluralistic ideas were validated by politicians, intellectuals, entertainers, and other leaders and molders of public opinion. The visibility of these minority group movements for cultural pluralism helped make it more respectable for European Americans to express their ethnicity and honor their heritage.

Ethnic Identity and Competition

A third reason for the resurgence of white ethnicity is political and economic in nature and brings us back to issues of inequality, competition, and control of resources. In the 1960s a European-American working class remained in the neighborhoods of the industrial Northeast and continued to keep the old networks and traditions of the earlier generations alive. Because of the pattern of ethnic succession, this group consisted largely of the descendants of the immigrant laborers from Ireland and from Southern and Eastern Europe.

At the same time that cultural pluralism was coming to be seen as more legitimate, this ethnic working class was feeling increasingly threatened by minority groups of color. In the industrial cities, it was not unusual for white ethnic neighborhoods to adjoin black and Hispanic neighborhoods, putting these groups in direct competition for housing, jobs, and other resources. Many members of the white ethnic working class saw racial minority groups as inferior and perceived the advances being made by these groups as unfair, unjust, and threatening.

The urban working-class descendants of European immigrants also reacted to what they saw as special treatment and attention being accorded to African Americans and Hispanic Americans. They had problems of their own (the declining number of good, unionized jobs, inadequate schooling, and deteriorating city services) and felt that their problems were being given lower priority and less legitimacy because they were white. They saw programs such as affirmative action and school desegregation as unfairly taking resources or opportunities from their communities. The enhanced sense of ethnicity in the urban, working-class neighborhoods was in large part a way of resisting racial reform and expressing resentment for the racial minority groups.

These conflicts can be illustrated by the attempt of Boston city schools to implement a busing plan to desegregate public schools in the 1970s. Part of the plan involved busing African-American children into the neighborhood of south Boston, an area that is heavily working-class Irish Catholic. The Irish saw the African-American children as outsiders and they deeply resented having to share what they saw as *their* schools. Like many working-class neighborhoods, south Boston suffered from poverty and unemployment, and the Irish were economically insecure as well as racially prejudiced. These feelings of being invaded and threatened erupted in a series of mass attacks on African Americans in south Boston and similar attacks on whites in some black neighborhoods (Lukas, 1985).

Thus, the Boston busing plan was an intergroup conflict in which race and ethnicity served as the primary dividing line. Members of white ethnic groups and racial minorities have clashed on a number of other occasions in which prejudice—blatant, ugly, and unapologetic—was commonly expressed by both sides. However, these racist sentiments and stereotypes are tangential to the more basic issues of control of jobs, neighborhoods, schools, and other resources. Although the language they use is racial and racist, the conflicts between white ethnics and the racial minorities are also about matters of social class: the distribution of power, prestige, and privilege (see Bell, 1975; Cummings, 1980).

Conclusion: The Future of White Ethnicity

Will the descendants of the European immigrants continue to identify with the nations from which their ancestors came? Will the white ethnic revival and the renewal of interest in roots and peoplehood continue? The results of a recent national survey suggest that ethnicity is alive and well. People were asked, "From what country or part of the world did your ancestors come?" More than 80% of the white respondents named a European country (not America or the United States), and fewer than 4% failed to answer the question (National Opinion Research Councils, 1994).

But given massive assimilation—the demise of the European mother tongues, extensive intermarriage across ethnic and religious lines, and generations of social and geographic mobility—how long can this ethnic identity last? Some analysts argue that the revival that began in the 1960s and 1970s was in fact the last gasp of white ethnicity and that the ethnic identity of these groups will soon fade (Steinberg, 1981).

Others propose that, rather than dying, white ethnicity is reshaping itself. Richard Alba argues that a process of ethnogenesis (see chapter 1) is under way and that a new ethnic group, based on the common experiences of immigration and Americanization, is emerging among the descendants of the European immigrants. The new ethnic identity stresses the victimization of the immigrants from Europe and the discrimination and exclusion that they and their descendants faced. These groups overcame these barriers because they worked hard, "played by the rules," and took responsibility for themselves. The United States may not have been completely open and fair but success was possible for anyone if he or she only worked hard enough (Alba, 1990, pp. 310–319).

We have encountered thoughts like these at several points in this text. They echo modern racism, the human capital theory of status attainment, and blaming the victim. They have strong political and moral content and, at some level, they are replies to the charges of the racial minority groups that the United States is racist, deeply unfair, and fundamentally unjust. While celebrating European-American heritage and tradition, these ideas defend the status quo and hold the larger society blameless for the persistence of racial stratification.

Thus, this new sense of ethnicity may be yet another manifestation of group competition over scarce resources and power and the need to defend the larger society from criticism. If so, we can be sure that it (or some variant) will persist as long as racial stratification and group conflict continue. As we have seen repeatedly, this is likely to be a very long time.

MAIN POINTS

- Mass immigration from Europe to the United States lasted for about a century, during which time almost 40 million people made the voyage. The immigrants supplied much of the labor force for the American industrial revolution.

- European immigrant groups varied in language, religion, social class, levels of education, motives for immigrating, and mode of incorporation into American society.

- The speed of assimilation and social class position of these groups were affected by the degree of dissimilarity with the dominant group, ethnic succession, and structural mobility.

- The pathways to integration followed by the European-American ethnic groups are generally not available to racial minority groups today.

- In the 1960s a revival of interest in and commitment to ethnic heritages occurred. The revival was in large part the result of increased competition with other minority groups.

FOR FURTHER READING

Alba, Richard. 1985. *Italian Americans: Into the Twilight of Ethnicity.* Englewood Cliffs, NJ: Prentice Hall.

Fallows, Marjorie R. 1979. *Irish Americans: Identity and Assimilation.* Englewood Cliffs, NJ: Prentice-Hall.

Higham, John. 1963. *Strangers in the Land: Patterns of American Nativism 1860–1925.* New York: Atheneum.

Lopata, Helena Znaniecki. 1976. *Polish Americans.* Englewood Cliffs, NJ: Prentice Hall.

Schoener, Allon. 1967. *Portal to America: The Lower East Side, 1870–1925.* New York: Holt, Rinehart & Winston.

Sklare, Marshall. 1971. *America's Jews.* New York: Random House.

Steinberg, Steven. 1981. *The Ethnic Myth: Race, Ethnicity, and Class in America.* New York: Atheneum.

Yans-McLaughlin, Virginia. (Ed.). 1990. *Immigration Reconsidered: History, Sociology, and Politics.* New York: Oxford University Press.

The issues raised in this text will continue to animate U.S. society for decades to come. Some of the old patterns of inequality and exclusion will continue, but new forms of diversity and unity will also emerge as we continue to debate what it means to be an American.

A field laborer on Long Island, New York.

Workers in a modern sweatshop.

Mexicans crossing the border illegally between Tijuana and San Ysidro, California.

Chinatown, San Francisco.

Native American women wearing the traditional garments of the tribe are transported to an ancient ceremony by bus.

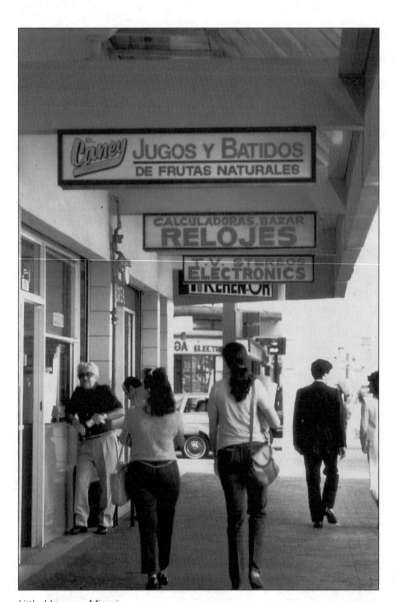

Little Havana, Miami.

A Chinese immigrant girl has her first experience with a fork while her Hispanic classmate observes.

College students share a meal. Separate or together?

CHAPTER 10

Minority Groups and U.S. Society
Themes, Patterns, and the Future

O ver the course of this text, we have analyzed ideas and theories about dominant-minority group relations and examined the historical and contemporary situations of minority groups in the United States. Now it is time to reexamine our major themes and concepts, conclude the analysis, and raise some speculative questions about the future. As we look backward to the past and forward to the future of America's minority groups, it seems appropriate to paraphrase the words of historian Oscar Handlin: Once I thought to write a history of the minority groups in America. Then, I discovered that the minority groups *were* American history (Handlin, 1951, p. 3).

The Importance of Subsistence Technology

Dominant-minority relations are shaped by the same social, political, and economic forces that shape the society as a whole. To understand the evolution of America's minority groups is to understand the history of the United States, from the earliest colonial settlements to the modern megalopolis.

Subsistence technology is the most basic force shaping the relationships between dominant and minority groups. In colonial times, minority relations were bent to the demands of a land-hungry, labor-intensive agrarian technology, and the early relationships among Africans, Europeans, and Native Americans flowed from the colonists' desire to control land and labor. In the mid-1800s, the same dynamics that had enslaved African Americans and nearly annihilated Native Americans made a minority group out of Mexican Americans.

The agrarian era came to an end in the 19th century as the new technologies of the industrial revolution increased the productivity of the economy and eventually changed every aspect of life in the

United States. The paternalistic, oppressive systems used to control the labor of minority groups in the agrarian system were abolished and replaced by competitive systems of group relations. These newer systems evolved from more rigid forms to more fluid forms as industrialization and urbanization progressed.

As the United States grew and developed, new minority groups were created and old minority groups were transformed. Rapid industrialization, combined with the opportunities available on the frontier, made the United States an attractive destination for immigrants from Europe, Asia, and Latin America. Immigrants helped to farm the Great Plains, mine the riches of the West, and, above all, supply the armies of labor required by industrialization.

The descendants of the immigrants from Europe benefited from U.S. industrialization, rising in the social class structure as the economy grew and matured. Immigrants from Asia and Latin America were not so fortunate. Chinese and Japanese immigrants constructed ethnic enclaves on the fringes of the mainstream society, while Mexican Americans and Puerto Ricans supplied low-paid manual labor for both the rural and urban economy. Both Asian Americans and Hispanic Americans were barred from access to dominant group institutions and higher paid jobs for much of the century.

African Americans, Mexican Americans, and Puerto Ricans began to enter the urban working class after European-American ethnic groups had begun to rise in the occupational structure. By that time, continuing industrialization and automation caused the supply of manual, unskilled jobs to dwindle. The processes by which European-American ethnic groups had achieved upward mobility faltered for the racial minority groups, large segments of which still confront urban poverty and bankrupt cities, continuing racial prejudice and institutional discrimination, and the prospect of permanent membership in an impoverished and powerless underclass.

We can only speculate about what the future holds, but the emerging information-based, high-tech society is unlikely to offer many opportunities to people with lesser educational backgrounds and lower occupational skills. It seems fairly certain that members of the racial and colonized minority groups will be participating in the mainstream economy of the future at lower levels than the dominant group and the descendants of European and some Asian immigrants. The grim scenario of continued exclusion might be altered by upgrading the urban educational systems, job training programs, and other community development programs. Current public opinion about matters of race and discrimination make it unlikely that such programs will be created, however.

Inaction and perpetuation of the status quo will bar a large percentage of the population from the emerging mainstream economy. Those segments of the African-American, Hispanic-American, and Asian-American communities currently mired in the urban underclass will continue to compete with recent immigrants for jobs in the low-wage, secondary labor market or in the alternative opportunity structures, including crime.

The Importance of the Contact Situation, Group Competition, and Power

The importance of the contact situation—the conditions under which the minority group and dominant group first came into contact with each other—has been stressed throughout this text. Blauner's distinction between colonized minority and immigrant groups is fundamental, a distinction so basic that it helps to clarify minority group situations centuries after the initial contact period. Our case studies of U.S. minority groups were arranged in rough accordance with this distinction, and the groups covered first (African Americans and Native Americans) are clearly at a greater disadvantage in contemporary society than the groups covered last (Asian Americans and white ethnics).

Noel's hypothesis states that if three conditions are present in the contact situation—ethnocentrism, competition, and the differential in power—ethnic or racial stratification will result. The relevance of ethnocentrism is largely limited to the actual contact situation but the other two concepts help to clarify the changes that occur after initial contact.

We have examined numerous instances in which competition—or even the threat of competition—between groups increased prejudice and led to greater discrimination and more repression. For example, in the 1880s, the labor movement and others led a campaign against Chinese immigrants. Legislation curtailing immigration from China was passed, the first significant restriction on immigration to the United States. There are parallels between this campaign for exclusion and some of the contemporary proposals to end or drastically curtail immigration. Clearly, some part of the current opposition to immigration is motivated by a sense of threat and the fear that immigrants are a danger not only to jobs and to the economy, but also to the cultural integrity of U.S. society.

Noel's third variable, the differential in power, determines the outcome of the initial contact situation: which group becomes dominant and which becomes minority. Following the initial contact, the superior power of the dominant group helps it to sustain the inferior position of the minority group. Minority groups by definition have fewer power resources, but they characteristically use what they have to attempt to improve their situation. The progress in minority group situations over the past half century has been due, in large part, to the fact that the minority groups finally acquired some power resources of their own. One important source of power for the civil rights movement in the South during the 1950s and 1960s was the growth of African-American voting strength in the North. After World War II, the African-American electorate became too sizable to ignore, and its political power helped pressure the federal government to take action and pass the legislation that ended the Jim Crow era.

Minority status being what it is, however, each of the groups we have discussed faces sharp limitations on its ability to pursue its own self-interest. Many of these limitations are economic and related to social class; many minority groups simply lack the monetary resources to finance campaigns for reform or to exert significant pressure on the political institution. Other limitations include small group size (e.g., Asian-American groups), language barriers (e.g., many Latino groups), and divided loyalties within the group (e.g., Native Americans separated by tribal allegiances).

At any rate, the relative powerlessness of minority groups today is a legacy of the contact situations that created the groups in the first place. In general, colonized groups are at a greater power disadvantage than immigrant groups. Contact situations set agendas for group relations that have impacts centuries after the initial meeting.

Given all that we have examined in this text, it requires no particular insight to conclude that competition and differences in power resources will continue to shape intergroup relations (including relations among minority groups themselves) well into the future. Because they are so basic and so consequential, jobs will continue to be primary objects of competition, but there will be plenty of other issues to divide the nation. Included on this divisive list will be debates over crime and the criminal justice system, welfare reform, national health care policy, school busing, bilingual education, and multicultural curricula in schools.

These and other public issues will continue to separate us along ethnic and racial lines because those lines have become so deeply embedded in the economy, in politics, in our schools and neighborhoods, and in virtually every other nook and cranny of U.S. society. These deep divisions reflect fundamental realities about who gets what in the United States. They will continue to reflect the distribution of power and stimulate competition along group lines for generations to come.

Diversity Within Minority Groups

All too often—and this text is no exception—minority groups are seen as unitary, undifferentiated entities. Although overgeneralizations are sometimes difficult to avoid, I want to stress again the diversity within each of the groups we have examined. Minority group members vary by age, sex, region of residence, levels of education, political ideology, and many other variables. The experience of one segment of the group (college-educated, fourth-generation, native-born, Chinese-American females) may bear very little resemblance to the experience of another segment (illegal Chinese male immigrants with less than a high school education), and the problems of some members may not be the problems of others.

I have tried to highlight the importance of this diversity by noting the gender differentiation within each minority group. The study of minority groups by U.S. social scientists has focused predominantly on males, and the experiences of minority women have been described in much less depth. All of the groups examined in this text tend to have cultures with strong patriarchal traditions. Women of the dominant group, as well as minority women, have had much less access to leadership roles and powerful positions and have generally occupied a subordinate status, even in their own groups. The experiences of minority group women and the extent of their differences with minority group males and dominant group women are only now being fully explored.

One clear conclusion we can make about gender is that minority group females are doubly oppressed and disempowered. Limited by both their minority and their gender roles, they are among the most vulnerable and exploited segments of the society. At one time or another, the women of every minority group have taken the least desirable, lowest status positions available in the economy, often while trying to raise children and attend to other family needs. They have been expected to provide support for members of their families, kinship groups, and communities, often sacrificing their own self-interest to the welfare of others.

In their roles outside of the family, minority women have encountered discrimination based on their minority group membership, which has been compounded by discrimination based on their gender. The result is, predictably, an economic and social status at the bottom of the social structure. When comparing income by gender and group status, minority women typically rank at the bottom. They are highly concentrated in the low-paid secondary labor market and are often employed in jobs that provide services to members of more privileged groups.

The inequality confronted by minority women extends beyond matters of economics and jobs: Women of color have higher rates of infant mortality, births out of wedlock, and a host of other health-related, quality-of-life problems (Zinn & Dill, 1994, p. 4). In short, there is ample evidence to document a pervasive pattern of gender inequality within America's minority groups. Much of this gender inequality is interconnected with rising rates of poverty and female-headed households, teenage pregnancy, and unemployment for minority males in the inner city.

Gender differentiation cuts through minority groups in a variety of ways. Specific issues might unite minority women with women of the dominant group (e.g., sexual harassment in schools and the workplace), and others might unite them with the men of their minority group (e.g., the enforcement of civil rights legislation). Their problems and grievances are the results of the patterns of inequality and discrimination in the larger society and within their own groups. Solving the problems faced by minority groups will not resolve the problems faced by minority women, and neither will resolving the problems of gender inequality alone. Articulating and addressing these difficulties requires a recognition of the complex interactions between gender and minority group status.

Assimilation and Pluralism

It seems fair to conclude that the diversity and complexity of minority group experiences in the United States are not well characterized by the traditional views of assimilation. For example, the idea that assimilation is a linear, inevitable process has little support. Immigrants from Europe probably fit that model better than other groups, but as the recent ethnic revival demonstrates, European-American ethnic groups and ethnic identity have survived, even if in attenuated form.

Equally without support is the notion that assimilation occurs in a series of ordered steps: acculturation, integration into public institutions, integration into the private sector, and so forth. We have seen that some groups integrated before they acculturated, others have become *more* committed to their ethnic and/or racial identity over the generations, and still others have been acculturated for generations but are no closer to full integration. No simple or linear view of assimilation can begin to make sense of the array of minority group experiences.

Indeed, the very desirability of assimilation has been called into question. Since the 1960s, many minority spokespersons have questioned the wisdom of further acculturation and integration with a society constructed by the systematic exploitation of minority groups. Pluralistic themes increased in prominence as the commitment of the larger society to racial equality faltered. Virtually every minority group proclaimed the validity of its own experiences, its own culture, and its own version of history. The consensus that assimilation was the best solution, the most sensible goal for all of America's minority groups, was shattered (if it ever really existed at all).

Let's review the state of acculturation and integration in the United States on a group-by-group basis. African Americans are highly acculturated but not highly integrated. In their residential and school attendance patterns, African Americans are about as separate today as they were a generation ago. The political power of the group has increased but remains disproportionately low. Unemployment and poverty in general remain serious problems and may even be more serious than they were a generation ago.

Native Americans are less acculturated than African Americans, and the strength and vitality of Native American cultures and languages may be increasing. On measures of integration, there is some indication of improvement but, by and large, this group (or, I should say, these groups) remains the most isolated and impoverished minority group in the United States.

Hispanic Americans are also less acculturated than African Americans. Hispanic traditions and the Spanish language have been sustained by isolation within the United States and have been continually renewed and revitalized by immigration. Cubans, on the one hand, have achieved greater equality than other Hispanic groups, but they did so by resisting assimilation and building an ethnic enclave economy. Mexican Americans and Puerto Ricans, on the other hand, share many of the problems of urban poverty that confront African Americans and, on the average, are far below national norms on measures of equality and integration.

Asian Americans, like Hispanic Americans, are highly variable in the extent of their assimilation. Some segments of these groups (e.g., fourth-generation Japanese and Chinese Americans) have virtually completed the assimilation process and are, on the average, remarkably successful. Other segments shatter the myth of Asian success and consist largely of recent immigrants with occupational and educational profiles that resemble colonized minority groups. Some Asian Americans have used their cohesiveness and solidarity to construct ethnic enclaves in which, like Cubans, they have achieved relative economic equality by resisting acculturation.

Only European-American ethnics (or, even more narrowly, only the Protestant old immigrants from Northern and Western Europe) seem to approximate the traditional model of assimilation. The development of even these groups, however, has taken unexpected twists and turns, and the recent upsurge of pluralism suggests that ethnic traditions and ethnic identity may withstand the pressures of assimilation for generations to come. These groups are the closest, culturally and racially, to the dominant group. If they still retain some sense of ethnicity after generations of acculturation and integration, what is the likelihood that the sense of group membership will fade in the racially identified minority groups?

Assimilation is far from accomplished. The group divisions that remain are real and consequential; they can't be willed away by pretending that we are all "just Americans." Group membership continues to be important, in large part because it continues to be linked to fundamental patterns of exclusion and inequality. The realities of pluralism, inequality, and ethnic and racial identity continue to persist to the extent that the American promise of a truly open opportunity structure continues to fail. The group divisions forged in the past and perpetuated over the decades by racism and discrimination will remain to the extent that racial and ethnic group membership continues to be correlated with inequality and position in the social class structure.

Besides economic and political pressures, other forces help to sustain the pluralistic group divisions. Some argue that ethnicity is rooted in biology and can never be fully eradicated (Van den Berghe, 1981). While this may be an extreme position, there is little doubt that many people find their own ancestry to be a matter of great interest. Some (perhaps most) of the impetus behind ethnic and racial identity may be caused by the most vicious and destructive intergroup competition. In other ways, though, ethnicity is a positive force that helps people locate themselves in time and space and understand their position in the contemporary world. Ethnicity remains an important aspect of self-identity and pride for many Americans from every group and tradition. It seems unlikely that this sense of a personal link to particular groups and heritages within U.S. society will soon fade.

Can we survive as a pluralistic, culturally and linguistically fragmented, racially and ethnically unequal society? What will save us from balkanization and fractionalization? How much unity is truly necessary? As we deal with these questions, we need to remember that diversity is no more "bad" in and of itself than unity is "good." Our society has grown to a position of global preeminence in spite of or, perhaps, because of our diversity. In fact, many have argued that our diversity is a fundamental and essential characteristic of U.S. society and a great strength to be cherished and encouraged rather than feared and repressed (Takaki, 1993).

We should also recognize that it is not cultural diversity per se that threatens the stability of U.S. society but the realities of split labor markets, racial and ethnic stratification, urban poverty, and institutionalized discrimination. Our society needs to focus on these issues guided by an honest recognition of the past and the economic, political, and social forces that have shaped present-day relationships between dominant and minority groups. Clearly, the one-way, Anglo-conformity model of assimilation of the past does not provide a basis for dealing with these problems realistically and is too narrow and destructive to be a blueprint for the future of U.S. society.

Minority Group Progress and the Ideology of American Individualism

There is so much sadness, misery, and unfairness in the study of minority groups that evidence of progress sometimes goes unnoticed. It should be firmly stated that, in many ways, U.S. minority groups are better off today than in the past. The United States has become more tolerant and open, and minority group members can be found at even the highest levels of success, affluence, and power.

One of the most obvious recent changes is the decline of traditional racism and prejudice. The strong racial and ethnic sentiments and stereotypes of the past are no longer the primary vocabulary for discussing race relations among dominant group members, at least not in public. However, recent research on American prejudices strongly suggests that negative feelings and stereotypes have not so much disappeared as changed form. The old racist feelings are now being expressed in other guises, specifically what we have called modern racism: the view that the routes of upward mobility were opened to all when Jim Crow–type segregation ended in the 1960s, and that the continuing problems of poverty and inequality are the results of choices made by individuals not to pursue improvement and success.

This individualistic view of social mobility is consistent with the human capital perspective and the traditional views of assimilation we have critiqued at various points throughout this book. Taken together, these ideologies present a powerful and widely shared perspective on the nature of minority group problems in modern American society. Proponents of these views tend to be unsympathetic to the plight of minorities and to programs such as school busing and affirmative action, and the overt bigotry of the past has been replaced by blandness and an indifference more difficult to define and harder to measure than "old-fashioned" racism.

This text has argued that the most serious problems facing contemporary minority groups are structural and institutional, not individual or motivational. For example, the paucity of jobs and high rates of unemployment in the inner cities are the result of economic and political forces beyond the control not only of the minority communities but also of local and state governments. The marginalization of the minority group labor force is a reflection of the essence of modern American capitalism. The mainstream, higher paying blue-collar jobs available to people with modest educational credentials are controlled by national and multinational corporations that maximize profits by automating their production processes and then moving the jobs that remain to areas with abundant supplies of cheaper labor, often outside the United States.

We also saw that some of the more effective strategies for pursuing equality require strong in-group cohesion and networks of cooperation, not heroic individual effort. Immigration to this country, for instance, was a group process that involved extensive, long-lasting networks of communication and chains of population movement, usually built around family ties and larger kinship groups. Group networks continued to operate in America and assist individual immigrants with early adjustments and later opportunities for jobs and upward mobility. A variation on this theme is the ethnic enclave found among so many different groups.

Survival and success in America for all minority groups have had more to do with group processes than with individual will or motivation. The concerted, coordinated actions of the minority community provided support during hard times and, when possible, provided the means to climb higher in the social structure during good times. Far from being a hymn to individualism, the story of minority groups in the United States is profoundly sociological.

A Final Word

U.S. society and its minority groups are linked in fractious unity, part of the same structures but separated by color and culture as well as long histories (and clear memories) of exploitation and unfairness. This society owes its prosperity and position of prominence in the world no less to the labor of minority groups than to that of the dominant group. By harnessing the labor and energy of these minority groups, the nation grew prosperous, but the benefits have flowed disproportionately to the dominant group.

Since midcentury, minority groups in the United States have demanded greater openness, fairness, equality, justice, and respect for their traditions. Increasingly, the demands have been made on the terms of the minority groups, not on those of the dominant group. Some of these demands have been met, at least verbally, and the society as a whole has rejected the oppressive racism of the past. Minority group progress has stalled well short of equality, though, and the patterns of poverty, discrimination, marginality, hopelessness, and despair remain as strong today as they were a generation ago.

As we approach the 21st century, the dilemmas of America's minority groups remain perhaps the primary unresolved issue facing the nation. The answers of the past—the faith in assimilation and an open society—have proved inadequate, even destructive and dangerous, because they help to sustain the belief that the important barriers to equality have been removed and that any remaining inequalities are the problems of the minority groups, not the larger society.

These problems of inequality and access will not solve themselves or simply fade away. They will continue to manifest themselves in myriad ways through protest activities, diffused rage, and pervasive violence. The solutions and policies that will carry us through these coming travails are not clear. Only by asking the proper questions, realistically and honestly, can we hope to find the answers that will help our society fulfill its promises to the millions who are currently excluded from the American dream.

The United States is one of many nations in the world today that are ethnically and racially diverse. As the globe continues to shrink and networks of communication, immigration, trade, and transportation continue to link all peoples into a single global entity, the problems of diversity will become more international in their scope and implications. Ties will grow with the nations of Africa, agreements between the United States and Latin American nations will have a direct impact on immigration patterns, Asian Americans will be affected by international developments on the Pacific Rim, and so forth. Domestic and international group relations will increasingly blend into a single reality.

In many ways, the patterns of dominant-minority relations discussed in this text have already been reproduced on the global stage. The mostly Anglo industrialized nations of the Northern Hemisphere have continuously exploited the labor and resources of the mostly nonwhite, underdeveloped nations of the Southern Hemisphere.

Thus, the tensions and resentments we have observed in U.S. society are mirrored in the global system of societies.

The United States is neither the most nor the least diverse society in the world. Likewise, our nation is neither the most nor the least successful in confronting the problems of prejudice, discrimination, and racism. However, the multigroup nature of our society, along with the present influx of immigrants from around the globe, does present an opportunity to improve our record and make a lasting contribution. A society that finds a way to deal fairly and humanely with the problems of diversity and difference, prejudice and inequality, and racism and discrimination can provide a sorely needed model for other nations and, indeed, for the world.

REFERENCES

Abalos, David. 1986. *Latinos in the United States: The Sacred and the Political.* Notre Dame, IN: University of Notre Dame Press.

Abrahamson, Harold. 1980. "Assimilation and Pluralism." In Stephen Thornstrom (Ed.), *Harvard Encyclopedia of Ethnic Groups* (pp. 150–160). Cambridge: Harvard University Press.

Acosta, Frank, & Kim, Bong Hwan. 1993. "Race Baiting in Sacramento: Anti-Immigrant Bills Ignore Reality: Our Multiracial Economy Is Dependent on Workers From Abroad." *Los Angeles Times*, May 4, p. B7.

Acosta-Belen, Edna, & Sjostrom, Barbara R. (Eds.). 1988. *The Hispanic Experience in the United States: Contemporary Issues and Perspectives.* New York: Praeger.

Acuna, Rodolfo. 1988. *Occupied America* (3rd ed.). New York: Harper & Row.

Adorno, T. W., et al. 1950. *The Authoritarian Personality.* New York: Harper & Row.

Alba, Richard. 1985. *Italian Americans: Into the Twilight of Ethnicity.* Englewood Cliffs, NJ: Prentice Hall.

———. 1990. *Ethnic Identity: The Transformation of White America.* New Haven, CT: Yale University Press.

Albers, Patricia, & Medicine, Beatrice. (Eds.). 1983. *The Hidden Half: Studies of Plains Indian Women.* Lanham, MD: University Press of America.

Allport, Gordon. 1954. *The Nature of Prejudice.* Reading, MA: Addison-Wesley.

Almaguer, Tomas. 1989. "Ideological Distortions in Recent Chicano Historiography: The Internal Model and Chicano Historical Interpretation." *Aztlan*, 18:7–28.

Almquist, Elizabeth M. 1979. "Black Women and the Pursuit of Equality." In Jo Freeman (Ed.), *Women: A Feminist Perspective* (pp. 430–450). Palo Alto, CA: Mayfield Publishing.

Alvarez, Rodolfo. 1973. "The Psycho-Historical and Socioeconomic Development of the Chicano Community in the United States." *Social Science Quarterly*, 53:920–942.

Amir, Yehuda. 1976. "The Role of Intergroup Contact in Change of Prejudice and Ethnic Relations." In Phyllis Katz (Ed.), *Towards the Eliminatiom of Racism* (pp. 245–308). New York: Pergamon Press.

Amott, Teresa, & Matthaei, Julie. 1991. *Race, Gender, and Work: A Multicultural History of Women in the United States.* Boston: South End Press.

Andersen, Margaret L. 1993. *Thinking About Women: Sociological Perspectives on Sex and Gender* (3rd ed.). New York: Macmillan.

Aronson, Eliot, & Gonzalez, Alex. 1988. "Desegregation, Jigsaw, and the Mexican-American Experience." In Phyllis Katz & Dalmas Taylor (Eds.), *Eliminating Racism: Profiles in Controversy* (pp. 301–314). New York: Plenum.

Ashmore, Richard, & del Boca, Frances. 1976. "Psychological Approaches to Understanding Group Conflict." In Phyllis Katz (Ed.), *Towards the Elimination of Racism* (pp. 73–123). New York: Pergamon Press.

Bahr, Howard, Chadwick, B., & Day, R. 1972. *Native Americans Today: Sociological Perspectives*. New York: Harper & Row.

Ball-Rokeach, Sandra, Grube, Joel, & Rokeach, Milton. 1981. " 'Roots: The Next Generation'—Who Watched and With What Effect?" *Public Opinion Quarterly*, 45:58–68.

Barber, Ben. 1994. "Howard University Flare-up." *Christian Science Monitor*, April 21, p. B1.

Barrera, Mario. 1979. *Race and Class in the Southwest: A Theory of Racial Inequality*. Notre Dame, IN: University of Notre Dame Press.

Barret, James R. 1992. "Americanization From the Bottom Up: Immigration and the Remaking of the Working Class in the United States, 1880–1930." *Journal of American History*, 79:996–1020.

Barringer, Herbert, Takeuchi, David, & Xenos, Peter. 1990. "Education, Occupational Prestige, and Income of Asian Americans." *Sociology of Education*, 63:27–43.

Bass, Bernard. 1955. "Authoritarianism or Acquiescence?" *Journal of Abnormal and Social Psychology*, November, pp. 616–623.

Becerra, Rosina. 1988. "The Mexican American Family." In Charles H. Mindel, Robert W. Habenstein, & Roosevelt Wright (Eds.), *Ethnic Families in America: Patterns and Variations* (3rd ed.) (pp. 141–159). New York: Elsevier.

Beck, E. M., & Tolnay, Stewart. 1990. "The Killing Fields of the Deep South: The Market for Cotton and the Lynching of Blacks, 1882–1930." *American Sociological Review*, 55:526–539.

Bell, Daniel. 1973. *The Coming of Post-Industrial Society*. New York: Basic Books.

———. 1975. "Ethnicity and Social Change." In Nathan Glazer & Daniel Moynihan (Eds.), *Ethnicity: Theory and Experience* (pp. 141–174). Cambridge: Harvard University Press.

Bell, Derrick. 1992. *Race, Racism, and American Law* (3rd ed.). Boston: Little, Brown.

Benedict, Ruth. 1946. *The Chrysanthemum and the Sword: Patterns of Japanese Culture*. Boston: Houghton Mifflin

Bennet, Lerone. 1962. *Before the Mayflower*. Baltimore: Penguin Books.

Berkowitz, Leonard. 1978. "Whatever Happened to the Frustration-Aggression Hypothesis?" *American Behavioral Scientist*, 21:691–708.

Berkowitz, Leonard, & Green, James. 1962. "The Stimulus Qualities of the Scapegoat." *Journal of Abnormal and Social Psychology*, April, pp. 293–301.

Biskupic, Joan. 1989. "House Approves Entitlement for Japanese-Americans." *Congressional Quarterly Weekly Report*, October 28, p. 2879.

Blassingame, John W. 1972. *The Slave Community: Plantation Life in the Antebellum South*. New York: Oxford University Press.

Blau, Peter M.,. & Duncan, Otis Dudley. 1967. *The American Occupational Structure*. New York: John Wiley.

Blauner, Robert. 1972. *Racial Oppression in America*. New York: Harper & Row.

Blessing, Patrick. 1980. "Irish." In Stephen Thornstrom (Ed.), *Harvard Encyclopedia of Ethnic Groups* (pp. 524–545). Cambridge: Harvard University Press.

Bluestone, Barry, & Harrison, Bennet. 1982. *The Deindustrialization of America*. New York: Basic Books.

Blumer, Herbert. 1965. "Industrialization and Race Relations." In Guy Hunter (Ed.), *Industrialization and Race Relations: A Symposium* (pp. 200–253). London: Oxford University Press.

Bobo, Lawrence. 1988. "Group Conflict, Prejudice, and the Paradox of Contemporary Racial Attitudes." In Phyllis Katz & Dalmas Taylor (Eds.), *Eliminating Racism: Profiles in Controversy* (pp. 85–114). New York: Plenum.

Bodnar, John. 1985. *The Transplanted.* Bloomington: Indiana University Press.

Bonacich, Edna. 1972. "A Theory of Ethnic Antagonism: The Split Labor Market." *American Sociological Review,* 37:547–559.

———. 1976. "Advanced Capitalism and Black/White Relations in the United States: A Split Labor Market Interpretation." *American Sociological Review,* 41:34–51.

Bonacich, Edna, & Modell, John. 1980. *The Economic Basis of Ethnic Solidarity: Small Business in the Japanese American Community.* Berkeley: University of California Press.

Borjas, George J. 1990. *Friends or Strangers: The Impact of Immigrants on the U.S. Economy.* New York: Basic Books.

Boswell, Thomas D., & Curtis, James R. 1984. *The Cuban American Experience.* Totowa, NJ: Rowman and Allanheld.

Bouvier, Leon F. 1992. *Peaceful Invasions: Immigration and Changing America.* Lanham, MD: University Press of America.

Bouvier, Leon F., & Gardner, Robert W. 1986. "Immigration to the U.S.: The Unfinished Story." *Population Bulletin,* November, p. 41.

Brandon, William. 1961. *Indians.* Boston: Houghton Mifflin.

Briggs, Vernon. 1992. *Mass Migration and the National Interest.* Armonk, NY: M. E. Sharpe.

Brody, David. 1980. "Labor." In Stephen Thornstrom (Ed.), *Harvard Encyclopedia of Ethnic Groups* (pp. 609–618). Cambridge: Harvard University Press.

Brown, Dee. 1970. *Bury My Heart at Wounded Knee.* New York: Holt, Rinehart & Winston.

Bureau of Indian Affairs. 1991. *American Indians Today: Answers to Your Questions.* Washington, DC: U.S. Department of the Interior.

Carmichael, Stokely, and Hamilton, Charles V. 1967. *Black Power: The Politics of Liberation in America.* New York: Vintage.

Carney, James. 1995. "Clinton Strongly Endorses Affirmative Action." *New York Times,* July 31, p. A35

"Casino Profits Help Indians Get Degree in Gambling." 1994. *New York Times,* March 2, p. B–8.

Chan, Sucheng. 1990. "European and Asian Immigrants Into the United States in Comparative Perspective, 1820s to 1920s." In Virginia Yans-McLaughlin (Ed.), *Immigration Reconsidered: History, Sociology, and Politics.* New York: Oxford University Press.

Chavez, Linda. 1991. *Out of the Barrio: Towards a New Politics of Hispanic Assimilation.* New York: Basic Books.

Chirot, Daniel. 1994. *How Societies Change.* Thousand Oaks, CA: Pine Forge Press.

Cho, Sumi. 1993. "Korean Americans vs. African Americans: Conflict and Construction." In Robert Gooding–Williams (Ed.), *Reading Rodney King, Reading Urban Uprising.* New York: Routledge.

Christie, R., & Yahoda, M. (Eds.). 1954. *Studies in the Scope and Method of the Authoritarian Personality.* Glencoe, IL: Free Press.

Churchill, Ward. 1985. "Resisting Relocation: Dine and Hopis Fight to Keep Their Land." *Dollars and Sense,* December, pp. 112–115.

Cohen, Steven M. 1985. *The 1984 National Survey of American Jews: Political and Social Outlooks.* New York: American Jewish Committee.

Colburn, David R., & Pozzetta, George. 1979. *America and the New Ethnicity.* Port Washington, NY: Kennikat Press.

Conner, Doug. 1994. "Tribe Elders Meet to Decide Youths' Fate." *Los Angeles Times*, September 2, p. A19.

Conot, Robert. 1967. *Rivers of Blood, Years of Darkness*. New York: Bantam.

Conzen, Kathleen N. 1980. "Germans." In Stephen Thornstrom (Ed.), *Harvard Encyclopedia of Ethnic Groups* (pp. 405–425). Cambridge: Harvard University Press.

Cornelius, Wayne A., & Bustamante, Jorge A. (Eds.). 1989. *Mexican Migration to the United States: Origins, Consequences, and Policy Options*. San Diego: Center for U.S.–Mexican Studies.

Cornell, Stephen. 1988. *The Return of the Native: American Indian Political Resurgence*. New York: Oxford University Press.

———. 1990. "Land, Labour and Group Formation: Blacks and Indians in the United States." *Ethnic and Racial Studies*, 13:368–388.

Cortes, Carlos. 1980. "Mexicans." In Stephen Thornstrom (Ed.), *Harvard Encyclopedia of Ethnic Groups* (pp. 697–719). Cambridge: Harvard University Press.

Cose, Ellis. 1993. *The Rage of a Privileged Class*. New York: HarperCollins.

Coughlin, Ellen K. 1993. "Sociologists Examine the Complexities of Racial and Ethnic Identity in America." *Chronicle of Higher Education*, March 24, pp. A7, A8.

Cox, Oliver. 1948. *Caste, Class, and Race: A Study in Social Dynamics*. New York: Modern Reader Paperbacks.

Cronon, Edmund D. 1955. *Black Moses: The Story of Marcus Garvey and the Universal Negro Improvement Association*. Madison: University of Wisconsin Press.

Cummings, Scott. 1980. "White Ethnics, Racial Prejudice, and Labor Market Segmentation." *American Journal of Sociology*, 85:938–950.

Curtain, Philip. 1990. *The Rise and Fall of the Plantation Complex*. New York: Cambridge University Press.

David, Paul A., et al. (Eds.). 1976. *Reckoning With Slavery: A Critical Study in the Quantitative History of American Negro Slavery*. New York: Oxford University Press.

Davis, David Brion. 1966. *The Problem of Slavery in Western Culture*. Ithaca, NY: Cornell University Press.

Davis, F. 1979. *Yearning for Yesterday*. New York: Free Press.

Davis, F. James. 1991. *Who Is Black: One Nation's Definition*. University Park: University of Pennsylvania Press.

de la Garza, R. O. (Ed.). 1987. *Ignored Voices: Public Opinion Polls and the Latino Community*. Austin, TX: Center for Mexican American Studies.

de la Garza, R. O., DeSipio, L., Garcia, F. C., Garcia, J., & Falcon, A. 1992. *Latino Voices: Mexican, Puerto Rican, and Cuban Perspectives on American Politics*. Boulder, CO: Westview.

Debo, Angie. 1970. *A History of the Indians of the United States*. Norman: University of Oklahoma Press.

Deloria, Vine. 1969. *Custer Died for Your Sins*. New York: Macmillan.

———. 1970. *We Talk, You Listen*. New York: Macmillan.

——— (Ed.). 1971. *Of Utmost Good Faith*. San Francisco: Straight Arrow Books.

——— (Ed.). 1985. *American Indian Policy in the Twentieth Century*. Norman: University of Oklahoma Press.

Deloria, Vine, & Lyttle, Clifford. 1983. *American Indians, American Justice*. Austin: University of Texas Press.

———. 1984. *The Nations Within: The Past and Future of American Indian Sovereignty*. New York: Pantheon.

Deutsch, Morton, & Collins, Mary Ann. 1951. *Interracial Housing: A Psychological Evaluation of a Social Experiment*. Minneapolis: University of Minnesota Press.

Dinnerstein, Leonard. 1977. "The East European Jewish Immigration." In Leonard Dinnerstein & Frederic C. Jaher (Eds.), *Uncertain Americans* (pp. 216–231). New York: Oxford University Press.

Dinnerstein, Leonard, Nichols, Roger, & Reimers, David M. 1979. *Natives and Strangers.* New York: Oxford University Press.

Dinnerstein, Leonard, & Reimers, David M. 1982. *Ethnic Americans: A History of Immigration and Assimilation.* New York: Harper & Row.

Dollard, John, Doob, Leonard, et al. 1939. *Frustration and Aggression.* New Haven, CT: Yale University Press.

Dovidio, John F., & Gartner, Samuel (Eds.). 1986. *Prejudice, Discrimination and Racism.* Orlando, FL: Academic Press.

Draper, Theodore. 1970. *The Rediscovery of Black Nationalism.* New York: Viking.

Driver, Harold. 1969. *Indians of North America* (2nd ed.). Chicago: University of Chicago Press.

D'Souza, Dinesh. 1995. *The End of Racism: Principles for a Multiracial Society.* New York: Free Press.

DuBois, W. E. B. 1961. *The Souls of Black Folk.* Greenwich CT: Fawcett Publications.

Duleep, Harriet O. 1988. *Economic Status of Americans of Asian Descent.* Washington, DC: U.S. Commission on Civil Rights.

Easterlin, Richard A. 1980. "Immigration: Economic and Social Characteristics." In Stephen Thornstrom (Ed.), *Harvard Encyclopedia of Ethnic Groups* (pp. 476–486). Cambridge: Harvard University Press.

Edwards, Harry. 1989. "Camouflaging the Color Line: A Critique." In Charles Willie (Ed.), *Round Two of the Willie/Wilson Debate* (2nd ed.) (pp. 101–105). Dix Hills, NY: General Hall.

Eitzen, D. Stanley, & Timmer, Douglas. 1985. *Criminology.* New York: John Wiley.

Elkins, Stanley. 1959. *Slavery: A Problem in American Institutional and Intellectual Life.* New York: Universal Library.

Embree, Edwin R. 1970. *Indians of the Americas.* New York: Collier.

Essien-Udom, E. U. 1962. *Black Nationalism.* Chicago: University of Chicago Press.

Evans, Sara M. 1979. *Personal Politics.* New York: Knopf.

———. 1989. *Born for Liberty: A History of Women in America.* New York: Free Press.

Fallows, Marjorie R. 1979. *Irish Americans: Identity and Assimilation.* Englewood Cliffs, NJ: Prentice Hall.

Farb, Peter. 1968. *Man's Rise to Civilization as Shown by the Indians of North America.* 1968. New York: E. P. Dutton.

Farley, John. 1995. *Majority-Minority Relations* (3rd ed.). Englewood Cliffs, NJ: Prentice Hall.

Farley, Reynolds, & Frey, William. 1994. "Changes in the Segregation of Whites from Blacks during the 1980s: Small Steps Towards an Integrated Society." *American Sociological Review,* February, pp. 23–45.

Feagin, Joe R., & Feagin, Clairece Booher. 1986. *Discrimination American Style: Institutional Racism and Sexism.* Malabar, FL: Robert E. Krieger.

Feshbeck, Seymour, & Singer, Robert. 1957. "The Effects of Personal and Shared Threats Upon Social Prejudice." *Journal of Abnormal and Social Psychology,* May, pp. 411–416.

Fishel, Leslie, & Quarles, Benjamin. 1970. *The Black American: A Brief Documentary History.* Glenview, IL: Scott, Foresman.

Fitzpatrick, Joseph P. 1976. "The Puerto Rican Family." In Charles H. Mindel & Robert W. Habenstein (Eds.), *Ethnic Families in America* (pp. 173–195). New York: Elsevier.

————. 1980. "Puerto Ricans." In Stephen Thornstrom (Ed.), *Harvard Encyclopedia of Ethnic Groups* (pp. 858–867). Cambridge: Harvard University Press.

————. 1987. *Puerto Rican Americans: The Meaning of Migration to the Mainland* (2nd ed.). Englewood Cliffs, NJ: Prentice Hall.

Fong, Eric, & Markham, William. 1991. "Immigration, Ethnicity, and Conflict: The California Chinese, 1849–1882." *Sociological Inquiry*, 61:471–490.

Forbes, Jack. 1990. "The Manipulation of Race, Caste, and Identity: Classifying AfroAmericans, Native Americans, and Red-Black People." *Journal of Ethnic Studies*, 17:1–51.

Forner, Philip S. 1980. *Women and the American Labor Movement: From World War I to the Present*. New York: Free Press.

Franklin, John Hope. 1967. *From Slavery to Freedom* (3rd ed.). New York: Knopf.

Franklin, John Hope, & Starr, Isidore. 1967. *The Negro in 20th Century America*. New York: Vintage.

Frazier, E. Franklin. 1957. *Black Bourgeoisie: The Rise of a New Middle Class*. New York: Free Press.

Freeman, Jo (Ed.). 1979. *Women: A Feminist Perspective*. Palo Alto, CA: Mayfield Publishing.

Gans, Herbert. 1962. *The Urban Villagers*. New York: Free Press.

————. 1979. "Symbolic Ethnicity: The Future of Ethnic Groups and Cultures in America." *Ethnic and Racial Studies*, 2:1–20.

Garcia, Jesus. 1993. *The Hispanic Population in the United States: March 1992*. (Current Population Reports, P20–465RV). Washington, DC: Government Printing Office.

Garcia, Mario T. 1976. "Merchants and Dons: San Diego's Attempts at Modernization, 1850–1860." In Carlos Cortes (Ed.), *Mexicans in California After the U.S. Conquest* (pp. 78–113). New York: Arno.

Garvey, Marcus. 1969. *Philosophy and Opinions of Marcus Garvey* (Vols. 1–2). (Amy Jacques Garvey, Ed.). New York: Atheneum.

————. 1977. *Philosophy and Opinions of Marcus Garvey* (Vol. 3). (Amy Jacques Garvey & E. U. Essien-Udom, Eds.). London: Frank Cass.

Genovese, Eugene D. 1974. *Roll, Jordan, Roll: The World the Slaves Made*. New York: Pantheon.

Georgakas, Dan. 1973. *The Broken Hoop*. Garden City, NY: Doubleday.

Gerth, Hans, & Mills, C. Wright. (Eds.). 1946. *From Max Weber: Essays in Sociology*. New York: Oxford University Press.

Geschwender, James A. 1978. *Racial Stratification in America*. Dubuque, IA: Wm. C. Brown.

Giago, T. 1992. "I Hope the Redskins Lose." *Newsweek*, January 27, p. 8.

Gladwell, Malcolm. 1995. "Personal Experience, the Primary Gauge." *Washington Post*, October 8, p. A–26.

Glazer, Nathan. 1983. *Ethnic Dilemmas, 1964–1982*. Cambridge: Harvard University Press.

Glazer, Nathan, & Moynihan, Daniel. 1970. *Beyond the Melting Pot* (2nd ed.). Cambridge: MIT Press.

————. 1975. *Ethnicity: Theory and Experience*. Cambridge: Harvard University Press.

Gleason, Philip. 1980. "American Identity and Americanization." In Stephen Thornstrom (Ed.), *Harvard Encyclopedia of Ethnic Groups* (pp. 31–57). Cambridge: Harvard University Press.

Goldstein, Sidney, & Goldscheider, Calvin. 1968. *Jewish Americans: Three Generations in a Jewish Community*. Englewood Cliffs: Prentice Hall.

Gooding-Williams, Robert. 1993. *Reading Rodney King, Reading Urban Uprising*. New York: Routledge.

Gordon, Leonard. 1986. "College Student Stereotypes of Blacks and Jews on Two Campuses: Four Studies Spanning Fifty Years." *Sociology and Social Research*, 70:200–201.

Gordon, Milton. 1964. *Assimilation in American Life*. New York: Oxford University Press.

———. 1975. "Toward a General Theory of Racial and Ethnic Group Relations." In Nathan Glazer & Daniel Moynihan (Eds.), *Ethnicity: Theory and Experience* (pp. 84–110). Cambridge: Harvard University Press.

———. 1978. *Human Nature, Class, and Ethnicity*. New York: Oxford University Press.

Goren, Arthur. 1980. "Jews." In Stephen Thornstrom (Ed.), *Harvard Encyclopedia of Ethnic Groups* (pp. 571–598). Cambridge: Harvard University Press.

Graham, Hugh D., & Gurr, Ted. 1969. *Violence in America: Historical and Comparative Perspectives*. New York: Signet.

Grebler, Leo, Moore, Joan W., & Guzman, Ralph C. 1970. *The Mexican American People*. New York: Free Press.

Greeley, Andrew M. 1974. *Ethnicity in the United States: A Preliminary Reconnaissance*. New York: John Wiley.

———. 1988. "The Success and Assimilation of Irish Protestants and Irish Catholics in the United States." *Sociology and Social Research*, 72:229–236.

Greeley, Andrew M., & McCready, William C. 1975. "The Transmission of Cultural Heritages: The Case of the Irish and Italians." In Nathan Glazer & Daniel Moynihan (Eds.), *Ethnicity: Theory and Experience* (pp. 209–235). Cambridge: Harvard University Press.

Greeley, Andrew M., & Sheatsley, Paul B. 1971. "Attitudes Towards Racial Integration." *Scientific American*, 225:13–19.

Greene, Victor. 1980. "Poles." In Stephen Thornstrom (Ed.), *Harvard Encyclopedia of Ethnic Groups* (pp. 787–803). Cambridge: Harvard University Press.

Griswold del Castillo, Richard. 1984. *La Familia: Chicano Families in the Urban Southwest, 1848 to the Present*. Notre Dame, IN: University of Notre Dame Press.

Gross, Emma. 1989. *Contemporary Federal Policy Towards American Indians*. New York: Greenwood Press.

Guttman, Herbert. 1976. *The Black Family in Slavery and Freedom, 1750–1925*. New York: Vintage.

Hacker, Andrew. 1992. *Two Nations: Black and White, Separate, Hostile, and Unequal*. New York: Charles Scribner's Sons.

Hagan, William T. 1979. *American Indians*. Chicago: University of Chicago Press.

Halbswach, Maurice. 1950. *The Collective Memory*. New York: Harper.

Hamer, Fannie Lou. 1967. *To Praise Our Bridges: An Autobiography of Fannie Lou Hamer*. Jackson, MS.: KIPCO.

Handlin, Oscar. 1951. *The Uprooted*. New York: Grosset & Dunlap.

Hansen, Marcus Lee. 1952. "The Third Generation in America." *Commentary*, 14:493–500.

Hardin, Garrett. 1993. *Living Within Limits*. New York: Oxford University Press.

Harris, Marvin. 1988. *Culture, People, Nature*. New York: Harper & Row.

Hartley, E. L. 1946. *Problems in Prejudice*. New York: Kings Crown Press.

Hawkins, Hugh. 1962. *Booker T. Washington and His Critics: The Problem of Negro Leadership*. Boston: Heath.

Heer, David M. 1980. "Intermarriage." In Stephen Thornstrom (Ed.), *Harvard Encyclopedia of Ethnic Groups* (pp. 513–521). Cambridge: Harvard University Press.

Herberg, Will. 1960. *Protestant–Catholic–Jew: An Essay in American Religious Sociology*. New York: Anchor.

Herrnstein, Richard J., & Murray, Charles. 1994. *The Bell Curve: Intelligence and Class Structure in American Life.* New York: Free Press.

Higham, John. 1963. *Strangers in the Land: Patterns of American Nativism, 1860–1925.* New York: Atheneum.

———. 1975. *Send These to Me: Jews and Other Immigrants in Urban America.* New York: Atheneum.

Hill, Robert. 1981. "The Economic Status of Black Americans." In *The State of Black America, 1981* (pp. 1–5). New York: National Urban League.

Hirschman, Charles. 1983. "America's Melting Pot Reconsidered." *Annual Review of Sociology*, 9:397–423.

Hirschman, Charles, & Wong, Morrison. 1981. "Trends in Socioeconomic Achievement Among Immigrant and Native-Born Asian Americans, 1960–1976." *Sociological Quarterly*, 22:495–513.

———. 1984. "Socioeconomic Gains of Asian Americans, Blacks, and Hispanics: 1960–1976." *American Journal of Sociology*, 90:584–607.

———. 1986. "The Extraordinary Educational Attainment of Asian-Americans: A Search for Historical Evidence and Explanations." *Social Forces*, 65:1–27.

Hodgkinson, Harold, Outtz, J., & Obarakpor, A. 1990. *The Demographics of American Indians: One Percent of the Population, Fifty Percent of the Diversity.* Washington, DC: IEL Publications.

Hostetler, John. 1980. *Amish Society.* Baltimore: Johns Hopkins University Press.

Houston, Jeanne Wakatsuki. 1994. "Manzanar, U.S.A." In Laurie Kirszner & Stephen Mandell (Eds.), *Common Ground: Reading and Writing About America's Cultures* (pp. 286–289). New York: St. Martin's Press.

Hovland, Carl I., & Sears, Robert R. 1940. "Minor Studies of Aggression: Correlation of Lynchings and Economic Indices." *Journal of Psychology*, 9:301–310.

Howe, Irving. 1976. *World of Our Fathers.* New York: Simon & Schuster.

"How to Tell Your Friends From the Japs." 1941. *Time,* October–December, p. 33.

Hoxie, Frederick. 1984. *A Final Promise: The Campaign to Assimilate the Indian, 1880–1920.* Lincoln: University of Nebraska Press.

——— (Ed.). 1988. *Indians in American History.* Arlington Heights, IL:Harlan Davidson.

Hraba, Joseph. 1979. *American Ethnicity.* Itasca, IL: F. E. Peacock.

Hur, Kenneth K., & Robinson, John P. 1978. "The Social Impact of Roots." *Journalism Quarterly,* 55:19–21, 83.

Hyman, Herbert, & Sheatsley, Paul. 1984. "Attitudes Towards Desegregation." *Scientific American*, 211:16–23.

Isaacs, Harold. 1975. "Basic Group Identity: The Idols of the Tribe." In Nathan Glazer & Daniel Moynihan (Eds.), *Ethnicity: Theory and Experience* (pp. 29–52). Cambridge: Harvard University Press.

Jackman, Mary. 1973. "Education and Prejudice or Education and Response Set." *American Sociological Review,* 40:327–339.

Jacoby, Russel, & Glauberman, Naomi. 1995. *The Bell Curve Debate: History, Documents, Opinions.* New York: Random House.

Jaffe, A. J., Cullen, R. M., & Boswell, T. D. 1980. *The Changing Demography of Spanish Americans.* New York: Academic Press.

James, Carney. 1995. "Clinton Strongly Endorses Affirmative Action." *Time,* July 31, p. 35.

Jarvis, Brian. 1993. "Against the Great Divide." *Newsweek,* May 13, p. 14.

Jibou, Robert M. 1988. "Ethnic Hegemony and the Japanese of California." *American Sociological Review,* 53:353–367.

John, Robert. 1988. "The Native American Family." In Charles H. Mindel, Robert W. Habenstein, & Roosevelt Wright (Eds.), *Ethnic Families in America: Patterns and Variations* (3rd ed.) (pp. 325–363). New York: Elsevier.

Jordan, Winthrop. 1968. *White Over Black: American Attitudes Towards the Negro: 1550–1812*. Chapel Hill: University of North Carolina Press.

Josephy, Alvin M. 1968. *The Indian Heritage of America*. New York: Knopf.

———— 1971. *Red Power: The American Indians' Fight for Freedom*. New York: McGraw-Hill.

Kallen, Horace M. 1915a. "Democracy Versus the Melting Pot." *The Nation,* February 18, pp. 190–194.

————. 1915b. "Democracy Versus the Melting Pot." *The Nation,* February 25, pp. 217–222.

Kamen, Al. 1992. "After Immigration, An Unexpected Fear: New Jersey's Indian Community Is Terrorized by Racial Violence." *Washington Post*, November 16, p. A1.

Karlins, Marvin, Coffman, Thomas, & Walters, Gary. 1969. "On the Fading of Social Stereotypes: Studies in Three Generations of College Students." *Journal of Personality and Social Psychology,* 13:1–16.

Karp, Abraham J. 1977. *Golden Door to America: The Jewish Immigration Experience*. New York: Penguin Books.

Kasarda, John D. 1989. "Urban Industrial Transition and the Underclass." *Annals of the American Academy*, 501:26–47.

Katz, Phyllis. 1976a. "The Acquisition of Racial Attitudes in Children." In Phyllis Katz (Ed.), *Towards the Elimination of Racism* (pp. 125–154). New York: Pergamon Press.

———— (Ed.).1976b. *Towards the Elimination of Racism*. New York: Pergamon Press.

Katz, Phyllis, & Taylor, Dalmas. (Eds.). 1988. *Eliminating Racism: Profiles in Controversy*. New York: Plenum.

Keefe, Susan E., & Padillo, Amado M. (Eds.). 1987. *Chicano Ethnicity*. Albuquerque: University of New Mexico Press.

Kephart, William, & Zellner, William. 1994. *Extraordinary Groups*. New York: St. Martin's Press.

Kessner, Thomas. 1977. *The Golden Door: Italian and Jewish Mobility in New York City, 1880–1915*. New York: Oxford University Press.

Killian, Lewis. 1975. *The Impossible Revolution, Phase 2: Black Power and the American Dream*. New York: Random House.

Kim, Kwang Chung, and Hurh, Won Moo. 1988. "The Burden of Double Roles: Korean Wives in the USA." *Ethnic and Racial Studies*, 11:152–167.

Kim, Kwang Chung, Hurh, Won Moo, & Fernandez, Marilyn. 1989. "Intra-group Differences in Business Participation: Three Asian Immigrant Groups." *International Migration Review,* 23:73–95.

Kinder, Donald R., & Sears, David O. 1981. "Prejudice and Politics: Symbolic Racism Versus Racial Threats to the Good Life." *Journal of Personality and Social Psychology,* 40:414–431.

King, Martin Luther, Jr. 1958. *Stride Toward Freedom: The Montgomery Story*. New York: Harper.

————. 1963. *Why We Can't Wait*. New York: Mentor.

————. 1968. *Where Do We Go From Here: Chaos or Community?* New York: Harper & Row.

Kitano, Harry H. L. 1969. *Japanese Americans*. Englewood Cliffs, NJ: Prentice Hall.

————. 1980. "Japanese." In Stephen Thornstrom (Ed.), *Harvard Encyclopedia of Ethnic Groups* (pp. 561–571). Cambridge: Harvard University Press.

Kitano, Harry H. L., & Daniels, Roger. 1988. *Asian Americans: Emerging Minorities.* Englewood Cliffs, NJ: Prentice Hall.

Kluegel, James R. 1990. "Trends in Whites' Explanations of the Black-White Gap in Socioeconomic Status, 1977–1989." *American Sociological Review,* 55:512–525.

Kluegel, James R., & Smith, Eliot R. 1982. "Whites' Beliefs About Blacks' Opportunities." *American Sociological Review,* 47:518–532.

Knowles, Louis L., & Prewitt, Kenneth. (Eds.). 1969. *Institutional Racism in America.* Englewood Cliffs, NJ: Prentice Hall.

Ko, Gilbert Kwok-Yiu, & Clogg, Clifford. 1989. "Earnings Differential Between Chinese and Whites in 1980: Subgroup Variability and Evidence for Convergence." *Social Science Research,* 18:249–270.

Kung, S. W. 1962. *Chinese in American Life.* Westport, CT: Greenwood Press.

Kwong, Peter. 1987. *The New Chinatown.* New York: Hill & Wang.

Labaton, Stephen. 1994. "Denny's Restaurants to Pay $54 Million in Bias Suits." *New York Times,* May 25, p. A1.

Lacy, Dan. 1972. *The White Use of Blacks in America.* New York: McGraw-Hill.

Ladner, Joyce A. 1971. *Tomorrow's Tomorrow: The Black Woman.* Garden City, NY: Doubleday.

Lai, H. M. 1980. "Chinese." In Stephen Thornstrom (Ed.), *Harvard Encyclopedia of Ethnic Groups* (pp. 217–234). Cambridge: Harvard University Press.

Lame Deer, John, & Erdoes, Richard. 1992. "Talking to the Owls and Butterflies." In Gary Colombo, Robert Cullen, & Bonnie Lisle (Eds.), *Rereading America* (pp. 128–134). Boston: Bedford Books of St. Martin's Press.

Lamm, Richard D., & Imhoff, Gary. 1985. *The Immigration Time Bomb: The Fragmenting of America.* New York: E. P. Dutton.

Landry, Bart. 1987. *The New Black Middle Class.* Berkeley: University of California Press.

LaPiere, Robert. 1934. "Attitudes vs. Actions." *Social Forces,* 13:230–237.

Lawson, Bill (Ed.). 1992. *The Underclass Question.* Philadelphia: Temple University Press.

Lee, Sharon M., & Yamanaka, Keiko. 1990. "Patterns of Asian American Intermarriage and Marital Assimilation." *Journal of Comparative Family Studies,* 21:287–305.

Lenski, Gerhard. 1966. *Power and Privilege: A Theory of Social Stratification.* New York: McGraw–Hill.

Lenski, Gerhard, Nolan, Patrick, & Lenski, Jean. 1995. *Human Society: An Introduction to Macrosociology* (7th ed.). New York: McGraw–Hill.

Levin, Jack, & Levin, William. 1982. *The Functions of Discrimination and Prejudice.* New York: Harper & Row.

Levine, Lawrence. 1977. *Black Culture and Black Consciousness.* New York: Oxford University Press.

Levy, Jacques. 1975. *Cesar Chavez: Autobiography of La Causa.* New York: Norton.

Lewis, Oscar. 1959. *Five Families: Mexican Case Studies in the Culture of Poverty.* New York: Basic Books.

———. 1965. *La Vida: A Puerto Rican Family in the Culture of Poverty.* New York: Random House.

———. 1966. "The Culture of Poverty." *Scientific American,* October, pp. 19–25.

Lewis, Rupert. 1988. *Marcus Garvey: Anti-Colonial Champion.* Trenton, NJ: African World Press.

Lieberson, Stanley. 1980. *A Piece of the Pie: Blacks and White Immigrants Since 1880.* Berkeley: University of California Press.

Lieberson, Stanley, & Walters, Mary C. 1988. *From Many Strands.* New York: Russell Sage Foundation.

Light, Ivan, & Bonacich, Edna. 1988. *Immigrant Entrepreneurs: Koreans in Los Angeles, 1965–1982.* Berkeley: University of California.

Lincoln, C. Eric. 1961. *The Black Muslims in America.* Boston: Beacon Press.

Locust, Carol. 1990. "Wounding the Spirit: Discrimination and Traditional American Indian Belief Systems." In Gail Thomas (Ed.), *U.S. Race Relations in the 1980s and 1990s: Challenges and Alternatives* (pp. 219–232). New York: Hemisphere Publishing.

"Looking for a Piece of the Action." 1994. *Newsweek,* June 13, p. 44.

Lopata, Helena Znaniecki. 1976. *Polish Americans.* Englewood Cliffs, NJ: Prentice Hall.

Lopreato, Joseph. 1970. *Italian Americans.* New York: Random House.

Lukas, Anthony. 1985. *Common Ground.* New York: Random House.

Lurie, Nancy Oestrich. 1982. "The American Indian: Historical Background." In Norman Yetman & C. Hoy Steele (Eds.), *Majority and Minority* (3rd ed.) (pp. 131–144). Boston: Allyn & Bacon.

Lyman, Stanford. 1974. *Chinese Americans.* New York: Random House.

Madrid, Arturo. 1990. "Official English: A False Policy Issue." In Courtney B. Cazden & Catherine E. Snow (Eds.), *The Annals of the American Academy of Political and Social Science* (Vol. 508, March 1990) (pp. 62–65). Newbury Park, CA: Sage.

Malcolm X. 1964. *The Autobiography of Malcolm X.* New York: Grove.

Mangiafico, Luciano. 1988. *Contemporary American Immigrants.* New York: Praeger.

Mann, Arthur. 1968. *Immigrants in American Life.* Boston: Houghton Mifflin.

Mannix, Daniel P. 1962. *Black Cargoes: A History of the Atlantic Slave Trade.* New York: Viking.

Margolis, Richard. 1989. "If We Won, Why Aren't We Smiling?" In Charles Willie (Ed.), *Round Two of the Willie/Wilson Debate* (2nd ed.) (pp. 95–100). Dix Hills, NY: General Hall.

Martin, Philip, & Midgley, Elizabeth. 1994. "Immigration to the United States: Journey to an Uncertain Destination." *Population Bulletin* (Vol. 47, No. 4). Washington DC: Population Reference Bureau.

Marx, Karl, & Engels, Friedrich. 1967. *The Communist Manifesto.* Baltimore: Penguin Books.

Masserik, Fred, & Chenkin, Alvin. 1973. "United States National Jewish Population Study: A First Report." In *American Jewish Year Book 1973* (pp. 264–306). New York: American Jewish Committee.

Massey, Douglas. 1993. "Latinos, Poverty, and the Underclass: A New Agenda for Research." *Hispanic Journal of Behavioral Science,* 15:449–475.

Massey, Douglas, et al. 1987. *Return to Aztlan: The Social Process of International Migration From Western Mexico.* Berkeley: University of California Press.

Massey, Douglas, & Denton, Nancy. 1992. "Residential Segregation of Asian-Origin Groups in U.S. Metropolitan Areas." *Sociology and Social Research,* 76:170–177.

———. 1993. *American Apartheid.* Cambridge: Harvard University Press.

McClelland, Katherine, & Austen, C. J. 1990. "Public Platitudes and Hidden Tensions." *Journal of Higher Education,* 61:607-642.

McConahy, John B. 1986. "Modern Racism, Ambivalence, and the Modern Racism Scale." In John F. Dovidio & Samuel Gartner (Eds.), *Prejudice, Discrimination and Racism* (pp. 91–125). Orlando, FL: Academic Press.

McConahy, John B., & Hough, Joseph C. 1976. "Symbolic Racism." *Journal of Social Issues,* 32:23–45.

McKay, James. 1982. "An Exploratory Synthesis of Primordial and Mobilizationist Approaches to Ethnic Phenomena." *Ethnic and Racial Studies,* 5:395–420.

McLemore, S. Dale. 1973. "The Origins of Mexican American Subordination in Texas." *Social Science Quarterly,* 53:656–679.

McNickle, D'Arcy. 1973. *Native American Tribalism: Indian Survivals and Renewals*. New York: Oxford University Press.

McWilliams, Carey. 1961. *North From Mexico: The Spanish Speaking People of the United States*. New York: Monthly Review Press.

Meier, Barry. 1994. "Casinos Putting Tribes at Odds." *New York Times,* January 13, p. D1.

Meier, Matt S., & Rivera, Feliciano. (Eds.). 1974. *Readings on La Raza*. New York: Hill & Wang.

Merida, Kevin. 1995. "Worry, Frustration Build for Many in Black Middle Class." *Washington Post*, October 9, pp. A1, A22–23.

Merton, Robert. 1968. *Social Theory and Social Structure*. New York: Free Press.

Miller, Kerby. 1990. "Class, Culture, and Immigrant Groups in the United States: The Case of Irish-American Ethnicity." In Virginia Yans-McLaughlin (Ed.), *Immigration Reconsidered: History, Sociology, and Politics* (pp. 96–129). New York: Oxford University Press.

Miller, Neal, & Bugleski, R. 1948. "Minor Studies of Aggression: The Influence of Frustrations Imposed by the Ingroup on Attitudes Expressed Towards Outgroups." *Journal of Psychology*, 25:437–442.

Miller, Norman, & Brewer, Marilyn. (Eds.). 1984. *Groups in Contact: The Psychology of Desegregation*. Orlando, FL: Academic Press.

Miller, Stuart. 1969. *The Unwelcome Immigrant: The American Image of the Chinese, 1785–1882*. Berkeley: University of California Press.

Mindel, Charles H., Habenstein, Robert W., & Wright, Roosevelt. (Eds.). 1988. *Ethnic Families in America* (3rd ed.). New York: Elsevier.

Mirande, Alfredo. 1985. *The Chicano Experience: An Alternative Perspective*. Notre Dame, IN: University of Notre Dame Press.

Mirande, Alfredo, & Enriquez, Evangelica. 1979. *La Chicana: The Mexican-American Woman*. Chicago: University of Chicago Press.

Model, Suzanne. 1990. "Work and Family: Blacks and Immigrants From the South and East Europe." In Virginia Yans-McLaughlin (Ed.), *Immigration Reconsidered: History, Sociology, and Politics* (pp. 130–159). New York: Oxford University Press.

———. 1992. "The Ethnic Economy: Cuban and Chinese Reconsidered." *Sociological Quarterly*, 33:63–82.

Montagu, Ashley. 1972. *Statement on Race* (3rd ed.). New York: Oxford University Press.

Moore, Joan W. 1970. *Mexican Americans*. Englewood Cliffs, NJ: Prentice Hall.

Moore, Joan W., & Pachon, Harry. 1985. *Hispanics in the United States*. Englewood Cliffs, NJ: Prentice Hall.

Moore, Robert B. 1988. "Racial Stereotyping in the English Language." In Paula Rothenberg (Ed.), *Racism and Sexism: An Integrated Study* (pp. 269–279). New York: St. Martin's Press.

Moquin, Wayne, & Van Doren, Charles. (Eds.). 1971. *A Documentary History of Mexican Americans*. New York: Bantam.

Morawska, Ewa. 1990. "The Sociology and Historiography of Immigration." In Virginia Yans–McLaughlin (Ed.), *Immigration Reconsidered: History, Sociology, and Politics* (pp. 187–238). New York: Oxford University Press.

Morin, Richard. 1994. "Study Cites Drop in Antisemitism." *Washington Post,* June 21, p. A8.

———. 1995. "A Distorted Image of Minorities." *Washington Post,* October 8, pp. A1, A27.

Morris, Aldon D. 1984. *The Origins of the Civil Rights Movement*. New York: Free Press.

Moskos, Charles. 1980. *Greek Americans: Struggle and Success*. Englewood Cliffs, NJ: Prentice Hall.

Moynihan, Daniel. 1965. *The Negro Family: The Case for National Action.* Washington, DC: U.S. Department of Labor.

Muller, Thomas, & Espenshade, Thomas. 1985. *The Fourth Wave: California's Newest Immigrants.* Washington, DC: Urban Institute.

Murguia, Edward. 1991. "On Latino/Hispanic Ethnic Identity." *Latino Studies Journal,* September, pp. 8–18.

Murphey, Dwight. 1991. "The Historic Dispossession of the American Indian: Did It Violate American Ideals?" *Journal of Social, Political, and Economic Studies,* 16:347–368.

———. 1993. "The World War II Relocation of Japanese Americans." *Journal of Social, Political, and Economic Studies,* 18:93–117.

Myrdal, Gunnar. 1944. *An American Dilemma: The Negro Problem and Modern Democracy.* New York: Harper & Row.

Nabakov, Peter. 1991. *Native American Testimony.* New York: Penguin Books.

Nagel, Joane, & Snipp, C. M. 1993. "Ethnic Reorganization: American Indian Social, Economic, Political, and Cultural Strategies for Survival." *Ethnic and Racial Studies,* 16:203–235.

National Advisory Commission. 1968. *Report of the National Advisory Commission on Civil Disorders.* New York: The New York Times Co.

National Opinion Research Council. 1994. "General Social Survey." Chicago: Author.

Nelli, Humbert S. 1980. "Italians." In Stephen Thornstrom (Ed.), *Harvard Encyclopedia of Ethnic Groups* (pp. 545–560). Cambridge: Harvard University Press.

Newman, William. 1973. *American Pluralism.* New York: Harper & Row.

Noel, Daniel. 1968. "A Theory of the Origin of Ethnic Stratification." *Social Problems,* 16:157–172.

Novak, Michael. 1973. *The Rise of the Unmeltable Ethnics: Politics and Culture in the 1970s.* New York: Collier.

———. 1979. "The New Ethnicity." In David R. Colburn & George Pozzetta (Eds.), *America and the New Ethnicity* (pp. 16–19). Port Washington, NY: Kennikat Press.

O'Hare, William P. 1992. "America's Minorities—The Demographics of Diversity." *Population Bulletin* (Vol. 47, No. 4). Washington, DC: Population Reference Bureau.

O'Hare, William P., & Felt, Judy C. 1991. *Asian Americans: America's Fastest Growing Minority Group.* Washington, DC: Population Reference Bureau.

O'Hare, William, et al. 1991. *African Americans in the 1990s.* Washington, DC: Population Reference Bureau.

O'Hare, William P., & Usdansky, Margaret. 1992. "What the 1990 Census Tells Us About Segregation in 25 Large Metros." *Population Today* (Vol. 20, No.9). Washington, DC: Population Reference Bureau.

Olson, James, & Wilson, R. 1984. *Native Americans in the Twentieth Century.* Provo, UT: Brigham Young University Press.

Olzak, Susan. 1983. "Contemporary Ethnic Mobilization." *Annual Review of Sociology,* 9:355–374.

Olzak, Susan, & Nagel, Joanne. (Eds.). 1986. *Competitive Ethnic Relations.* New York: Academic Press.

Omi, Michael, & Winant, Howard. 1986. *Racial Formation in the United States From the 1960s to the 1980s.* New York: Routledge.

Ortiz, Vilma. 1994. "Women of Color: A Demographic Overview." In Maxine Baca Zinn & Bonnie Thorton Dill (Eds.), *Women of Color in U.S. Society* (pp. 13–40). Philadelphia: Temple University Press.

Osborne, Richard H. (Ed.). 1971. *The Biological and Social Meaning of Race.* San Francisco: Freeman.

Osofsky, Gilbert. 1969. *Puttin' on Old Master.* New York: Harper & Row.

Owen, Carolyn, Eisner, Howard, & McFaul, Thomas. 1981. "A Half Century of Social Distance Research: National Replication of the Bogardus Studies." *Sociology and Social Research,* 66:80–98.

Paisano, Edna. 1993. *We the American Asians.* Washington, DC: U.S. Bureau of the Census.

Parish, Peter J. 1989. *Slavery: History and Historians.* New York: Harper & Row.

Park, Robert E., & Burgess, Ernest W. 1924. *Introduction to the Science of Society.* Chicago: University of Chicago Press.

Parker, Linda. 1989. *Native American Estate: The Struggle Over Indian and Hawaiian Lands.* Honolulu: University of Hawaii Press.

Parrillo, Vincent N. 1996. *Diversity in America.* Thousand Oaks, CA: Pine Forge Press.

Patterson, Orlando. 1982. *Slavery and Social Death: A Comparative Study.* Cambridge: Harvard University Press.

Pavalko, Ronald M. 1980. "Racism and the New Immigration." *Sociology and Social Research,* 65:56–77.

Pellett, Lea B. 1990. "Sojourners in Aztlan: Mexican Women Who Go North to Work." Presented to the 25th International Conference of Schools of Social Work, Lima, Peru. August.

Perez, Lisandro. 1980. "Cubans." In Stephen Thornstrom (Ed.), *Harvard Encyclopedia of Ethnic Groups* (pp. 256–261). Cambridge: Harvard University Press.

Petersen, William. 1971. *Japanese Americans.* New York: Random House.

Pettigrew, Thomas. 1971. *Racially Separate or Together?* New York: McGraw-Hill.

———. 1980. "Prejudice." In Stephen Thornstrom (Ed.), *Harvard Encyclopedia of Ethnic Groups* (pp. 820–829). Cambridge: Harvard University Press.

Phillips, Ulrich B. 1918. *American Negro Slavery.* New York: Appleton.

Pienkos, Donald. 1977. "Ethnic Orientation Among Polish Americans." *International Migration Review,* 11:350–362.

Pinkney, Alphonso. 1993. *Black Americans.* Englewood Cliffs, NJ: Prentice Hall.

Pitt, Leonard. 1970. *The Decline of the Californios: A Social History of the Spanish-Speaking Californians, 1846–1890.* Berkeley: University of California Press.

Poe, Janita. 1993. "Multiracial People Want a Single Name That Fits." *Chicago Tribune,* May 3, p. 1.

Polner, Murray. 1993. "Asian Americans Say They Are Treated Like Foreigners." *New York Times,* March 7, p. 1.

Portes, Alejandro. 1990. "From South of the Border: Hispanic Minorities in the United States." In Virginia Yans-McLaughlin (Ed.), *Immigration Reconsidered: History, Sociology, and Politics* (pp. 160–184). New York: Oxford University Press.

Portes, Alejandro, & Bach, Robert L. 1985. *Latin Journey: Cuban and Mexican Immigrants in the United States.* Berkeley: University of California Press.

Portes, Alejandro, & Manning, Robert. 1986. "The Immigrant Enclave: Theory and Empirical Examples." In Susan Olzak & Joanne Nagel (Eds.), *Competitive Ethnic Relations* (pp. 47–67). New York: Academic Press.

Portes, Alejandro, & Rumbaut, Ruben. 1990. *Immigrant America: A Portrait.* Berkeley: University of California Press.

Portes, Alejandro, & Schauffler, Richard. 1994. "Language and the Second Generation: Bilingualism Yesterday and Today." *International Migration Review,* 28:640–641.

Portes, Alejandro, & Zhou, Min. 1992. "Gaining the Upper Hand: Economic Mobility Among Immigrant and Domestic Minorities." *Ethnic and Racial Studies,* 15:491–518.

Potter, George. 1973. *To the Golden Door: The Story of the Irish in Ireland and America.* Westport, CT: Greenwood Press.

Raab, Earl, & Lipset, Seymour. 1959. *Prejudice and Society.* New York: Anti-Defamation League.

Rabinowitz, Jonathon, Kim, Israel, & Lazerwitz, Bernard. 1992. "Metropolitan Size and Participation in Religio-Ethnic Communities." *Journal for the Scientific Study of Religion*, 31:339–345.

Rader, Benjamin G. 1983. *American Sports: From the Age of Folk Games to the Age of Spectators.* Englewood Cliffs, NJ: Prentice Hall.

Rawick, George P. 1972. *From Sunup to Sundown: The Making of the Black Community.* Westport, CT: Greenwood Press.

Raymer, Patricia. 1974. "Wisconsin's Menominees: Indians on a Seesaw." *National Geographic*, August, pp. 228–251.

Reich, Michael. 1986. "The Political-Economic Effects of Racism." In Richard Edwards, Michael Reich, & Thomas Weisskopf (Eds.), *The Capitalist System: A Radical Analysis of American Society* (3rd ed.) (pp. 381–388). Englewood Cliffs, NJ: Prentice Hall.

Reilly, R. 1991. "Let's Bust Those Chops." *Sports Illustrated*, October 28, p. 110.

Reinhold, Robert. 1993. "A Welcome for Immigrants Turns to Resentment." *New York Times*, August 25, p A1.

Rivkin, Steven G. 1994. "Residential Segregation and School Integration." *Sociology of Education*, October, pp. 279–292.

Rodriquez, Clara. 1989. *Puerto Ricans: Born in the USA.* Boston: Unwin Hyman.

Rodriquez, Clara, & Cordero-Guzman, Hector. 1992. "Placing Race in Context." *Ethnic and Racial Studies*, 15:523–542.

Roos, Patricia, & Hennessy, Joyce F. 1987. "Assimilation or Exclusion? Japanese and Mexican Americans in California." *Sociological Forum*, 2:278–304.

Rose, Peter I. 1970. *Slavery and Its Aftermath.* New York: Atherton.

Rosenfield, Geraldine. 1982. "The Polls: Attitudes Toward American Jews." *Public Opinion Quarterly*, 46:431–443.

Ruiz, Vicki L., & Tiano, Susan. (Eds.). 1987. *Women on the U.S.-Mexico Border: Responses to Change.* Boston: Allen & Unwin.

Rumbaut, Ruben. 1991. "Passage to America: Perspectives on the New Immigration." In Alan Wolfe (Ed.), *America at Century's End* (pp. 208–244). Berkeley: University of California Press.

Sanchez-Ayendez, Melba. 1988. "The Puerto Rican American Family." In Charles H. Mindel, Robert W. Habenstein, & Roosevelt Wright (Eds.), *Ethnic Families in America* (3rd ed.) (pp. 173–195). New York: Elsevier.

Sanders, Jimy, & Nee, Victor. 1987. "Limits of Ethnic Solidarity in the Enclave Economy." *American Sociological Review*, 52:745–773.

Schaefer, Richard T. 1993. *Racial and Ethnic Groups.* New York: HarperCollins.

Schlesinger, Arthur. 1992. *The Disuniting of America: Reflections on a Multicultural Society.* New York: Norton.

Schoener, Allon. 1967. *Portal to America: The Lower East Side, 1870–1925.* New York: Holt, Rinehart & Winston.

Schuman, Howard. 1982. "Free Will and Determinism in Public Beliefs About Race." In Norman Yetman & C. Hoy Steele (Eds.), *Majority and Minority: The Dynamics of Race and Ethnicity in American Life* (pp. 345–350). Boston: Allyn & Bacon.

Sears, David. 1988. "Symbolic Racism." In Phyllis Katz & Dalmas Taylor (Eds.), *Eliminating Racism: Profiles in Controversy* (pp. 53–84). New York: Plenum.

Seattle, Chief. 1994. "A Change of Worlds." In Laurie Kirszner & Stephen Mandell (Eds.), *Common Ground: Reading and Writing About America's Cultures* (pp. 286–289). New York: St. Martin's Press.

See, Katherine O'Sullivan, & Wilson, William J. 1988. "Race and Ethnicity." In Neil Smelser (Ed.), *Handbook of Sociology* (pp. 223–242). Newbury Park, CA: Sage.

Segura, Denise. 1989. "Chicana and Mexican Immigrant Women at Work: The Impact of Class, Race, and Gender on Occupational Mobility." *Gender and Society*, 3:37–52.

Seller, Maxine S. 1987. "Beyond the Stereotype: A New Look at the Immigrant Woman." In Ronald Takaki (Ed.), *From Different Shores: Perspectives on Race and Ethnicity in America* (pp. 197–203). New York: Oxford University Press.

Selzer, Michael. 1972. *"Kike"—Anti-Semitism in America*. New York: Meridian.

Selznik, G. J., & Steinberg, S. 1969. *The Tenacity of Prejudice*. New York: Harper & Row.

Shannon, William V. 1964. *The American Irish*. New York: Macmillan.

Sherif, Muzafer, et al. 1961. *Intergroup Conflict and Cooperation: The Robbers Cave Experiment*. Norman, OK: University Book Exchange.

Shils, E. A. 1954. "Authoritarianism: Right and Left." In R. Christie & M. Yahoda (Eds.), *Studies in the Scope and Method of the Authoritarian Personality* (pp. 123–147). Glencoe, IL: Free Press.

Shinagawa, Larry, & Pang, Gin Yong. 1988. "Intraethnic, Interethnic, and Interracial Marriages Among Asian Americans in California, 1980." *Berkeley Journal of Sociology*, 33:95–114.

Sigelman, Lee, & Welch, Susan. 1993. "The Contact Hypothesis Revisited: Black-White Interaction and Positive Racial Attitudes." *Social Forces*, 71:781–795.

Simcox, David E. (Ed.). 1988. *U.S. Immigration in the 1980s: Reappraisal and Reform*. Boulder, CO: Westview Press.

Simon, Julian. 1989. *The Economic Consequences of Immigration*. Cambridge, MA: Basil Blackwell.

Simpson, George, & Yinger, Milton. 1985. *Racial and Cultural Minorities: An Analysis of Prejudice and Discrimination*. New York: Plenum.

Sklare, Marshall. 1971. *America's Jews*. New York: Random House.

Slaughter-Defoe, Diana, Takanishi, Ruby, & Johnson, Deborah. 1990. "Toward Cultural/ Ecological Perspectives on Schooling and Achievement in African and Asian American Children." *Child Development*, 61:363–383.

Smedley, Audrey. 1993. *Race in North America: Origin and Evolution of a World View*. Boulder, CO: Westview Press.

Smith, Tom, & Dempsey, Glenn. 1983. "The Polls: Ethnic Social Distance and Prejudice." *Public Opinion Quarterly*, 47:584–600.

Snipp, C. Matthew. 1989. *American Indians: The First of This Land*. New York: Russell Sage.

Snipp, C. Matthew. 1992. "Sociological Perspectives on American Indians." *Annual Review of Sociology*, 18:351–371.

Sowell, Thomas. 1983. *The Economics and Politics of Race: An International Perspective*. New York: Quill.

Spicer, Edward H. 1980. "American Indians." In Stephen Thornstrom (Ed.), *Harvard Encyclopedia of Ethnic Groups* (pp. 58–122). Cambridge: Harvard University Press.

Stampp, Kenneth. 1956. *The Peculiar Institution: Slavery in the Ante-Bellum South*. New York: Random House.

Staples, Robert. 1988. "The Black American Family." In Charles Mindel, Robert Habenstein, & Roosevelt Wright (Eds.), *Ethnic Families in America* (3rd ed.) (pp. 303–324). New York: Elsevier.

Staples, Robert (Ed.). 1994. *The Black Family*. Belmont, CA: Wadsworth.

Steele, Shelby. 1990. *The Content of Our Character*. New York: St. Martin's Press.

Stein, Howard F., & Hill, Robert. 1977. *The Ethnic Imperative*. University Park: Pennsylvania State University Press.

Steinberg, Stephen. 1981. *The Ethnic Myth: Race, Ethnicity, and Class in America*. New York: Atheneum.

———. 1995. *Turning Back: The Retreat From Racial Justice in American Thought and Policy.* Boston: Beacon.

Steiner, Stan. 1968. *The New Indians.* New York: Dell.

———. 1979. *Fusang: The Chinese Who Built America.* New York: Harper & Row.

Stember, C. H. 1961. *Education and Attitude Change.* New York: Institute of Human Relations Press.

Stoddard, Ellwyn. 1973. *Mexican Americans.* New York: Random House.

Strategy Research Corporation. 1991. *U.S. Hispanic Market.* Miami: Author.

Stuckey, Sterling. 1987. *Slave Culture: Nationalist Theory and the Foundations of Black America.* New York: Harper & Row.

Sung, Betty Lee. 1990. "Chinese American Intermarriage." *Journal of Comparative Family Studies,* 21:337–352.

Szapocznik, Jose, & Hernandez, Roberto. 1988. "The Cuban American Family." In Charles H. Mindel, Robert W. Habenstein, & Roosevelt Wright (Eds.), *Ethnic Families in America* (3rd ed.) (pp. 160–172). New York: Elsevier.

Takaki, Ronald. 1993. *A Different Mirror: A History of Multicultural America.* Boston: Little, Brown.

Tauber, Karl E. 1975. "Racial Segregation: The Persisting Dilemma." *Annals of the American Academy of Political and Social Sciences,* 442:87–96.

Tauber, Karl E., & Tauber, Alma. 1964. "The Negro as an Immigrant Group: Recent Trends in Racial and Ethnic Segregation." *American Journal of Sociology,* 69:374–382.

———. 1969. *Negroes in Cities: Residential Segregation and Neighborhood Change.* New York: Atheneum.

Tidwell, Billy J. (Ed.). 1994. *The State of Black America 1994.* New York: National Urban League.

Tienda, Marta. 1989. "Looking to the 1990s: Mexican Immigration in Sociological Perspective." In Wayne A. Cornelius & Jorge A. Bustamante (Eds.), *Mexican Migration to the United States: Origins, Consequences, and Policy Options* (pp. 109–147). San Diego: Center for U.S.-Mexican Studies.

Tilly, Charles. 1990. "Transplanted Networks." In Virginia Yans-McLaughlin (Ed.), *Immigration Reconsidered: History, Sociology, and Politics* (pp. 79–95). New York: Oxford University Press.

Tsai, Shih-Shan Henry. 1986. *The Chinese Experience in America.* Bloomington: Indiana University Press.

Tsukashima, Ronald T. 1991. "Cultural Endowment, Disadvantaged Status and Economic Niche: The Development of an Ethnic Trade." *International Migration Review,* 25:333–354.

Turner, Ralph, & Killian, Lewis. 1987. *Collective Behavior* (3rd ed.) Englewood Cliffs, NJ: Prentice Hall.

Tyler, Gus (Ed.). 1975. *Mexican-Americans Tomorrow.* Albuquerque: University of New Mexico Press.

United States Bureau of the Census. 1972. *Statistical Abstract of the United States: 1972* (93rd ed.). Washington, DC: Government Printing Office.

———. 1977. *Statistical Abstract of the United States: 1977* (98th ed.). Washington, DC: Government Printing Office.

———. 1988. *Statistical Abstract of the United States: 1988* (108th ed.). Washington, DC: Government Printing Office.

———. 1990. *Summary Population and Housing Characteristics: United States.* Washington, DC: Government Printing Office.

————. 1992. *Statistical Abstract of the United States: 1992* (112th ed.). Washington, DC: Government Printing Office.

————. 1993. *Statistical Abstract of the United States: 1993* (113th ed.). Washington, DC: Government Printing Office.

————. 1994. *Statistical Abstract of the United States: 1994* (114th ed.). Washington, DC: Government Printing Office.

United States Commission on Civil Rights. 1976. *Puerto Ricans in the Continental United States: An Uncertain Future.* Washington, DC: Government Printing Office.

————. 1979. *Window Dressing on the Set: An Update.* Washington, DC: Government Printing Office.

————. 1992. *Civil Rights Issues Facing Asian Americans in the 1990s.* Washington, DC: Government Printing Office.

United States Immigration and Naturalization Service. 1992. *Statistical Yearbook of the Immigration and Naturalization Service, 1991.* Washington, DC: Government Printing Office.

————. 1993. *Statistical Yearbook of the Immigration and Naturalization Service, 1992.* Washington, DC: Government Printing Office.

Valdivieso, Rafael, & Davis, Cary. 1988. *U.S. Hispanics: Challenging Issues for the 1990s.* Washington, DC: Population Reference Bureau.

Valentine, Charles A. 1968. *Culture and Poverty: Critique and Counter-Proposals.* Chicago: University of Chicago Press.

Van den Berghe, Pierre. 1967. *Race and Racism: A Comparative Perspective.* New York: John Wiley.

————. 1978. *Man in Society.* New York: Elsevier.

————. 1981. *The Ethnic Phenomenon.* New York: Elsevier.

Vidmar, Neil, & Rokeach, Milton. 1974. "Archie Bunker's Bigotry." *Journal of Communication,* 24:36–47.

Vincent, Theodore G. 1976. *Black Power and the Garvey Movement.* San Francisco: Ramparts Press.

Vogel, Virgil (Ed.). 1972. *This Country Was Ours: A Documentary History of the American Indian.* New York: Harper & Row.

Waddel, Jack, & Watson, O. M. 1971. *The American Indian in Urban Society.* Boston: Little, Brown.

Wagley, Charles, & Harris, Marvin. 1958. *Minorities in the New World: Six Case Studies.* New York: Columbia University Press.

Walzer, Michael. 1980. "Pluralism: A Humanistic Perspective." In Stephen Thornstrom (Ed.), *Harvard Encyclopedia of Ethnic Groups* (pp. 772–787). Cambridge: Harvard University Press.

Ward, David. 1980. "Immigration Settlement Patterns and Spatial Distribution." In Stephen Thornstrom (Ed.), *Harvard Encyclopedia of Ethnic Groups* (pp. 496–508). Cambridge: Harvard University Press.

Washburn, Wilcomb. 1975. *The Indian in America.* New York: Harper & Row.

Washington, Booker T. 1965. *Up From Slavery.* New York: Dell.

Waters, Mary. 1990. *Ethnic Options.* Berkeley: University of California Press.

Wax, Murray. 1971. *Indian Americans: Unity and Diversity.* Englewood Cliffs, NJ: Prentice Hall.

Wax, Murray, & Buchanan, R. 1975. *Solving "the Indian Problem": The White Man's Burdensome Business.* New York: The New York Times Co.

Weeks, Philip. 1988. *The American Indian Experience.* Arlington Heights, IL: Forum Press.

Wellman, David. 1993. *Portraits of White Racism.* Cambridge: Cambridge University Press.

Wertheimer, Barbara M. 1979. " 'Union Is Power': Sketches From Women's Labor History." In Jo Freeman (Ed.), *Women: A Feminist Perspective* (pp. 339–358). Palo Alto, CA: Mayfield Publishing.

Whitaker, M. 1995. "Whites v. Blacks." *Newsweek,* October 16, pp. 28–35.

White, Deborah Gray. 1985. *Ar'n't I a Woman? Female Slaves in the Plantation South.* New York: Norton.

Wilkens, Roger. 1992. "L.A.: Images in the Flames—Looking Back in Anger: 27 Years After Watts, Our Nation Remains Divided by Racism." *Washington Post,* May 3, p. C1.

Williams, Juan. 1987. *Eyes on the Prize: America's Civil Rights Years, 1954–1965.* New York: Penguin Books.

Williams, R. 1964. *Strangers Next Door.* Englewood Cliffs, NJ: Prentice Hall.

Willie, Charles (Ed.). 1989. *Round Two of the Willie/Wilson Debate* (2nd ed.). Dix Hills, NY: General Hall.

Wilson, Kenneth, & Portes, Alejandro. 1980. "Immigrant Enclaves: An Analysis of the Labor Market Experience of Cubans in Miami." *American Journal of Sociology,* 86:295–319.

Wilson, Terry. 1993. "People of Mixed Racial Descent: The Issue of Marginality." In Young I. Song & Eugene C. Kim (Eds.), *American Mosaic.* Englewood Cliffs, NJ: Prentice Hall.

Wilson, William J. 1973. *Power, Racism, and Privilege: Race Relations in Theoretical and Sociohistorical Perspectives.* New York: Free Press.

———. 1980. *The Declining Significance of Race.* Chicago: University of Chicago Press.

———. 1987. *The Truly Disadvantaged: The Inner City, the Underclass, and Public Policy.* Chicago: University of Chicago Press.

——— (Ed.). 1992. *The Ghetto Underclass.* Newbury Park, CA: Sage.

Winsberg, Morton. 1994. "Hispanics Dominate Miami's Demography." *Population Today,* 22:4.

Wirth, Louis. 1945. "The Problem of Minority Groups." In Ralph Linton (Ed.), *The Science of Man in the World* (pp. 347–372). New York: Columbia University Press.

Witt, Gretchen, & Kalish, Susan. 1995. "Black Households: How Are They Doing Economically?" *Population Today* (Vol. 23, No. 10). Washington, DC: Population Reference Bureau.

Wolfenstein, Eugene V. 1993. *The Victims of Democracy: Malcolm X.* New York: Guilford.

Wong, Jade Snow. 1993. "Fifth Chinese Daughter." In Dolores LaGuardia & Hans Guth (Eds.), *American Voices.* Mountain View, CA: Mayfield.

Woodward, C. Vann. 1971. *American Counterpoint: Slavery and Racism in the North-South Dialogue.* Boston: Little, Brown.

———. 1974. *The Strange Career of Jim Crow* (3rd ed.). New York: Oxford University Press.

Worsnop, Richard. 1992. "Native Americans." *CQ Researcher,* May 8, pp. 387–407.

Wright, Bobby, & Tierney, W. 1991. "American Indians in Higher Education: A History of Culture Conflict." *Change,* March/April, pp. 11–26.

Yans-McLaughlin, Virginia (Ed.). 1990. *Immigration Reconsidered: History, Sociology, and Politics.* New York: Oxford University Press.

Yetman, Norman, & Steele C. Hoy. (Eds.). 1992. *Majority and Minority: The Dynamics of Race and Ethnicity in American Life.* Boston: Allyn & Bacon.

Yinger, J. Milton. 1985. "Ethnicity." *Annual Review of Sociology,* 11:151–180.

Zhou, Min. 1992. *Chinatown*. Philadelphia: Temple University Press.

Zhou, Min, & Logan, John R. 1989. "Returns on Human Capital in Ethnic Enclaves: New York City's Chinatown." *American Sociological Review*, 54:809–820.

Zinn, Maxine Baca, & Dill, Bonnie Thornton. 1994. *Women of Color in U.S. Society*. Philadelphia: Temple University Press.

Zinn, Maxine Baca, & Eitzen, D. Stanley. 1990. *Diversity in Families*. New York: HarperCollins.

Zunz, Olivier. 1985. "American History and the Changing Meaning of Assimilation." *Journal of American Ethnic History*, Spring, pp. 53–72.

Numbers in brackets refer to the chapter in which the term is introduced.

institutional discrimination *(continued)*
"doing" dimension of, 15
individual vs. group, 13
modern, 108–111
past-in-present, 109–110
See also discrimination

integration [1] the process by which a
minority group enters the social
structure of the dominant society
in labor market, 137–139
process of, 18–19
residential, 134–135
school, 135–136
without acculturation, 22

intergroup contacts
equal status contact hypothesis on, 48–
50
initial contact, 66–69
recent trends in, 50–52
situation of, 269–270

intermarriage
of Latino Americans, 199
of Native Americans, 166
as third stage of assimilation, 19

interracial marriage, 5

invisible minority, 207. *See also* Chinese
Americans

Issei [8] first-generation immigrants
from Japan, 213, 215–216

Italians
as sojourners, 94
WASPs compared to, 92
See also European immigrants

J

Jackson, Jesse, 137

Japanese Americans
after World War II, 215–216
as enclave minority, 213
immigration of, 89, 211–213
internment of, 214–215
second generation (Nisei) of, 213
stereotypes of, 30–31
See also Asian Americans

Jewish immigrants, 30–31, 93, 237–238,
243–246. *See also* European immigrants

jigsaw method [2] a learning technique
that requires cooperation among
students, 51–52

Jim Crow system, 96–97, 118. *See also*
civil rights movement

jobs. *See* occupations

K

Kallen, Horace, 22

King, Martin Luther, Jr., 119, 124

King, Rodney, 127

Kitano, Harry L. L., 210

Klamath tribe, 151

Korean Americans, 217

Korean War, 106

Ku Klux Klan, 90, 98, 118, 246

L

labor market
Asian immigrants and, 220–222
globalization of, 106–107
integration within, 137–139
labor unions and, 249–250
Mexican immigration and U.S., 175–
176
modern institutional discrimination in,
108–111
primary/secondary, 105–106
Puerto Ricans and, 181–182
See also occupations

labor movement, 249–250, 254

labor unions, 249–250

LaPiere, Robert, 40

La Raza Unida party, 179

Latin American immigration, 188–192

Latino Americans
Asian Americans compared to, 229–231
Cuban Americans, 184–188
description of, 170
Puerto Rican, 181–184
relations with dominant group, 192–
199
See also Hispanic Americans; Mexican
Americans

Lenski, Gerhard, 8

levels of development [1] the stages of
evolution of society. The stages
discussed in this text relate to
agrarian and industrial subsistence
technology, 8

Lieberson, Stanley, 100

Lincoln, Abe, 30–31

Little, Malcolm, 124

M

machismo [7] a cultural value stressing
male dominance, virility, and honor,
172

Malcolm X, 124

**manufacturing (secondary) occupa-
tions** [4] occupations involving the
transformation of raw materials into
finished products ready for the
marketplace. An example would be
an assembly line worker in an
automobile plant, 103

March on Washington (1963), 119